CADOGAN   David J J Evans & Kamin Mohammadi

Portugal:
the Algarve

Cadogan Guides
West End House, 11 Hills Place, London W1R 1AG
becky.kendall@morrispub.co.uk

The Globe Pequot Press
246 Goose Lane, PO Box 480, Guilford,
Connecticut 06437–0480

Copyright © David J. J. Evans and Cadogan Guides 1996, 2000
with additional text by Kamin Mohammadi
Illustrations © Charles Shearer 1996

Book and cover design by Animage
Cover illustrations: front: Alex Robinson
                back: The Travel Library, Stuart Black
Maps © Cadogan Guides, drawn by Map Creation Ltd

Editorial Director: Vicki Ingle
Series Editor: Linda McQueen

Editing: Linda McQueen
Indexing: Isobel McLean
Production: Rupert Wheeler Book Production Services

**A catalogue record for this book is available from the British Library
ISBN 1–86011–957–3**

Printed and bound in Great Britain by Cambridge University Press.

*The author and publishers have made every effort to ensure the accuracy
of the information in the book at the time of going to press. However, they
cannot accept any responsibility for any loss, injury or inconvenience
resulting from the use of information contained in this guide.*

Please Help Us Keep This Guide Up to Date

We have done our best to ensure that the information in this guide is correct at the time of going to
press. But places and facilities are constantly changing, and standards and prices in hotels and restaurants fluctuate. We would be delighted to receive any comments concerning existing entries or
omissions. Significant contributions will be acknowledged in the next edition, and authors of the best
letters will receive a copy of the Cadogan Guide of their choice.

'It is difficult to praise the Cadogan Guides series too highly. Portugal by David J. J. Evans is typical of the series' blend of good writing, amusing comment and invaluable advice.'

The Independent

'With his highly readable text on Portugal, Evans has added a replete, witty and wonderfully lucid volume to the Cadogan Series. This is an essential tote-along guidebook... Think of a question to ask vis-à vis your travel planning and Evans, an inveterate roamer with a richly entertaining style, will no doubt have addressed it.'

Travel Publishing News, USA

'An exceptional guide, unique in the English language.'

Jornal de Notícias

'Cadogan Guides: Portugal by David J. J. Evans offers a good blend of cultural and practical information and, like the best companions, challenges assumptions and constantly keeps one amused.'

The Daily Telegraph

'A smooth blend of practical, historical and cultural information, spiced with a dash of wit and irreverance... The author is sharp-eyed and does not flinch from telling what he has seen on his journeys around the country.'

The Anglo-Portuguese News

'Keeping the best to last, we come finally to Cadogan Guides' Portugal: the perfect marriage of cultural and practical information, but not confined to the budget end of the scale. Evans' guide is a marvellous collection of treasure and trivia...description...and humour. Once again the Cadogan Guide is the pick of the bunch.'

The Daily Telegraph

David Evans

David Evans roamed Mediterranean Europe, India, Egypt and Southeast Asia before Portugal seduced him. He studied at Eton and read History at Cambridge. He has lived in New York and London on and off since he was a baby, and has worked as a freelance writer on both sides of the Atlantic. In 1993 he joined the Society of St Francis, an Anglican Franciscan order and donned a voluminous brown habit. He enjoys going for walks amongst trees, making soup, and following his curiosity (which is as omnivorous as a Portuguese goat).

Acknowledgements

I could not have undertaken this project, or completed it, without the encouragement and support of Susan and John Mayo. Michael and Rosita Simpson-Orlebar became my fairy godparents and my mother, Louise Evans, lent me a house to write in. I am grateful to Maria Emília Ribeiro for all the transport arrangements and to Christopher Cramer for his driving skills. I would like to thank Paula Levey and Lorna Horsfield for their superb work on the original edition of Portugal, Rachel Fielding for caring enough to be patient with me, and meticulous Linda McQueen.

The Portuguese National Tourist Office have been unstintingly generous with their time and their hospitality. This book would have been impossible without the help of Alberto Marques and Luís Cancela de Abreu. I would also very much like to thank António Serras Pereira, Pilar Pereira, Álvaro de Sousa, Celestino Domingues, Gabriela Ferreira, João Custódio, Isabel Terenas and Alice Martin. I am grateful to the regional Tourist Office in Faro, and to Enatur and the town hall in Évora.

Kamin Mohammadi

Kamin Mohammadi left a revolution for the chaos of a London childhood, the city where she is still based. After years of a random and freelance lifestyle wandering the Iberian Peninsula, she now runs a stable of glossy magazines in London and wears spike heels. She does, however, put on her trainers to go back to her European loves: Portugal, especially the rugged west coast of the Algarve and the bullrings of Spain. Most frequently, she dons a chador to return to her first love, Iran, where she still has much to learn.

Acknowledgements

I would like to thank the Portuguese National Tourist Office in London for their help as always, especially Pilar Pereira for, among other things, her definitive knowledge of seafood. Many thanks go to Mr Crawford-Ricks and Emilia Saunders of TAP Air Portugal for their help and also to Maria Elisabete Máximo of Região de Turismo do Algarve. Thanks to Claire at Marketeer PR for her help with car rentals in many countries, but particularly in the Algarve. Permanently resounding thanks to my parents for providing love, food and a roof, with little return. The customary hugs to Maria Lagôas for making a trip to Tavira like going home. Thanks to Charles Shearer for his pictures, and to Katrina Burroughs, my first editor, for being so supportive then and still being my friend now. Many thanks go to Linda McQueen for her hard work and for always being available to exchange information, news and a laugh. Most thanks to Rachel Fielding, just for all of it: the opportunity, the encouragement, the support, the discipline and her unsuspected talent as a travel agent. Finally, deep gratitude to Klaus Mörtel for shelter and sympathy at the edge of the world—may your nails never break. I dedicate my work on this book to him: *For Klaus, with love.*

About the Updaters

Algarve chapters: **Paul Murphy** is a full-time travel writer, editor and photographer. He has written 35 books as sole author and has contributed to as many again. He also writes regularly for national magazines. Although he travels worldwide the Algarve is one of his favourite and most frequently covered destinations.

Alentejo chapter: **John and Madge Measures** have lived in southern Portugal since 1968 and are well-known for their local artisan and natural history lectures. They are regular contributors to magazines such as *Algarve Resident*, and have published several books (see p.189) on the wildlife and crafts of the region they love.

Contents

Maps

The Algarve is a separate region proud of its distinctive identity, yet as diverse as Portugal itself, packing into its small space an impressive range of land- and seascapes.

The inland landscape encompasses lush wooded mountain peaks, acres of citrus groves and gently rolling hills

Introduction

dappled with umbrella pines and arid, amber tracts of windswept land stabbed with the spindly trunks of century plants. The scent of rosemary mingles with the sweet aroma of cistus until both give way to the cool smell of eucalyptus and a haze of pine. Glorious beaches are never far away: the coast changes from the drama of high, black, tightly compressed cliffs to mellower sandstone cliffs punctuated by coves and grottoes, to sheltered spits of sand stretching for miles.

Tourism is the main industry, and has mushroomed at the expense of aesthetic appeal on parts of the coast, leading some to view the Algarve as simply a motley collection of resorts offering predictable delights. But it's too easy and smug to dismiss the popular resorts; after all, they are popular for a reason. The range of activities on offer is a great attraction, including the chance to play golf on championship courses above pounding Atlantic waves.

Fortunately, the coast will never suffer from the worst excesses of tourism witnessed in the popular Mediterranean resorts, as the government now exerts tight building controls. Adventurous and independent travellers can take heart: there is not much development west of Lagos, east of Faro, or inland. Stand on Albufeira's Fishermen's Beach at sunset, look out to sea and you'll understand why so many people flock here. The sinking sun sends salmon-pink wisps across the sky while the ocean hardens to slate blue and the red-tinged cliffs are bathed in soft, forgiving light. People can construct their buildings all around, but they can never spoil the natural beauty of the seascape.

In two weeks spent in the Algarve it is possible to have several different types of holiday and still to have only scratched the surface of this tiny region. Much fun is to be had in the cosmopolitan resorts, while minuscule villages show rural life as it has always been—and it's not necessary to travel any great distance between the two. Often, just five or ten kilometres away from a busy tourist centre a few shambling houses huddle together on the beach, chickens peck the soil while a couple of fishermen mend their nets and goats devour the bushes. Families travelling in carts drawn by elaborately head-dressed horses edge along the main highway; inland, women wear distinctive pinafores and scarves under straw hats. The Algarvians are friendly souls, kind and lighthearted; those in the smallest hamlets are unused to tourists and may regard you with amazement. Resist self-consciousness and smile— you'll see their faces break into the widest grins.

While in the Algarve, do consider making a foray into the neighbouring province of the Alentejo. Its very different character derives from its vast, flat, arid spaces, brilliant colours and fiery climate; it covers nearly a third of the country but supports just 12% of the population. You may like to spend a day meandering up the stunning River Guadiana, or plan an expedition covering a couple of nights. Typically, the people of the Alentejo are as open and friendly as the Algarvians, though outside Èvora they will be less familiar with tourists—and perhaps more bemused by them.

Tourism is not the Algarve's only moneyspinner. Fishing is a buoyant source of revenue, as well as brick manufacture and the cultivation of hothouse tomatoes, strawberries and avocados for export. Inland, dry-stone walls pen sheep with pendulous undocked tails, a breed that originated in west Africa, whose coarse wool is used for stuffing mattresses and weaving into heavy blankets. The shepherds wear ex-army swallowtail caps, surplus from the African wars.

Prices here are fast catching up with the rest of Europe, but there are still some great bargains to be had at all price levels—particularly out of high season. Accommodation is plentiful and wide-ranging, and the public transport system is good along the coast, though a little more unpredictable inland. If you don't fall in love with the Algarve at first sight, give it a day or two and slowly, gently, it will work its magic on you; you'll find yourself enamoured without realizing quite how.

Travel

By Air

From the UK and Ireland

In peak season, scheduled flights to Faro in the Algarve can get booked up, so you may also consider Lisbon as a destination; there are connecting flights to Faro but it is better to continue to the Algarve by train or express bus.

To Lisbon: TAP Air Portugal (the Portuguese national airline) flies daily direct from London (Heathrow and Gatwick), and also from Dublin on Thursday, Saturday and Sunday. From other parts of the UK it operates alongside British Midland. **British Airways** flies from London (Heathrow), connecting with a British Airways flight from Glasgow and Manchester and an Aer Lingus flight from Dublin.

To Faro: TAP Air Portugal flies daily from London (Heathrow in the summer). It also flies from Dublin on Thursday and Saturday. From other parts of the UK it flies under a code-share agreement with British Midland. **British Airways** flies from London (Gatwick), connecting with Air UK and British Airways flights from Glasgow and Dublin. **Go,** ✆ (0845) 605 4321, the budget airline from British Airways, fly to Faro, from Stansted, daily in summer, winter Saturdays only. There is a small discount for on-line booking, *www.go-fly.com.*

A steady stream of charter flights lands in Faro all year round. The cheapest flights are off-season although some good last-minute bargains can be had in the summer.

TAP Air Portugal's subsidiary, **Caravela**, handles bookings for *pousadas* and *Solares de Portugal (Turismo de Habitação) (see* p.30), as well as organizing a number of fly-drive alternatives (London ✆ (020) 7630 9223 and Dublin ✆ (01) 679 8809; *www.caravela.co.uk*).

TAP Offices in the UK and Ireland

UK:	Gillingham House, 38–44 Gillingham St, London SW1V 1JW, ✆ (0845) 601 0932.
Ireland:	54 Dawson St, Dublin 2, ✆ (3531) 679 8844.
Scotland:	TAP have no offices in Scotland.

From the USA and Canada

The frequency of flights to Portugal from the USA and Canada is increasing rapidly, though there are no direct flights to Faro as yet; fly to Lisbon and change planes there. TAP Air Portugal offers non-stop services to Lisbon from Newark and JFK (6½hrs) with an additional ¾hr onward flight to Faro from there. However, connecting flights can involve a long wait and it's often worthwhile taking an express bus from Lisbon. TWA flies to Lisbon from New York, with connections from San Francisco (5½hrs plus 6½hrs).

Many European airlines fly to Lisbon from Montreal and Toronto, via London.

For cut-price flights try **Globus and Cosmos Group Voyagers**, 5301 South Federal Circle, Middleton, Colorado 80123 (toll-free ✆ 800 851 0728, or ✆ (303) 703 7000), who are the leading budget tour operators for Europe in North America.

It can work out cheaper to fly from the USA or Canada to Madrid or London, and head on to Portugal from there, if you have the time.

TAP Offices in the USA and Canada

Boston: 1 Exeter Plaza, Boston, MA 02116, ✆ (1) 800 221 7370 toll free, or ✆ 617 262 8585.

Newark: 399 Market St, Newark, NJ 07105, ✆ (1) 800 221 7370 toll free, or ✆ 973 344 4490.

Los Angeles: 9841 Airport Boulevard, Suite 1104, CA 90245–0916, ✆ (1) 800 221 7370 toll free, or ✆ 310 322 9222.

TAP does not fly from Canada.

By Rail

From the UK

A daily rail and ferry service operates between London (Victoria) and Lisbon (30–40hrs), via Paris and Irún/Hendaye. In Paris and at the Spanish border passengers must change stations. For full details of times and fares contact **Connex Rail**, ✆ (0870) 6030 405, *www.connex.co.uk.*

Much quicker, though more expensive, is the **Eurostar** from London Waterloo to Paris Gare du Nord through the Channel Tunnel, which connects up with the train to Lisbon. The price is the same for all travellers at £278 return, and the ticket is valid for two months. Details and reservations are available from **Rail Europe**, 179 Piccadilly, London W1V 0BA, ✆ (0990) 848 848, *www.raileurope.co.uk*, or, in the USA, 226 Westchester Avenue, White Plains, NY 100604, ✆ (1800) 438 7245, *www.raileurope. com.*

From Spain

Trains from Madrid to Lisbon take around 10hrs, with connections from Barcelona. Most recently this service only operated during the summer; this is liable to change again so please check. Other trains run from Vigo (via Oporto) and from Salamanca. There is no direct train from Seville to Faro, though express buses go from to Seville to Sagres.

From Lisbon

Semi-frequent trains run to the Algarve from Barreiro (take the ferry from Lisbon's Terreiro do Paço), via Setúbal, Ermidas-Sado (change from Santiago do Cacém and Sines), Tunes (3hrs; change at Tunes for Silves and Lagos, 1¼hrs), Albufeira (4hrs), Faro (4½hrs), Olhão, Tavira (5hrs), Conceicão, Cacela, Castro Marim, and Vila Real de Santo António (5¾hrs). For the complete Portuguese train timetable, go to *www.cp.pt.*

The Algarve is such a compact area that buying a special ticket for sole use in the region does not really offer value for money. However, if you are visiting the Algarve as part of a European tour, the following options are worth considering. EU citizens who have been resident for the past six months in the European country in which they wish to buy their ticket are eligible for the **InterRail** pass (currently £279 if you're over 26, from British Rail or any travel agent), which gives one month's unlimited travel on all European, Moroccan and Turkish railways, as well as up to 30 per cent discounts on trains in Britain, cross-Channel ferries, and ferries between Spain and Morocco. The equivalent North American **EurRail** pass can be bought in the USA, for 7, 15, 21, 30, 60 or 90 days; it too saves the hassle of buying numerous tickets, but it will only pay for itself if you use it every day, everywhere. Supplementary fares are required on many express trains. **Eurotrain** offers anyone under the age of 26 inexpensive tickets to a fixed destination. These are valid for two months, and allow travellers to stop off at any stations along the preplanned route. Eurotrain's London office is at 52 Grosvenor Gardens, London SW1W 0AG, ✆ (0870) 240 010, *www.usitcampus.co.uk*; in the USA, contact Rail Europe (*see* p.3).

By Bus

There are no direct bus or coach services to the Algarve.

Eurolines, ✆ (0990) 143 219, *www.eurolines.co.uk*, offers services from London's Victoria coach station on Monday, Wednesday, Thursday, Friday and Saturday nights to Lisbon (41hrs), requiring a long stopover in Paris. Change at Villa Formoso for the Algarve/Alentejo service stopping at Evora, Beja, Loulé, Portimão, Lagos and Faro. This runs every Monday and Friday and also Saturday in August. The direct service to Oporto leaves on Monday, Wednesday, Friday and Saturday mornings and takes 39hrs. This route is only available during the summer and over Christmas.

Tickets are available from any National Express agent, or by credit card booking over the phone. An under-25 discount is available on both services.

By Car

More than 2,000km of main roads separate Faro from Calais. If you prefer a short Channel crossing and a long stint on the *autoroute*, take the ferry from Dover/Folkestone to Calais/Boulogne, and continue to Paris, where you join the toll *Autoroute de l'Aquitaine* to just beyond Bordeaux. Enter Spain at Irún and go via Burgos and Salamanca.

For a longer Channel crossing and less *autoroute*, take a night ferry from Portsmouth, and head south via Rennes, Nantes, and La Rochelle before joining the *autoroute*. If you want to take it comfortably, reckon on two overnight stops *en route*. A hop across the Channel via Eurotunnel is another alternative: call ✆ (0990) 35 35 35 for details.

There are a couple of options for cutting down on driving times. A Motorail service operates between Paris and Madrid (daily all year round). Passengers and their cars travel on different trains. The car is loaded on to a train during the day. Passengers take an overnight train, arrive in Madrid the next day and collect their cars. For details, contact French Railways, ☎ (0870) 584 8848, *www.sncf.fr*.

Alternatively, Brittany Ferries, Milbay Docks, Plymouth PL1 3EW, ☎ (0990) 360 360, *www.brittanyferries.com*, operates a twice-weekly 24-hour service from Plymouth to Santander in northern Spain. There is a special rate for 5- and 10-day returns. Santander is approximately 1,300km from Faro.

Specialist Tour Operators

in the UK

Caravela, 38–44 Gillingham Street, London SW1V 1HU, ☎ (020) 7630 9223; Dublin ☎ (01) 679 8844, TAP's tour arm, books *pousadas* and *Solares de Portugal*, and arranges various fly-drive options.

Destination Portugal, Madeira House, 37 Corn Street, Witney, Oxfordshire, ☎ (0870) 774 0050 or ☎ (01993) 773269, is an excellent agency offering options from flights only to *pousada* tours.

Simply Portugal (Simply Travel), King's House, Wood Street, Kingston-upon-Thames, Surrey KT1 1SG, ☎ (020) 8541 2207, ✉ 8541 2282, offers high-quality self-catering properties in unspoilt rural or quiet parts of southern Portugal.

in the USA

Abreu Tours, 25 West 45th Street, New York, NY 10036, toll-free ☎ (1) 800 223 1580 or ☎ (212) 869 1840, is a Portuguese-run agency with many years of experience.

Special-interest Holidays

Abreu Travel, 109 Westbourne Grove, London W2 4UL, ☎ (020) 7229 9905, offers golf holidays, wine tours and pilgrimages, using *pousadas* and *Solares de Portugal*.

Let's Walk, ☎ (00 351) 282 698 676, mobile ☎ (07936) 575 3033, is a local Portuguese company run by Julie Statham, an expert on the flora, fauna and history of the region. She covers a broad chunk of the Algarve, from the Cape St Vincent Natural Park in the far west to Alte in the heart of the region, and offers long walking holidays and 3-day packages.

Mundi Color, 276 Vauxhall Bridge Road, London SW1V 1BE, ☎ (020) 7828 6021, organizes tailor-made and *pousada* holidays, and golf holidays.

Portugal Travel Club, 15 Harrow View Road, London W5 1NA, ☎ (020) 8810 6010, will book golf and tennis holidays and self-catering accommodation.

Portugala Holidays, 1–3 Princes Lane, London N10 3LU, ☎ (020) 8444 1857, offers self-catering accommodation and tailor-made, golf, walking and *pousada* holidays.

Roger Taylor Tennis Holidays, 85 High Street, London SW19 5EG, ☎ (020) 8947 9727, books tennis holidays at the prestigious centre.

Entry Formalities

Holders of British, Irish and EU passports or identity cards can enter Portugal without a visa and stay as long as they wish. Holders of US and Canadian passports can enter Portugal for up to 60 days without a visa. These periods may be extended, before they expire, on application to the Foreigners' Registration Service, 22 Rua Conselheiro José Silvestre Ribeiro, Lisbon 1600, ✆ (217) 141 027. In practice, visitors are very unlikely to be challenged over how long they have been in the country. Customs are usually polite and present few problems.

Getting Around

Better is the ass that carries me than the horse that throws me.

Portuguese proverb

By Air

Portugal is such a small country that there should be no need to fly. If you're in a hurry, TAP Air Portugal's Airbus fleet wing their way several times daily from Lisbon to Faro. TAP's office in Faro is at 8 Rua Dom Francisco Gomes, ✆ (808) 205 700; or, at the airport, ✆ (289) 800 731.

By Rail

Travelling by train is inexpensive, cheaper than travelling by bus, and generally the routes are more picturesque, though connections are sparser. A railway line stretches from Lagos to Vila Real de Santo António, a 4–4½hr trip serviced by frequent trains; note that some trains do not stop at the smaller stations. Portugal's trains are nationalized, and are operated by **CP** (*Caminhos de Ferro Portugueses*), *www.cp.pt.*

Train **timetables** are generally available, and are usually posted on station walls. If you plan to travel a lot by train, it's worth asking in the main stations for a copy of CP's official timetable (*Guia Horário Oficial*), which costs 600$00 and gives full details of routes and schedules throughout the country. Alternatively, the *Thomas Cook European Timetable*, published monthly, covers the main services. In the UK this can be purchased from any Thomas Cook Travel Shop and good bookshops.

Tickets must be purchased at the railway station in advance, rather than on the train—otherwise you are liable to be fined. Allow time to queue for buying a ticket.

discount tickets

The Algarve is so small, and train connections so much sparser than bus routes, that it's not really worth buying season or discount tickets; however, various discount schemes are available from major railway stations. CP sell *Bilhetes Turísticos* (railcards for tourists) valid for 7, 14 or 21 days. Travellers over the age of 60 are entitled to 30 per cent off the full fare, on production of their passport or other ID proving their age. Families are eligible for the *Cartão de Família*, which entitles a married couple and at least one of their children under the age of 18 to discount travel. Young people aged 12–26 are eligible for the *Cartão Jovem*, which allows 50 per cent discounts on journeys over 50km during limited periods. Children under 4 travel free if they do not occupy a seat, and from 4 to 12 pay half-fare.

Mainline rail travel is always less expensive on 'Blue Days': Monday afternoons to Friday mornings (excluding national holidays and the previous day to a national holiday), Saturdays and Sunday mornings.

By Bus

Buses are a quick and painless way to get around the province. Tickets are cheaper than in northern Europe. There are now two private bus companies operating in the Algarve, Rede Expressos and EVA, although EVA is the main company on all routes. EVA runs a twice-daily Alta Qualidade service, complete with stewardess, drinks and video, from Lisbon stopping at Albufeira, Vilamoura, Quarteira, Almansil and Faro (4½hrs).

For **Express travel**, check that you're standing in the correct line before queueing to buy your ticket at the bus station. Most Express buses depart from a (fume-laden) central depot. On longer journeys, buses stop for a coffee break every couple of hours. Ask at a travel agent for more details of services.

For **local buses**, buy your ticket on board. If you travel in the early morning or mid-afternoon you'll probably have to scramble for a seat with the children who travel to and from school on local buses (some local bus timetables are devised especially to suit school-children, so if you want to get somewhere out-of-the-way, those are the best times to try). In a way, travelling by public transport is simpler here than in other provinces because the bus and train stations are accustomed to baffled foreigners, and make allowances.

By Car

The charms of the Algarve are best appreciated by car, though you pay for the increased convenience of travel: **petrol** costs around 165$00 per litre for super or unleaded. Street **parking** is usually no problem, other than in the major towns and resorts.

The Algarve's **road network** is improving rapidly but there is still work to be done. All secondary roads are excellent; others are riddled with potholes (not to mention flocks of sheep and figs laid out to dry). In spring, delightful roadside flowers are sufficient compensation for the slowest of roads. Allow plenty of time when travelling inland, because although traffic is rarely heavy, some roads—particularly in Monchique and parts of the Barrocal—are almost entirely composed of hairpin bends. The bridge/border crossing between Ayamonte in Spain and Vila Real de Santo António is now open constantly. The 'Via do Infante' motorway runs just west of Albufeira, following a route 2–10km inland, with feeder roads to the coast. It will eventually continue to Sagres, and then to Lisbon via the Alentejo coast. Feeder roads branch out from there.

Beware Portuguese drivers. Portugal has one of the highest accident rates in Europe (most accidents occur on the Lisbon–Algarve highway, or the EN125). Few people think twice before drinking and driving; most show a general disregard for basic rules of the road, often choosing to overtake on blind bends.

Foreign-registered cars may enter Portugal for up to 6 months if accompanied by a registration document (log book) and a green card proving limited liability insurance. British and international driving licences are valid; the latter are available through the AA, RAC, or any auto club in the USA.

Portugal uses the international road sign system. Drive on the right and overtake on the left; give way to cars approaching from the right. Seatbelts are obligatory outside built-up areas in the front and back of the car. **Speed limits** for cars are: 60kph (37mph) in built-up areas; 90kph (55mph) outside built-up areas; 120kph (75mph) on motorways. There are no toll roads in the Algarve. For more information, contact the Automóvel Clube de Portugal, 24 Rua Rosa Araújo, Lisbon, ✆ (219) 425 095.

Hitch-hiking is demoralizing because few of the many motorists stop, as most are tourists and already on unfamiliar ground.

car hire

Car hire is cheap by European standards. In Faro, all the major firms are represented at the airport. In the UK, **Holiday Cars Direct**, ✆ (01892) 833 366, and generally have good rates, franchising out to local companies. They are always flexible about changing drop-off dates and destinations, not imposing an extra charge for picking up and dropping off at different places. You could also try **Holiday Autos**, ✆ (0990) 300 400. The minimum age for hiring a car is usually 23, and customers must have held a full driving licence for one year.

By Taxi

Taxis are black, with greeny-turquoise roofs. Most are metered; there is no official rate. As an example, the average fare from Faro airport to the town, 6km away, is 1,400$00 (excluding luggage). It is difficult to hail a cab from the street; you're much better off going to a taxi rank, or phoning for a radio taxi.

Practical A–Z

Beaches

The Algarve is a distinct geographical region, shaped like a huge amphitheatre on the sea at the extreme southwest edge of Europe. The region is about 155km long and 50km deep with the Atlantic bounding it in the south and west and low mountain ranges separating it from the rest of Portugal in the north. The River Guadiana forms the boundary with Spain in the east. The population of 350,000 is concentrated along the south coast.

The coast changes geological character just west of Faro, with the eastern half, the *sotavento* (leeward) strip, comprising long sandy strands sheltered by spits, sand bar islands and lagoons, with calmer and warmer waters. The western part, the *barlavento* (windward), between Faro and Sagres, is a more varied coastline with ochre cliffs, fantastical rock formations, and grottoes, and beefier waves. From Sagres northwards up the west coast, the cliffs soar to 60m and turn an impressive shade of slate-black; the sea is colder and choppier, sometimes dangerous, and many beaches are almost deserted. Don't swim where flags warn you not to, and always be aware of the undertow.

Climate and When to Go

The Algarve is blessed with a combination of Atlantic and Mediterranean climates, with hot summers that never get unbearable—rarely above 30-odd °C—and delightfully mild winters that never plunge much below 10°C. You can reckon on an average of 300 sunny days per year, and in summer expect a minimum of 12½hrs of sunshine each day (wearing a hat staves off headaches, and remember to bring an effective sunscreen or sunblock for yourself and the children). It rains occasionally, though almost never in summer and always less than the crops would like. A light northwesterly wind takes the edge off the heat, and the wooded mountains of Monchique offer a refreshing alternative to the coast and other inland areas. Spring and autumn are the best times to visit the Algarve; if you can, aim for April or early May when the warm and sunny weather coincides with the wild roadside flowers and hotels' winter rates. The closest the Algarve gets to snow is in February or March, when 'Algarvian snow' arrives in the shape of almond blossoms that cover the region in a white canopy of flowers, shedding a carpet of blooms.

The table below gives the average conditions which may be encountered during the year.

	air temp °C	sea temp °C	dry days per month	sunshine per day (hrs)
Jan	15	14	22	6
April	21	17	24	9
July	35	22	31	13
Oct	23	20	25	8

Disabled Travellers

There are few special facilities for disabled travellers, though the Portuguese will always rush to aid anyone who has trouble getting around. There are parking spaces reserved for disabled people in the main cities, and adapted WCs and wheelchair facilities at the airport and main train stations. The Portuguese National Tourist Office produces some literature for disabled travellers, including a list of hotels with facilities. In Britain, contact **RADAR** (**Royal Association for Disability and Rehabilitation**) at 12 City Forum, 250 City Road, London EC1V 8AF, ✆ (020) 7250 3222. They publish *Holidays and Travel Abroad: A Guide For Disabled People* at £5. In the USA, **Mobility International** can be contacted at PO Box 10767, Eugene, OR 97440, ✆ (503) 343 1284, *www.miusa.org*. Also in the USA is **SATH** (**Society for the Advancement of Travel for the Handicapped**) at 347 Fifth Ave, Suite 610, New York, NY 10016, ✆ 212 447 7284, *www.sath.org*.

In Portugal itself, useful associations are: the **Portuguese Handicapped Persons Association**, Largo do Rato, 1250 Lisbon, ✆ 1 388 9883; **ACAPO** (**Association of the Blind and Partially Sighted of Portugal**), 1st Floor, 86 Rua de José, 15000 Lisbon, ✆ 1 342 2001; **Centro Nacional de Reabilitação**, Avda Conde Valbom 63, 1000 Lisbon, ✆ 1 793 6517; **Portuguese Association of the Deaf**, Avda Liberdade 157, 1250 Lisbon, ✆ 1 355 7244. Try also David Player's organization, **Wheeling Around the Algarve**, Rua 5 de Outoubro 181, Apartado 3421, ✆ 289 393 636, which inspects holiday accommodation, transport and leisure facilities before making its recommendations.

Electricity

The current is 220V, 50Hz, which takes a continental two-pin plug. Some fancy hotels have adaptors—otherwise, bring your own.

Embassies and Consulates

embassies

UK: 33 Rua São Bernardo, Lisbon, ✆ 213 961 191.
USA: Avenida das Forças Armadas, Lisbon, ✆ 217 273 300.
Canada: 144 Avenida da Liberdade, 3rd Floor, Lisbon, ✆ 213 474 892.

consulates

UK: 7 Largo Francisco A. Maurício, Portimão, ✆ 282 417 800.
Ireland: 1 Rua da Imprensa à Estrela, 4th Floor, Lisbon, ✆ 213 929 440.
Canada: 1 Rua Frei Lourenço de Santa Maria, 1st Floor, PO Box 79, Faro, ✆ 289 803 757.

Entertainment and Nightlife

Films are cheap (800$00 or under) and are never dubbed. Foreign films are released at the same time as in their native country. All performances have a 10-minute interval, during which 90 per cent of the audience lights up a cigarette. Remember to tip the usherette (20$00). If it's **Portuguese cinema** you're after, watch out for the films of Manuel de Oliveira, João Botelho and Paulo Rocha.

Nightlife is full and energetic, especially in the tourist areas around Albufeira, Vilamoura and Lagos. Most discos are open from around 11 to about 5 or 6 in the morning, though in the summer most establishments are allowed to add an extra hour to their usual closing times. Some places charge an admission fee, with which you'll get a drink or two for free, but there are so many special offers around in the summer that it's unlikely you'll ever have to pay. Aside from these, all bars are open to about 2am, some till 4, and all play their own favoured brand of music, often loudly.

If they're going to gamble, most Portuguese gamble on the lottery, but there are three **casinos** in Monte Gordo (*see* p.77), Vilamoura (*see* p.92) and Praia da Rocha (*see* p.109). You need to be over 21 and to take your passport with you. Ask at the local tourist office for details of **concerts**, which increase in frequency in the summer months when the Algarve music festival stages a series of recitals, operas and ballets in a variety of venues all around the region.

Festivals

The Algarvians aren't as big on festivals as their compatriates, perhaps because the coastal resorts have elbowed out traditional Catholicism, or because the summer season already feels like a four-month party so there's no need for an excuse to celebrate. Things are different inland: almost every weekend in the summer there will be a *baile* in most towns and large villages. These family celebrations are held in honour of various saints. For a small fee, you'll be served a dinner of chicken and snails. Afterwards everyone dances to traditional bands; energetic teenagers sweep up granny and twirl her until she's quite giddy. Tourists are rare at these splendid occasions.

Enquire at a tourist office for the exact dates of festivals, which vary from year to year, or pick up a monthl;y guide detailing sporting events, music and festivals.

February	Loulé	Carnival (the long weekend before Lent)
spring	Silves	Orange festival
May–July	Region-wide	The Algarve classical music festival
Easter	Loulé	Procession of Senhora da Piedade
May	Portimão	Algarve film festival (nothing like Cannes)
1st May	Alte	May Day folk celebrations ending with a celebration of water
July	Silves	Week-long beer festival
July	Loulé	International jazz festival
August	Lagoa	*Fatacil*, the region's biggest trade, handicrafts and agricultural fair
August	Olhão	Seafood festival
September	Praia da Rocha	Final venue of the Algarve folk music and dance festival

Food and Drink

Eating Out

The early 18th-century traveller Mrs Marianne Baillie noted that 'the courtly whisper of the highest bred *fidalgo*, loaded with garlic and oil, differed not at all from the breath of the humblest peasant'. Today garlic makes only muted appearances, and Portuguese cooking is not particularly oily, but the gist of her observation holds true: tastes are remarkably democratic, and the best food in Portugal is peasant fare. Fancy restaurants may have extensive wine lists, but for a good meal you'd be better off at an upmarket *tasca* (tavern) or a **restaurante típico** (*see* 'Salir', p.86, for the meaning of '*típico*'). If in doubt, eat where the locals eat and choose the *prato do dia* (dish of the day).

You don't have to be cutting your second set of teeth to ask for a half-portion; helpings tend to be enormous. All restaurants are obliged by law to provide a **set menu**, called an *ementa turística*. This consists of the cover (*see* below), three courses, bread, olives and a drink and is usually pretty good value. In most restaurants the *ementa turística* is a mixture of the simplest dishes possible—vegetable soup, hake or pork fillets or sardines or roast chicken, and ice-cream or *flan* (crème caramel)—but you will often be surprised by the choices offered. Where the *ementa turística* is especially good value or particularly delicious, it has been mentioned in the appropriate restaurant review.

In most budget and average-price establishments the **couvert** (cover) generally comprises chewy white bread, a plastic tub of butter, a plastic tub of sardine paste, and some fairly tasteless dried-out olives. It is often plonked on the table as a *fait accompli*. If you don't want it, either refuse it when the waiter brings it or just push it to one side and make sure it does not appear on the bill. In some of the better restaurants the *couvert* can be a delightful medley of home-made sardine dip, crudités, fresh-baked bread, marinated herbed olives, a small round of delicious cheese and so on.

Dom Duarte (1433–8) advised his subjects to have an interval of 8 hours between their main meals, and his suggestion has been heeded, more or less. Breakfast is usually a cup of coffee with a bread roll and butter, followed by another cup of coffee in the middle of the morning. Lunch begins at about 12.30, and lasts until 2 or 2.30. After a mid-afternoon cup of coffee or tea, dinner gets under way at around 8.

Restaurant price categories: average main course for one person, no wine	
expensive	over 1,600$00
moderate	1,000$00–1,600$00
cheap	under 1,000$00

Portuguese Food

Most Portuguese food is simple and heavy; it's well worth seeking out the more complicated dishes, as these are often the richest and most tasty (particularly the bean stews and the coastal fish stews). Regional dishes are the closest you're likely to get to Portuguese home cooking; the best-known are detailed below. Vegetables often find their way into soups, but rarely into side dishes or salads, and the selection is limited. Spices are little used, which is surprising given Portugal's role in the 16th-century spice trade. Vegetarians may strike it lucky in urban areas, but veggie-consciousness has a long way to go. Vegans will find eating anything more nutritious than salads almost impossible.

Algarvian meals invariably kick off with a thick vegetable or fish and pasta **soup**. Sometimes inland you find *canja de galinha*, a rice and chicken broth which precedes simple meals. Algarvian *gaspacho* differs from its Spanish cousin in that the ingredients are diced rather than puréed, leaving the soup pleasantly crunchy. The only other soup you're likely to come across is *caldo verde*, a shredded cabbage soup with potatoes and the ubiquitous *chouriço* (spicy sausage) imported from the north of Portugal. The Alentejan *açorda de mariscos* is a bread-based broth full of delicious seafood, garlic, herbs and a couple of fried eggs; it sometimes makes an appearance on Algarvian menus.

Superb fresh **fish** is the joy of Algarvian cooking, and in the country as a whole fish and shellfish account for 40% of the protein intake. The emphasis on sardines (*sardinhas*) and tuna (*atum*), each utterly different in taste and texture from their tinned brothers and sisters. Sardines are charcoal-grilled with chunks of sea salt, and are at their best in the summer months when they are fat enough (*see* p.105). Tuna is normally served grilled in thick, firm steaks, with a sauce of butter, tomato and onion. With most fish you will be given separate flasks of oil and vinegar, but feel free to ask for a squeeze of lemon.

Clams (*amêijoas*) and cockles (*conquilhas*) are popular, perhaps cooked with smoked pork sausage, cured ham, tomatoes and onions in a *cataplana* (a sealed wok-like vessel used for steaming food, *see* p.74). Several different types of fish and crustacean are used to make *xarém*, a kind of maize mash with garlic and parsley—very filling. One of the most enjoyable fish dishes is the *caldeirada*, a stew of mixed fush and potatoes, often iincluding the succulent white meat of the monkfish (*tamboril*) and some shellfish too. A mixture of seafood makes *arroz de mariscos*, a big pot of rice, tomatoes and herbs—unbeatable when cooked to perfection. Keep an eye out for *Lulas recheadas*, squid stuffed with a mixture of rice, herbs and pork. It's uncommon, but worth seeking out. barnacles (*perceves*) are a delicacy worth trying if you have the chance. They're more common on the wqest coast. try not to be put off by their monstrous appearance, but twist off the shells to reveal chewy pink flesh that tastes like a fusion of squid and mussels.

With such a large variety of fish and seafood available, Algarvian menus frequently disagree on the English names. *See* **Language**, pp.186–8, for the definitive guide to help you get round confusing translations.

Another regional speciality is the delicious **white bean stews** (*feijoada*) cooked with a variety of seafood, bacon and sausages. In the Algarve they favour *feijoada com polvo* (with octopus) or *búzios* (whelks), though you may see *feijoada à trasmontana* on some menus: this is the northern version and is best enjoyed with eyes shut—the recipe calls for the ear, snout and trotters of a pig. The northern province of Trás-os-Montes is also responsible for *cozido à portuguesa*, a boiled medley of blood, spiced and pork sausages, ribs, pigs' ears, kale, carrots and potatoes.

Meat is excellent, particularly inland. In 1726 Brockwell wrote that Portuguese pork was the most delicious in Europe: 'their swine are small, short-legged, and generally black, their Bellies oft reaching to the Ground.' The kid is a treat too—it's especially flavourful braised with onions, tomatoes and herbs; *cabrito estufado* is a regional speciality. Inland, you'll also find **hare and partridge** served during the hunting season; *coelho assado* is rabbit roasted with onions, white wine and spices. *Espetada mista* is beef, lamb and pork cubes served on a skewer, often attached to gallows-like metal bars that grip the side of your table. One famous inland dish, imported from Portugal's former colony of Mozambique, is chicken *piri-piri*, chicken grilled and served with the popular hot chilli sauce (*see* p.118); for those fond of spices, *piri-piri* sauce can soon become addictive.

For **snacks**, the Portuguese favour the *prego* (steak sandwich), *bifana* (pork steak sandwich) *rissóis* (deep-fried envelopes of meat or seafood, sometimes lightly curried), or *pastéis de bacalhau* (codfish croquettes).

It's an understatement to say that the Portuguese have a sweet tooth; they have a mouthful of sweet teeth. This may be one of the Moors' most persistent legacies, and has been kindled over the centuries by the kitchens of numerous convents—the nuns used to sell **confections** to supplement their income. Hence some of the more picturesque names: *barriga de freira* (nun's belly) or *papos de anjo* (angel's breasts). All are made from egg yolks, sugar and little else. *Pastéis de nata* (custard tarts), *pão-de-ló* (sponge cake) and *bolos de mel* (honey cakes) are some of the most enjoyable. The marzipan sweets of the Algarve, shaped like fruits and filled with sugared egg yolk, may have Moorish origins, since they resemble those sold in North Africa. If you do crave some of these dental nightmares you will have to go to a *pastelaria* or a café, rather than a restaurant. When it comes to restaurant **desserts** the choice is usually limited to *flan* (crème caramel), ice-cream or fresh fruit salad. More enterprising establishments may also offer local specialities such as *tarte de amendoa* (almond tart), *tarte de natas* (a creamy cake dessert) or *quiejo de figo* (layers of dried figs, ground almonds, cinammon and chocolate). Figs and almonds are variously combined to make other delicious sweets and desserts. The Moors introduced citrus fruits to the Peninsula; the oranges of the Algarve are the succulent, juicy navel variety.

bacalhau

It seems perverse that a people whose shores are favoured by so many fish should adopt *bacalhau* as their national dish. This dried, salted codfish looks like ossified grey cardboard, and is cut with a saw before being soaked and cooked in one of (a reputed) 365 different ways. The first official *bacalhau* fleet set sail during the reign of Dom João I (1385–1433), and subsequent fleets made around 150 voyages to Newfoundland during the reign of Dom Manuel (1495–1521); now *bacalhau* is imported from Norway and Iceland.

We unfortunate foreigners are often incapable of appreciating the delights of *bacalhau*; it's only palatable when heavily disguised, as in *bacalhau à bras*, whipped up with cream, shrimps, mushrooms, eggs and potatoes.

Drink

The Portuguese drink a great deal of alcohol, but very rarely get drunk. **Wine** is extremely cheap—from around 150$00 per litre in the supermarket—and makes a highly enjoyable communion with Portugal. Locally produced wine is regarded as therapeutic, so you may opt for the *vinho da casa* (house wine)—in some restaurants this might arrive in a pottery jug. However, if you want quality it is always worth paying a little more.

Vines flourished in the south of Portugal under the Moors. Today, the Algarve is a 'demarcated region', with the major wine-producing towns being Tavira, Lagos and Lagoa, but the wines are undistinguished. All but 3 per cent are reds, with a hefty 13° of alcohol stemming from the grapes' high sugar content. It's acceptable to drink the reds diluted with sparkling water or lemonade as the locals do, but there won't be any need with quality wines labelled *reserva* or *garrafeira*. *Vinho verde* is one of the delights of Portugal, produced only in the Minho region in the north. The 'verde' refers to the young age at which the wine is drunk. It's light and pétillant, with a slight acidity balanced by its fruitiness. Stick to the whites, and drink it very cool as an aperitif or with shellfish or grilled fish.

It's certainly worth trying the Algarvian dry white apéritif wine, matured in wood and similar to an amontillado. Meals can be chased down with *aguardente*, at its best a brandy-like spirit distilled from wine; clear *bagaceira*, a throat-burning firewater distilled from the leftovers of pressed grapes; *figo*, made from figs; or the cough-syrupy *licor beirão*, made from aromatic plants. The fiery but flavourful *medronho* is distilled from arbutus berries in the Monchique hills (*see* **To Portimão and Monchique**, p.113). *Brandymel* is a sweet brandy flavoured with honey, and *amêndoa armaga* is flavoured with almonds. To take the edge off the sweetness, ask for a few drops of lemon to be squeezed on top.

The nice thing about drinking **port** in Portugal is that you can leave behind its crustier connotations, whiskers and all. Good port is like a liquid symphony playing upon the palate; anyone who thinks of it as a dark and sticky drink to send you to sleep after Christmas lunch is in for a surprise. All port is grown, harvested and made in the north of Portugal, around Oporto and the Douro valley. It's widely available in the Algarve as white, red or tawny wines. Red and ruby ports are young and sweet; the tawny are older and less sweet while the white ports are good apéritifs. Vintage port is the product of a single harvest of outstanding quality and LBV (late bottled vintage) ports stand in oak casks for up to six years before bottling.

All **shots** are at least double the volume of their British equivalents.

As for **beer** (*cerveja*), you'll see *Sagres* all over the place; it's brewed in Lisbon and has the cleanest taste. Keep an eye out for blue-labelled *Super Bock*, and creamy, dark brown *Sagres Preta*. A small draft measure is called an *imperial* and a large one, just under a pint, is a *caneca*.

Tea (*chá*) is drunk rarely, and then black, by the Portuguese. This is somewhat surprising since they introduced 'tea time' to Britain; Catherine of Bragança popularized the drinking of tea and the ritual of tea parties to keep an eye on her ladies-in-waiting—her husband was the philandering Charles II. The Portuguese are hooked on **coffee**, their preferred fix being a *bica* (espresso) taken with sugar and often a shot of brandy. Walk into any railway café early in the morning and watch manic workers line up at the counter for the first *bica* of the day, gulped down in one, always with a cigarette. A long glass of milky coffee (latte) is called a *galão*, and a normal cup of coffee with milk is *um café com leite*, or try a *bica pingada*, a *bica* with just a dash of milk (espresso macchiato).

With so many spas, Portugal produces a flood of **bottled waters**: chalky Carvalhelhos is particularly distinctive. The waters of Monchique and Luso are especially good. Fresh **orange juice** is easy to get in most bars and cafés along the coast. The rapid development of the Algarve has put great strains on the water supply; it's best not to drink tap water in the summer months, when water levels run low. Delicious bottled water is always available.

Golf

'Algarve, Land of Golf', screams the tourist office's brochure with some justification. Half of mainland Portugal's 45 golf courses are in the Algarve. It makes perfect sense: the weather is beautiful throughout the year, and good locations are plentiful.

The golfing high season runs from October and April, helping the local economy to tick over outside the summer months. Despite the wealth of golfing facilities, the Portuguese have never produced a disinguished golfer of international ranking, possibly because the green fees are prohibitive for locals and it is difficult to gain a toehold as a caddy, as most of the clubs don't supply them.

You can play until nightfall at all courses, with the last tee-off about two hours prior. All the courses are open to all comers as long as you hold the maximum handicap or under— 28 for men and 36 for women—though in the busier months many clubs quietly give preference to lower handicaps. The usual maximum time allowed per course is 4½ hours and all clubs advise booking at least a couple of days in advance to be assured of your desired tee-off time. This is imperative in high season and some clubs, if given prior warning, will try to arrange a caddy.

Prices vary wildly. They start at around 4,500$00 (at Vale de Milho) soaring to over 24,000$00 at San Lorenzo. There aren't many courses where you can play 18 holes for under 10,000$00. However, with so much competition there are usually special offers available, particularly at quieter times of the tourist season. Some clubs also offer special twilight-hour prices after a certain time. If you intend playing more than a couple of rounds you should think about a package; many of the mainstream tour operators include this in their ordinary brochure. Several of the more expensive hotels offers discounts on green fees at local clubs and other golfing privileges, such as reserved tee-off times. *See* the table on p.20 for a complete comparative list of prices on the Algarve's courses.

Do pick up a copy of the excellent free newspaper *Algarve Golf Guide*, which lists all the Algarve courses, gives pros' playing tips, the latest course developments and lots of other information. Local tourist offices should have a copy. The Portuguese National Tourist Office in London (*see* p.27) also holds a lot of information. Here is a run-down of the facilities at all the major courses; *see* also the map on the inside back cover of this guide.

Alto Golf, Quinta do Alto do Poço, Alvor, forms part of the Alto Club tourist development but is open to all. The last course designed by Sir Henry Cotton, it is near the sea with the purple mountains of Monchique stretching across the horizon. The front nine holes have good views over the Bay of Lagos while the back nine include the longest par 5 in Europe, at 604 metres. The convivial restaurant and bar are on the 18th green.

In 2000, **Benamor** became the first golf course to open in the Algarve east of Faro. Situated opposite the EN125 turn-off to Cabanas, this 18-hole course enjoys views both to the ocean and to the striking hills and fertile valleys of Tavira's hinterland. It is challenging, particularly the par-3 8th hole and the last hole, but not as daunting as many of the more famous courses to the west, and is described by the pros as 'user-friendly'.

Carvoeiro Pestana Golf Club offers two 18-hole courses: the Gramacho and Pinta. The Gramacho is a double-nine layout but has one set of greens for the first round and a different set for the second. The par 71 Pinta course is laid out around glades of almond, fig and olive trees. Both Gramacho and Pinta offer special twilight-hour prices when visitors are allowed to play as much as they can (before the light fails completely!) from 4.30pm onwards for 3,800$00.

The 18-hole **Palmares** golf course, Monte Palmares, is situated near Meia Praia with five holes almost on the beach and with views over the bodies on the beach, the Bay of Lagos, and the Monchique mountains in the background. In February and March the course is canopied by snow-white almond blossoms, which flutter on to golfers and make them feel positively bridal.

The **Parque da Floresta** course is 16km west of Lagos, near Budens in the hills above Salema. This most westerly course in the Algarve offers some dramatic landscape: the first hole demands an accurate shot over a chasm and the club boasts a 577-yard 9th hole. The par-3 11th is stunning with the green overhanging a lake. No handicap is necessary.

Five kilometres west of Portimão lies the famous **Penina Golf Club**, Montes de Alvor. It is a landmark in the development of golf in the Algarve, being the first course designed by the sculptor of Algarve golf courses, Sir Henry Cotton. The 36 holes of the two main courses are spread over sloping and carefully landscaped and wooded grounds, with views of Monchique. The course has been upgraded in recent years and hosted the Portuguese Open in 1998 and 1999.

Pinheiros Altos, Quinta do Lago, has an unusual layout over 250 acres of pine woods. It combines two nine-hole loops of very different character. The first nine are backed by pines and orange groves—the par-3 5th provides panoramic views. The second nine holes are set against the marshy lakes and lagoons of the Ria Formosa nature reserve; a relentless splash of balls landing in water can be heard above the fluttering of birds' feathers. Should you despair of your abilities, there is a golfing academy and practice tee. They also have a video playback facility—after viewing, retreat to the bar to come to terms with your game.

Quinta do Lago offers 36 holes divided into four nine-hole loops, all demanding great skill and precision to avoid the lakes and bunkers. The course covers some 600 acres of the Quinta do Lago estate and is proud of the international acclaim it receives for its design and maintenance, which is regularly confirmed by the number of tournaments held here. The Portuguese Open has graced the course on seven occasions and many pro/am contests ensure an annual sprinkling of British celebrities; much-aired one-liners seem to hover over each hole. There is a posh restaurant and a separate pizzeria.

The links-style 18-hole **Salgados** course was opened in 1994, located between Pêra and Albufeira, near the long Galé beach. The first nine holes travel anti-clockwise and end close to the friendly clubhouse. The back nine holes all have water hazards, with the exception of the par-3 17th, and migratory birds are already adapting to the brackish water lakes.

The championship **San Lorenzo** course, Quinta do Lago, is frequently ranked among the top five courses in Europe. The 18-hole par-72 course is set against some great views: the water-edged par-4 6th hole borders the Ria Formosa reserve, and the 11th has views of distant mountains. Play is straightforward until the 16th hole where things get hairy with the green besieged by bunkers. The par-4 17th takes you over water and the 18th hole has the biggest challenge: the green is on an island. Staff claim the course is 'hard but fair'.

Sheraton Pine Cliffs, Praia da Falésia, has probably the most spectacular nine holes you can play in southern Europe. Set on the amber cliffs overlooking the long beach, the undulating course demands accuracy from players tackling its narrow, tree-lined fairways; the ever-present Atlantic winds are a force to contend with. The course belongs to the Sheraton hotel, whose guests can play at a discount price.

Vale de Milho, a couple of kilometres east of Carvoeiro, is a small nine-hole par-3 course, nestling amongst villas. As no handicap is necessary, this is a good course for novices or for more experienced players as a way of sharpening up their short game (holes range from 60 metres to 164 metres). Vale de Milho claims to be the best-value golf in the Algarve and is certainly one of the cheapest courses: 3,250$00 for nine holes, 5,000$00 for 18 holes, and widely available 10–15% discount coupons reduce this further. It has the same characteristics as a full-size course and an advanced coaching system using the video playback facility, which will either improve your game or reduce you to an uncoordinated mess. Maximum time allowed to complete the course is 1½ hours.

Vale do Lobo was originally designed by the great Sir Henry Cotton, to include 27 holes. It was enlarged in 1997 and now comprises two 18-hole courses. The courses are peaceful and splendid, with the ocean always in sight and the beach tempting away uncommitted golfers. The par-3 7th hole is one of the most photographed in Europe; the green lies 220m from the tee across two deep ravines gashed to reveal ochre rocks. Good directional play is needed throughout the course as all the fairways are tight and demand concentration.

Vilamoura has four golf courses, the newest of which is the nine-hole **Millennium** course which opened to the public in June 2000. The other courses (all 18-holes), formerly known as I, II and III, have all been recently revamped and re-named, The Old Course, Pinhal and Laguna respectively. The **Old Course** is a classic of course design, built in 1969 by Frank Pennink. It has tight fairways, lots of character and is one of the most respected courses in the Algarve. All the par-3s are difficult with the most memorable being the 4th; the green and tee are elevated, with a small lake and lone umbrella pine acting as hazards in between. Brain not brawn is the key to this one! **Pinhal**, like the Old

Course, is distinguished by its umbrella-pine-lined fairways. The first nine meander through a residential complex; the back nine are built on more open, undulating land with occasional glimpses of the sea. Beware: the very first hole is a tricky par 5 with the initial drive 'blind'. Not recommended if you are the nervous type. **Laguna**, as its name suggests, is devoid of pines, largely flat, with *lagunas* (lakes) to swallow stray shots.

The **Vila Sol Club**, Alto do Semino, was chosen as the venue for the Portuguese Open a few months after opening in 1991, and in 1996 received a special Green Flag award for its high standard of environmental management. The 18-hole course makes good use of the naturally undulating countryside, with the first nine holes weaving around pine, cork and fig trees. The second nine-hole loop is spread over a valley of umbrella pines and affords good views. The first four holes are, according to experienced golfers, the most daunting. As well as the usual facilities, the clubhouse offers Turkish baths.

Golf Courses in the Algarve: Prices and Contact Details

All prices below are for public rates for 18 holes unless otherwise stated.

Alto Golf, Alvor, ✆ 282 401 047	9,950$00
Benamor, near Cabanas, ✆ 281 320 880	9,000$00
Carvoeiro Club (Pinta and Gramacho), Carvoeiro, ✆ 282 340 900	6,500–9,000$00
Palmares Golf, Lagos, ✆ 282 762 953	7,500–10,000$00
Parque da Floresta, Budens, ✆ 282 690 054	10,000$00
Sheraton Pine Cliffs Golf (9 holes), Falésia, ✆ 289 500 100	8,000$00
Pinheiros Altos, Quinta do Lago, ✆ 289 359 910	10,000$00
Penina Golf, Alvor, ✆ 282 420 200	Championship Course 7,500–10,000$00 Resort Course (9 holes) 4–6,000$00 Academy Course (9 holes) 3–5,000$00
Quinta do Lago Golf, ✆ 289 390 700	10,000$00
San Lorenzo, Quinta do Lago, ✆ 289 396 522	24,500$00
Salgados Golf, Praia da Galé, ✆ 289 591 111	10,000$00
Vale do Lobo Golf, ✆ 289 39 39 39	Ocean Course 15,000$00 Royal Course 20,000$00
Vale de Milho, Carvoeiro, ✆ 282 358 502	3,100$00 for 9 holes 4,500$00 for 18 holes
Vilamoura Old Course, ✆ 289 310 341	19,000$00
Vilamoura Pinhal, ✆ 289 310 390	12,000$00
Vilamoura Laguna, ✆ 289 310 180	11,000$00
Vilamousa Millennium, ✆ 289 310 341	18,000$00
Vila Sol Club, Quarteira, ✆ 289 300 505	11,000$00

Health and Emergencies

A fair proportion of doctors speak English, because they have been trained abroad. The Algarve's hospitals and local health centres are detailed in the text. Pharmacies (*farmácias*) are open Monday to Friday from some time after 9 until 1 and 3–7, if you're lucky, plus Saturday mornings. Keep all medical and pharmacy receipts. Dial ✆ 112 for an **ambulance**. The British Consulate in Portimão, ✆ 282 417 800, can provide numbers of English doctors and dentists.

Crime

The vast majority of foreign visitors to the Algarve will come and go without a hitch. The further you are from other foreigners, the less likely you are to get hustled. In the main resorts the appearance of recreational drugs has occasioned an increase in theft, so watch out for pick-pocketing, theft from parked cars, and dodgy property deals. Should you for any reason feel the long arm of the law, contact the appropriate embassy or consulate immediately (*see* p.11).

To call the **police** (and/or ambulance) in an emergency, dial ✆ 112.

Insurance

No vaccinations are required for visitors to Portugal from Britain, Ireland, the USA or Canada (though if you are coming from somewhere with a cholera or smallpox epidemic you must have an International Certificate of Vaccination).

Portugal has a reciprocal health agreement with Britain; fill in form E111 and get it stamped at a post office. This entitles you to free emergency medical treatment while visiting Portugal, on production of it and your passport. Some charges are made for prescribed medicines and dental treatment. The British National Health Service will not reimburse medical expenses. Travel insurance is advisable for everyone.

Maps and Publications

The tourist offices' most useful hand-outs are their town plans. These vary from illegible photocopies to glossy productions the size of a desktop.

The Automóvel Clube de Portugal produces the best road maps; one side represents the whole country, while the reverse depicts the north, centre or south of Portugal in fine detail. Both Michelin and Lascelles produce acceptable maps, should you wish to buy one in advance. Hildebrand's Travel Maps' *Algarve 1:100,000* provides good detail.

Media

Newspapers

The Portuguese are not great newspaper-readers, and yet there are ten major national weeklies—of which only a few can scrape together a circulation of more than 100,000. This situation has its roots in Salazar's dictatorship, when the Press was heavily censored.

When the Revolution came, the newspapers were filled with turgid revolutionary propaganda. Thus were the most stalwart of readers turned off their daily or weekly paper.

Before the Revolution of 1974, most newspapers were owned by banks. When the banks were nationalized, the newspapers were tagged on too—which explains the high proportion of state-owned publications. These state-owned newspapers include some of the most prestigious, among them the long-established Lisbon daily *Diário de Notícias*, which is noted for its editorial independence. Independent *Expresso* is the leading privately owned weekly, while the highest circulation goes to *Correio da Manhã*, a tittle-tattle tabloid.

Major British newspapers and the *International Herald Tribune* are available in all resorts and large towns. They arrive in Lisbon the day after publication, and take a while to be distributed from there. *Newsweek* and the European edition of *Time* arrive in Portugal a couple of days after publication. English publications produced for the British community are *The Entertainer*, free, and *The Algarve Resident*, both published weekly.

Television

Go into any bar or cheap eating place in the evening and the patrons are bound to be transfixed in front of a soap opera or a football match. There are 6½ million peak-time viewers in a population of 10 million. The two oldest TV channels are both state-run and state-funded. They are not as independent as the state-owned newspapers, so the private channels were a welcome addition when they arrived a few years ago. Satellite dishes are not uncommon around the main towns.

Radio

For 13 years the Roman Catholic Church had the only non-state radio station, Radio Renascença. In 1988 this stranglehold was broken, and dozens of new private local stations have appeared, all sharing, it seems, the same playlist. KissFM on 101.2 FM broadcasts some programmes in English.

Money

The unit of Portuguese currency is the *escudo*, made up of 100 *centavos*. A '$' sign is placed between the *escudos* to the left and the *centavos* to the right. Portuguese currency circulates in notes of 10,000$00, 5,000$00, 2,000$00, 1,000$00 and 500$00. Coins are issued for 200$00, 100$00, 50$00, 25$00, 20$00, 10$00, 5$00, 2$50 and 1$00.

Exchange rates vary from day to day, though unless drastic shifts occur it's convenient to reckon on 300–350$00 to the pound, or 180–190$00 to the dollar—which makes those brownish 1,000$00 notes worth around £3 or $5.50.

There are banks in every town, and all will change foreign currency or travellers' cheques. You may have to look around a bit harder if you wish to cash a Eurocheque (issued by UK banks and guaranteed by a Eurocheque card, these draw money on your UK account in the same way as a normal cheque). Most banks are open Mon–Fri, 8.30am–3pm. The rate of exchange varies between them, but not significantly. Some fancy hotels and travel agencies will cash traveller's cheques or exchange foreign currency, but the rates sting. Go to an exchange bureau rather than a bank when changing travellers' cheques as the latter charge higher interest plus a service charge.

Credit cards—American Express, Diner's Club, MasterCard and Visa—will be useful for booking airline tickets, car hire, and peace of mind in case of emergency. They are accepted by all the upmarket hotels and restaurants. However, the further you get off the beaten track, the more redundant your plastic will become.

National Holidays

In 1736 Dom Luís de Cunha estimated that there were only 122 working days in the Portuguese year, because of the number of religious festivals. Things have tightened up somewhat, but everything closes on:

1 January (New Year's Day)
Shrove Tuesday
Good Friday
25 April (Liberation Day)
1 May (May Day)
late May/early June (Corpus Christi)
10 June (Camões Day)
15 August (Assumption)
5 October (Republic Day)
1 November (All Saints' Day)
1 December (Independence Day)
8 December (Immaculate Conception)
25 December (Christmas Day)

In addition, every region, town and village finds some excuse for at least one annual holiday.

Opening Hours

shops

Some shops open at 9, but most unlock their doors at 9.30 or even 10. If they close for lunch it will be from 1 to 3; the Portuguese do not take a siesta as such, but prefer long, slow, discursive lunches. On weekdays, shops usually close at 6.30 or 7, though shopping centres stay open till midnight. Most establishments close at 1pm on Saturday. In the summer months, shops are often open until 9 in the evening and seven days a week with shorter hours on the weekends.

banks

Most banks are open Mon–Fri, 8.30am–3pm.

museums and churches

The majority of public museums are open Tues–Sun, 10–12.30 and 2–6. Some do not close for lunch. Admission charges for museums and archaeological sites are low, usually around 250$00.

Smaller churches are kept locked; the keys—giant or otherwise—are with the sacristans or caretakers, almost invariably old ladies living nearby, who shuffle over and are delighted to help.

Photography

To have your pictures developed in the Algarve, go to one of the many small shops in every town, resort and even larger villages, usually operated by Kodak or Fuji. They develop your films in an hour and throw in a matching new film besides, accounting for the high costs: around 2,000$00 for a 24-exposure film and 3,000$00 for 36.

Post Offices

Dom Manuel created Portugal's first postal system before 1520, which makes it one of the longest-running institutions in the country. Portugal's post offices (*correios*)—open Mon–Fri, 8 or 9–12.30 and 2.30–6, with main post offices open at lunchtime and Saturday mornings—are always a hive of activity, partly because they incorporate public telephones. If you're buying stamps, be sure to stand in the correct queue.

Standard air mail (*por avião*) letters and postcards to EU countries cost 100$00 and 90$00, and to countries outside Europe they cost 140$00 and 180$00 respectively. Reckon on mail taking 5–7 days to Britain, and 7–10 days to North America. There is a faster air mail service called *correio azul* which will only take a couple of days to reach Britain and about four to reach North America. Your letters have to be weighed and the price depends on this; a standard letter or postcard will cost 350$00. Use the blue post-boxes for *correio azul* and the red ones for normal post. Post offices also handle telegrams.

The *poste restante* system works well (letters should be marked '*Lista do Correios*', and will be held for the addressee at the designated post office; bring your passport when you collect letters, for which there is a small fee).

Shopping

Leaving aside the hideous pottery cockerels, there are some good buys in the Algarve—but if it's quality you want, you'll have to pay for it. At the upper end of the market are gold and silver filigree (Portimão), leather goods (Monchique and Loulé), large *azulejo* panels (which can be commissioned as a copy of a photograph in Loulé or Porches), copperwork and *cataplanas* (Loulé) and embroidery and lace work from Madeira.

Less pricy alternatives include fun ceramic crockery (Porches), pottery figures (Porches and all around), basketwork (Loulé, Monchique and elsewhere), chunky-knit sweaters (Portimão, Lagos, Sagres), and a supply of olive oil.

If you've brought the car, you could pick up a carved wooden ox-yoke to serve as a bedhead or, with a couple of pegs attached, as a coat rack. You could fix a lightbulb in an Algarvian chimney to make a night light, or suspend a plant from half a copper *cataplana*.

All towns and some of the larger villages have fruit and vegetable markets, sometimes with fresh fish and meat too. They're useful if you plan to picnic, as the choice is greater and prices are lower than at supermarkets.

Most markets are open on weekday mornings until lunchtime; some function on Saturdays, too. There are also monthly markets that sweep in and set up overnight, selling dresses, pots and pans, ox yokes, you name it. Sometimes you'll get lucky and find a bargain; it's OK to haggle.

Times and locations are detailed in each chapter.

Sports and Activities

For **golf**, *see* pp.17–20.

For **walking**, *see* pp.27–8.

The Portuguese are crazy about **football**, and tend to support one of three clubs: Porto, from Oporto, which won the European Cup in 1987; or Sporting Lisbon or Benfica from the capital (though the latter isn't what it was when Eusébio played for the side). Loyal Algarvians support Farense, Faro's first division team, which finished high enough in the league to qualify for the 1995 UEFA Cup competition for the first time in the team's history.

Tiny Rosa Mota may have won the 1988 Olympic gold medal for **marathon running**, but few of her compatriots follow in her footsteps.

Watersports make a big splash in summer, with every variety of activity on offer somewhere along the coast. Most major resort beaches offer water-skiing, sailing, scuba diving and windsurfing tuition on the beach. Vilamoura is the main water-sports centre of the region and you can hire boats at its marina too.

Monstrous water parks have sprung up throughout the Algarve, including three around Lagoa, and they are great fun for kids (*see* pp.103 and 104). Many resort hotels have **tennis courts**, but public courts are hard to come by.

Big game fishing trips depart from major resorts and Portimão.

For **bullfighting**, travel up to the Ribatejo. The bullfights staged in the Algarve are put on solely for tourists.

Telephones

Phoning from your hotel room or a bar can be expensive.

You have two alternatives: buy a phonecard from the post office or a paper shop; or make your call from a post office. Each post office has a pay phone, and the larger ones have a row of booths. Queue in the appropriate line, get allocated a particular booth, make your call and then pay the teller.

On weekdays, peak rates apply 9am to 7pm. the cheapest time to phone is at weekends.

To call the UK from Portugal, first dial 00 44; for Ireland 00 353; for the USA and Canada 00 1. To phone Portugal from the UK, first dial 00 351 (cheap rate 8pm–8am); from the USA dial 011 351.

Time

Portugal's clocks follow UK time and are 5–6 hours ahead of Eastern Standard time and 7–8 hours ahead of Pacific time.

Toilets

All the places to stay listed in this book have Western-style toilets rather than squatters, so there's no need to limber up before your visit. In most establishments you are requested to put used toilet paper in a bin.

Public facilities are uncommon except at bus and train stations but in an emergency nobody will mind if you ask to use the toilets of a hotel or restaurant without being a customer, though you'll often have to collect the key from behind the bar.

Tourism and Tourist Offices

You may hear the Portuguese saying that 'The Algarve is not Portugal'. This used to be true because the southern province was Moorish; today it is German, Scandinavian, British and French. The 85km stretch of coast between Faro and Lagos is jam-packed with high-rise hotels, apartment blocks, villa complexes, shopping centres and water parks—and more are on the way. Concrete-mixer trucks throw up clouds of dust along roads lined with rubble, supplying building sites bustling under the midday sun and the midnight floodlights.

When Faro airport opened in the early 1960s, the Algarve was something of a secret. The Salazar government kept such planning applications as there were under tight control, until the Revolution of 1974 toppled both the government and the controls. Tourism would bring employment to a poor region, so opportunist local councils adopted a more *laissez-faire* approach. Building did not really take off until the mid-1980s, when Spanish hoteliers upped their prices and British tour operators looked for new pastures. Most of the funding for the development in the 1980s came from Britain so the industry is very dependent on the British economy, bringing a new dimension to the ancient co-operation and interdependence of the two countries. To break this stronghold, over the past decade the government has succeeded in attracting more Scandinavian and German money.

In 1964 the Algarve offered 1,000 tourist beds; by 1988 this had reached 58,500, and by 1997 it had risen to 84,000, accounting for just under half the tourist beds in the entire country. And this is only the tip of the iceberg, as unofficial accommodation arrangements multiply this figure several times over. Visitor numbers tell a similar story, with 10.7 million out of a total of 23.6 million visitors to Portugal from abroad holidaying in the Algarve. But, by the 1990s (if not before), things were perceived as having gone too far; growth in visitor numbers to the Algarve slowed down in the mid-1990s and restrictions were imposed to control development in areas where there was growing concern for the quality of Portuguese tourism. People are increasingly aware of conservation, and new laws mean that those in the middle of building need to reapply for planning permission to ensure they comply with new regulations. Today visitor numbers are slightly up again, with a growth in the number of independent travellers looking for bargains. Still, tourism remains the biggest money-spinner in the Algarve, generating more money than fishing and farming combined.

Tourist Offices

There are tourist offices throughout the Algarve, operated by the Região de Turismo do Algarve, and signposted as *Turismo*. Generally tourist offices try hard to be helpful; you'll always find someone who speaks English. All know up-to-date hotel prices, and they tend to post timetables for public transport on noticeboards. In theory, opening hours are Mon–Sat 9–6; in fact it varies seasonally, geographically and according to staff availability. Few tourist offices will open before 10, some close for lunch 12.30–2, and Saturday afternoon can be a long shot, though during the summer season offices in the major towns are open on Sundays too.

Portuguese National Tourist Offices offer potential visitors numerous maps, fact sheets, and glossy brochures. Do pick up a copy of *Welcome to The Algarve* from the tourist office. It is full of excellent tourist information.

UK: 22–25a Sackville Street, London W1X 1DE, ✆ (020) 7494 1441.

Ireland: 54 Dawson Street, Dublin 2, ✆ (01) 670 9133.

USA: 590 Fifth Ave, 4th floor, New York, NY 10036, ✆ (212) 719 3985; 1900 L Street NW, Suite 310, Washington DC 20036, ✆ (202) 331 8222.

Canada: 60 Bloor Street West, Suite 1005, Toronto, Ontario M4W 3B8, ✆ 416 921 7376.

Walking

Despite the heavy commercialisation along the coast, much of the Algarve still cries out for slow exploration by foot; lonely beaches backed by tiny whitewashed settlements, lush valleys with streams trickling through an abundance of scarlet poppies, eucalyptus, pine and cork-oak-studded mountains—all this and much more lies beyond the well-known coast and is often inaccessible by car. The main thing to remember before setting out on a walk is to take plenty of water and wear loose-fitting light clothes. Sturdy shoes are a must and mountain boots are necessary if you plan on serious walking. You may get away with trainers for the easiest walks but remember they give no ankle support and will slip on steep and/or loose ground. Never wear open sandals in the countryside as there are vipers and scorpions here. The latter's sting is more painful than dangerous to most people but a viper bite can be serious. Don't let this put you off walking however—after all, the chances of having an accident on the EN125 are far greater than being bitten by a snake! So, where to walk? The simple answer is that, away from the resorts, and usually on the northern side of the EN125, there are infinite possibilities all the way from the Rio Guadiana in the east to the magnificent windswept coastal walks of the far west.

Ask the tourist office if they have any materials on walking, or to recommend a local guide. Monchique is far and away the most popular walking centre in the Algarve (*see* pp.115–18), but most should be able to help: even the offices in high-rise labyrinths like Monte Gordo carry relevant leaflets.

A recommended UK walking tour operator is **Let's Walk**, ✆ 282 698 676, mobile 07936 575 3033, run by Julie Statham, an expert on the flora, fauna and history of the region. She covers a broad chunk of the Algarve, from the Cape St Vincent Natural Park in the far west to Alte in the heart of the region. In addition to fully fledged walking holidays Julie runs a regular programme of easy half-day walks every Monday, Tuesday and Wednesday which will cost you around 2,000$00.

There are a small number of walking tour guide books, the best of which is *Algarve* by Sunflower Landscapes, which you can buy in Britain or locally. First-timers will find a number of walks (graded 'easy' or 'easy-moderate') but it is important to note the author's *caveat* that if you are a beginner or simply out for a stroll (pausing for pictures and picnics) then a walk may take up to twice the stated time. On average this would mean the time doubles from 2 hours to 4 hours—which is still within the remit of most people. Another good walking book is *Algarve Let's Walk*, published by VIP (Vista Ibérica Publications), available in all bookshops and many gift shops too.

Some tourist offices also sell an old-fashioned booklet called *Algarve Guide to Walks*. This covers 20 walks but only in very brief detail, so first-timers should approach it with caution.

The best months for walking are March to May and September to October, though as long as you are kitted out for rain, all the winter months are suitable.

Where to Stay

> *Wide not narrow be my cell*
> *That I may dance therein at will.*

Thus spake the hermit in Gil Vicente's 16th-century *Tragicomédia Pastoril da Serra da Estrêla*. This guide is intended to help you ferret out accommodation that will offer you the very best value for money. There are still a few bargains around, but prices for accommodation in 'undiscovered' Portugal are catching up with the rest of Europe.

Hotels

Most hotels and *pensões* are decent enough, and you are unlikely to have cause for complaint. Hotels are, however, obliged to provide an official complaints book (*Livro Oficial de Reclamações*). Hoteliers are not permitted to oblige guests to accept full- or half-board.

Accommodation is divided into a bewildering range of categories, which are allocated according to facilities: hotels (1 star to 5 star); apartment-hotels (2 star to 4 star); *pousadas*; *estalagems* (4 and 5 star); *albergarias* (4 star); *residenciais* (sing. *residencial*) and *pensões* (sing. *pensão*; 1 to 4 star). The system is not very helpful, and there are plenty of anomalies. Three-star *residenciais* are often more comfortable than one- or two-star hotels. The distinction between *estalagems* and *albergarias* is very slight; both are inns, and usually pleasant. Generally, *residenciais* are incorporated within larger buildings, and include breakfast in the tariff (unlike some *pensões*).

prices

Establishments are obliged to display prices in their lobbies and guest rooms. Unless listed or agreed otherwise, single occupancy of a double room is charged at the full rate less the cost of one breakfast. An extra bed installed in a double room will cost 30 per cent of the room rate, though children under the age of eight are charged half that. Single rooms are usually charged at 60–75 per cent of the rate for a double.

Accommodation in this book is listed under six price categories, which are intended as guidelines and nothing more: prices may vary in high and low season or during festivals; and rates vary within some hotels, depending, for example, on the view. Inflation is currently running at roughly 5 per cent per annum, and establishments are free to raise their prices from year to year as they wish.

Price ranges for a double room with bath in high season	
luxury	over 20,000$00
expensive	15,100$00–20,000$00
moderate	11,100$00–15,000$00
inexpensive	8,100$00–11,000$00
cheap	4,100$00–8,000$00
very cheap	4,000$00 and below. Shared bathroom.

Pousadas

Pousadas are government-owned hotels, installed either in monasteries, convents, castles or palaces, or in places of outstanding historic or scenic interest. They vary from opulent to modestly comfortable. *Pousadas* in the Algarve and the Alentejo are reviewed in the text. Their restaurants usually provide good, well-presented food, and are open to non-residents. All *pousadas* are very well signposted.

booking and prices

Book direct or through: Pousadas de Portugal, ✆ (218) 442 001, ✉ (218) 442 085, *www.pousadas.pt*, or in the UK through Caravela, ✆ (020) 7630 9223.

Expect to pay around 32,00$00 per night (35,000$00 at Évora) for a good *pousada*, or 25,000$00 for somewhere simpler.

Solares de Portugal (Turismo de Habitação)

A number of private farmhouses in the Algarve and the Alentjo have been comfortably adapted to receive paying guests under the aegis of the excellent *Solares de Portugal* scheme (also known by its former name of *Turismo de Habitação*). This gives a highly personal view of rural life and is a great antidote to all things associated with mass toursim—at very reasonable rates. Most hosts are charming, forthcoming and not averse to a bit of company; how much you see of them will depend upon the set-up. Some enthuse in English or French at the breakfast table; many will provide an evening meal if it is requested in advance. If you're in doubt about how to find the houses, do pick up direcions from the local tourist office.

booking and prices

Rooms should be booked at least three days in advance, and for a minimum of three nights. Fifty per cent of the total rate should be paid at the time of reservation.

Reservations should be made with the owners of the houses (who may not speak English) or with an agency representing them if there is one. Reservations for the majority of manor houses in Portugal can be made with the Associação do Turismo de Habitação, Praça da República, 4990 Ponte de Lima, ✆ (258) 741 672, ✉ (258) 741 444, *www.solares-de-portugal.com*. **Information** can be obtained from the Portuguese National Tourist Office in Britain, the United States or Canada.

Resort Accommodation

Most of Portugal's resort accommodation has been built in the last 20 years and, with the exception of some upmarket 'tourist villages', offers about as much atmosphere as an unpainted *azulejo*. Expect block bookings from package-tour operators; to get away from them, head for the west coast. The Algarve has great price variants between high and low seasons, so you can make substantial savings on accommodation by booking out of season.

Cheap Accommodation

Shoestring travellers can find their own kind of *Turismo de Habitação*; ask at local tourist offices for rooms to rent in people's houses, or look in windows for signs advertising *quartos*. You may end up with a scrupulously clean little room complete with a religious icon, a lace runner on the chest of drawers and homemade bread for breakfast.

Some of the cheaper *pensões* are a bit unsavoury; you can save money by asking for a room without a private shower room, but pack a pair of flip-flops to wear in the public one. It's advisable to ask to see a room before you commit yourself to renting it. You'll be asked to submit your passport and may have to pay a day in advance. Check whether breakfast is included in the room rate.

youth hostels

There are five youth hostels in the Algarve, and another four in the Alentejo as far north as Évora. Standards have improved from the bad old days and some are very comfortable, with good facilities. Guests must have a valid Youth Hostel Association membership card available in the UK from YHA, 8 St Steven's Hill, St Albans, AL1 2DY, Hertfordshire, ✆ (01727) 855215. In the USA, these can be obtained from the American Youth Hostels, Inc, Suite 840, Washington DC 20005, ✆ (202) 783 6161. In Portugal, contact the Associação Portuguesa da Pousadas de Juventude, Duque d'Avila 137, 1000 Lisbon, ✆ 213 558 820.

Camping is a low-key affair, and can work out remarkably cheap. Ask the tourist office for a list of campsites. Unofficial camping is frowned on, and with the number of campsites peppering the Algarve it seems churlish to ignore official regulations. Wherever you are, don't light firest in the summer. All campsites display daily prices per person, tent, car and caravan. You will have to leave your passport at reception when registering, and most sites will only admit pass-holders.

All campsites include the usual facilities of showers, washing up and laundry sinks; snack bar and restaurant; electric lighting with power points for caravans and for razors; and a small supermarket with basic supplies. Some of the more expensive sites have sports facilities such as swimming pools and tennis courts. All the campsites listed in the text are officially recognized.

Wildlife

The Algarve has a surprisingly varied landscape and plant life. The landscape changes from the thickly wooded Serra de Monchique (902m) and the rounded, cultivated hills of the Serra do Caldeirão (577m), to a zone of crests running parallel to the coast, cut by the valleys of rivers flowing down from the hills. Here are the orchards of the Algarve—the almonds, the carobs, the olives, and the figs which the Romans lauded and which, in the 17th century, were dried and exported to Flanders and the Levant. The Algarve is also laden with orange trees. The almond trees' pale pink blossom clouds the province from the middle of January to the end of February, above a mantle of bright yellow Bermuda buttercups. In March and April, the roads of the Algarve are fringed by quince trees' large white blossoms tinged with pink, as well as irises, golden yellow narcisci, jonquils, and tall, freely branched asphodels whose white flowers are veined with red.

Towards the west you'll see century plants, distinguished by their fleshy, yucca-like leaves radiating from a low-lying centre through which the slim tree trunk eventually grows. They have a sparse bunch of boughs at the top tipped with fresh green leaves. Every ten years they die and grow again on the spot where their seeds scattered; you'll spot these Mexican plants in varying stages of growth and decay, underlining the aridity of the area.

The salt lagoons of the eastern coast support a plethora of wading birds; here are the nature reserves of Ria Formosa and Castro Marim. The marshes around Alvor are also ripe for conservation, as is the protected zone of the West Coast; all these areas are covered in greater detail in the text. There is no reason why tourism and natural beauty shouldn't continue to co-exist in harmony if some common-sense guidelines are adhered to: walk or drive on existing tracks; don't collect plants, fruit or minerals; take your litter with you; and don't start fires or camp outside of campsites.

Women and Children

Sexual harassment is nothing compared with that in some Latin countries: in rural areas, single women travellers are a cause of amazement rather than anything else; however, in large towns and cities you may well encounter infuriating men on the street who hiss or cluck their approval. Steer clear of the areas around bus and train stations at night. For those interested in the feminist movement in Portugal, the *Comissão da Condição Feminina*, 2nd Floor, 32 Avenida da República, Lisbon, © (217) 983 000, has links with feminist groups throughout the country. It also organizes conferences and meetings, relating to every aspect of women's lives, and is active in social and legal reform.

Portugal is an excellent country in which to travel with small children because the Portuguese are entirely tolerant of their ways and, though there are few separate amusements for children, most bars and restaurants indulge them.

History

If you want to touch the history of the Algarve, feel the callouses on the hands of a fisherman; the ebb and flow of the province's history are echoed in those contours. For the Algarve has always looked first to the sea, and only after scanning the horizon—for fish, or continents undiscovered—have its eyes turned to the mainland.

The Moors made the Algarve their home for 500 years, and their influence is still pervasive. During the Age of Discoveries, Henry the Navigator assembled the world's most knowledgeable maritime men at Sagres, to quest beyond the boundaries of the known world. Now the tide has turned again, and the Algarve lures visitors across the oceans.

The history of the Algarve is inextricably bound up with that of its mother country, through the centuries in which Portugal gained and lost and regained her independence. It is a rich history, peopled with visionaries, eccentrics and flops.

Prehistory, the Romans, the Suevi and the Visigoths

When the Celts invaded the Iberian Peninsula in the first millennium BC, they mingled with the Iberians—who had been putting down roots since c. 8000 BC—and became **Celt-Iberians**. More influential on southern Portugal were the **Phoenicians**, who, drawn by the mineral wealth of the Peninsula, settled there in c. 1364 BC and founded the city of Ossonoba (possibly on the site now occupied by Faro) as an important base for their trade in marble and amber. Their empire passed to the Carthaginians, and in 202 BC the Romans occupied Hispania Ulterior (Andalucía).

The **Romans** marched inland, where the fierce **Lusitanian** tribespeople of central Portugal waged a successful guerrilla war against them north of the Tagus. South of the river, Julius Caesar founded the Pax Julia (c. 60 BC) to bolster the port of Olissipo (Lisbon) and the towns of Ebora (Évora) and Myrtilis (Mértola). Roman *latifundia* established the pattern of landholding in the Alentejo between 202 BC and 139 BC; the Romans built 18 dams in southern Portugal; Roman roads were used until the Middle Ages; and their bridges are still in use, for example in Tavira in the Algarve. They also introduced vines, olives, figs and almonds.

At the beginning of the 5th century, barbarian hordes entered the Peninsula. The Romans enlisted the aid of the **Visigoths**, who disposed of all but the **Suevi**, or Swabians. The Suevi based themselves between the northern Rivers Minho and Douro, and were converted to Christianity by St Martin. The Swabian monarchy was suppressed by the Visigothic ruler Leovigild in 585. Neither of these peoples made much of a mark on southern Portugal; the race who left an indelible mark on the region were the **Moors**.

The Moorish Occupation and the Christian Reconquest

The Moors were invited into Spain in 711 and nominally conquered the Peninsula within two years. They were a mixed salad of races—Arabs, Syrians, Persians, Jews, Berbers from Morocco and Copts from Egypt, who had been Christian—all of whom preferred the sunny climate of the south. Christians rallied together in northern Portugal and Galicia. Ferdinand I, King of Castile, drove the Moors from the north of Portugal, as far down as the city of Coimbra (1064). His successor, Alfonso VI, revived the metropolitan see of Braga in northern Portugal—which reinforced the integrity of the province that was to become Portugal. However, the Algarve remained Moorish for another two centuries, ensuring its separation from the rest of Portugal.

Alfonso's son-in-law, Henry of Burgundy, ruled the territory between the Rivers Minho and Douro from his northern capital at Guimarães. Later his widow, **Teresa**, governed Portugal as regent for their son, **Dom Afonso Henriques**. When Alfonso VII, King of Galicia, invaded Teresa's lands, her barons united behind Dom Afonso Henriques. He defeated his mother at São Mamede in 1128, and the reign of the first King of Portugal began.

In the Alentejo the Moors made few changes to the pattern of landholding; the towns became settlements owned by absentee landlords. When the Alentejo was reclaimed from the Moors, vast tracts of land were doled out to the military orders, though the king retained all the important cities and towns. Urban Moslems were compelled to reside outside the town walls and rural Moslems were milked by heavy taxes—most fled to southern Spain. **Dom Sancho I** (1185–1211), the second king of Portugal, tried to offset this depopulation by encouraging immigration from Flanders. He also undertook the reconquest of the Algarve, which remained incomplete until Dom Afonso III's military successes of 1249. In the 12th and 13th centuries, Christians labelled the part of the country that remained in Moorish hands 'Algarve'. For the Moors themselves, the province of el-Gharb encompassed the western part of the Peninsula as well as the coast of North Africa at Ceuta, Tangier and Fez. Thus when Tangier surrendered to Dom Afonso V, he styled himself 'King of Portugal and the Algarves, both on this side and beyond the sea'.

The House of Burgundy

Although the Pope did not recognize the kingdom of Portugal until 1179, the country had asserted its independence from Spain, helped by the fact that none of its rivers were navigable into Spain, and the Spaniards had no need of Portuguese ports. Moorish chroniclers refer to **Dom Afonso Henriques** (1128/39–85) as 'the cursed of Allah'; aided by strife amongst the Moors he crusaded southwards and captured Lisbon in 1147. But the reconquest was not completed until 150 years later, when the Algarve was taken. His son Dom Sancho I (1185–1211) continued the subjugation, but in 1191 was driven back north of the Tagus, except for a foothold in Évora. Dom Afonso III (1248–79) captured Faro; his *Cortes* at Leiria in 1254 was the first at which the commons were represented.

Afonso's son, **Dom Dinis** (1279–1325), became one of the greatest Burgundian kings. He ruled with great foresight—earning Dante's praise in *Paradiso*. Dom Dinis strengthened the nation's defences by building or rebuilding most of her castles, and established the Order of Christ to take the place of the suppressed Knights Templar. Forests were planted, and the king authorized at least 40 fairs. Dom Dinis founded Portugal's first university, the General Studies, in Lisbon in 1290; he also required deeds and official documents to be written in the vernacular. In all this, he was assisted by his peacemaking queen, Isabel, canonized for her devoted service to the poor. Once Dom Dinis, suspicious that she was secreting away bread in her clothing to give to the poor, asked her to unfurl her skirts. The bread she had been carrying was transformed into roses and petals floated to the king's feet.

The later Burgundian kings, both Dom Pedro I (1357–67) and his heir, Dom Fernando (1367–83), became embroiled in a series of **Castilian marriage alliances**. Dom Fernando obeyed his queen, Leonor, and married his heiress, Beatriz, to Juan, King of Castile; if this union produced no fruit, Juan would become King of Portugal.

When Dom Fernando died, Juan ordered the Portuguese townships to proclaim Beatriz queen. He received the backing of the entrenched nobility, who stood to benefit from Castilian-style government—but the spectre of absorption by Castile fired the towns and coastal regions in their support for a bastard son of Dom Pedro, **João of Avis**. In Lisbon he was 'accompanied by the common people as if he were dropping precious treasures for them all to grab', and in 1385 João was declared king (1385–1433). Shortly afterwards he and his lieutenant, **Nun' Álvares Pereira**, defeated Juan at Aljubarrota. This secured Portugal's independence for nearly 200 years. An Anglo-Portuguese alliance was cemented with the king's marriage to Philippa of Lancaster, sister of England's future Henry IV.

The House of Avis and the Age of Discoveries

Having made peace with Spain, Portugal turned her attention seawards. Fired by the desire for glory, piety and distraction, Dom João I took advantage of a civil war in the Magrib to capture **Ceuta** in 1415. But it was his third son, **Henry the Navigator** (*see* Topics, pp.49–50), who did most to foster Portugal's maritime exploits. He set up a school of navigation at Sagres, and channelled his funds into a succession of expeditions from the Algarvian port of Lagos to the west coast of Africa; local boy **Gil Eanes** rounded Cape Bojador in 1434. Madeira and the Azores were rediscovered, but were not colonized until 1445, during the reign of Henry's elder brother, the lawmaker Dom Duarte (1433–8).

Another brother, Dom Pedro, served as regent during the minority of Dom Duarte's heir, Dom Afonso V (1438–81). This riled the young king's half-uncle, the first Duke of Bragança, who fought and killed the regent in 1449.

Like his father and grandfather, Dom Afonso V fought in Morocco, storming to victory at Alcácer-Seguir in 1458. Also like his forebears, he strengthened the power of the *Cortes*, since expensive expeditions obliged the kings to woo the towns' resources. His son, Dom João, negotiated peace with Castile. As king (João II, 1481–95) he beheaded the over-mighty Duke of Bragança and received some 60,000 Jews fleeing persecution in Spain.

Overseas explorations resumed. In 1487 **Bartolomeu Dias** rounded the Cape of Good Hope without seeing land, and Pêro de Covilhã was dispatched to India and Ethiopia. The Portuguese Crown refused to finance Columbus' plan to find a westward route to the Indies; he took his idea to Ferdinand and Isabella of Spain, sailed in 1492, and discovered America. Now that Spain had a stake in the rest of the world, she and Portugal negotiated its partition. The Treaty of Tordesillas (1493) allocated to Spain all lands west, and to Portugal all lands east, of a line running north to south 360 leagues west of the Cape Verde Islands. The Portuguese lands just happened to include Brazil, prompting suspicions that the Portuguese already knew of its existence before the signing of the treaty.

The Crown passed to Dom João II's impatient cousin, **Dom Manuel** (1495–1521), whose arms were so long that his hands dangled beside his knees. During his reign, Portugal's position in Morocco and the Congo was consolidated (the former partly because Portugal had begun importing wheat and looked to the wide Moroccan plains). Looking further afield, **Vasco da Gama** set sail in 1497, and returned two years later having discovered a sea route to India and its spices. Pedro Álvares Cabral was dispatched towards India, but sailed too far west and discovered Brazil, in 1500. Following da Gama's discovery, Portugal established an administrative capital at Goa, and set about destroying the Indian Ocean's complex web of trading links, to secure the supremacy of her own commerce. A crew sailing under a Spanish flag completed the first circumnavigation of the globe, though their Portuguese captain, Fernão de Magalhães (Magellan), was killed *en route.*

The profits of the spice trade made Dom Manuel the wealthiest ruler in Europe—but Portugal's zenith was shortlived. The prospect of quick profit in Africa, India or Brazil lured the nation's entrepreneurs, leaving the home economy and agricultural productivity fatally weakened. The new wealth was not invested productively. Portugal lost most of her banking and economic expertise in 1496, when the king expelled his Jewish subjects—a prerequisite for his marriage to Princess Isabel of Castile. Those of the merchant classes who stayed put were hit very badly by the royal monopoly, established in 1506.

Dom João III (1521–57) and Charles V of Spain married each other's sister (thus providing the basis for Philip II's claim to the Portuguese throne 50 years later). Portugal settled Brazil, and in 1557 was granted Macau to enable her to trade with Canton. But already the prices of spices in Europe were falling, and the mother country was drained of men, ships and money defending the lines of communication that held together her global empire.

Dom João III's heir became king while still in his mother's womb; his great uncle, Cardinal Henrique, served as regent. **Dom Sebastian** (1557–78) was an odd fish, coupling a clear idea of his military calling with a childish impetuosity. The result was disastrous; in 1578 he led an ill-prepared expedition into Morocco from Lagos, where 15,000 Portuguese were captured at the battle of **Alcácer-Quivir**. Dom Sebastian was killed (*see* **Topics,** p.45), and fewer than 100 escaped; the ransom payments beggared the nation. The elderly cardinal was proclaimed king (1578–80) but died shortly afterwards. In desperation he was replaced by António, Prior of Crato (1580), bastard nephew of Dom João III.

The Spanish Usurpation

Philip II of Spain saw his opportunity. Wealthy Portuguese supported his entry into their country because they wished to avoid the expense of protracted warfare; he may also have had the support of the Jesuits. In addition Portugal's weakening economy needed Spain's American silver. The new king (Philip I of Portugal, 1580–98) abided by his promises to preserve the autonomy of Portugal. He closed the Portuguese ports to English and, later, Dutch ships. Undeterred, the Dutch made their own way to the East, where they snatched the spice trade from the Portuguese. In 1588 the Spanish Armada set sail for England from Lisbon with many Portuguese as crew. In retaliation, England's Elizabeth I sent forces which included the Algarve in their attacks: Sir Francis Drake razed all traces of Henry the

Navigator's headquarters from Sagres and the Earl of Essex sacked Faro. Philip's indolent son, Philip III (Philip II of Portugal; 1598–1621), had little contact with Portugal, and Philip IV (Philip III of Portugal, 1621–40) was distracted by the Catalan rebellion.

The Entrenchment of the House of Bragança

The Catalan rebellion gave the Portuguese a chance to rally round the Duke of Bragança, Dom João III's great-nephew. They crowned him King **João IV** (1640–56). Treaties were signed with the Dutch, who had occupied Brazil and had been attacking Portuguese shipping, and with the English, whose **Commonwealth Treaty** of 1654 set out privileges which held for nearly two centuries. At that time, approximately 14 per cent of Portugal's 1½ million souls were nobility or clergy, qualifying for the attendant financial privileges.

Dom Afonso VI (1656–67) was partly paralysed and partly stupid. Fighting against the Spanish dragged on until 1665; they made incursions into Évora in 1663. Alarmed by Spain's peace with France, Portugal was desperate to strengthen its alliance with England. Thus **Catherine of Bragança**, Dom Afonso's sister, married King Charles II. Her massive dowry included two million cruzados, the right to trade with Portuguese colonies, and the cession of Tangier (Bombay was an afterthought). England agreed to defend Portugal (and its overseas territories) 'as if it were England itself'. The king married Marie-Françoise of Savoy. Shortly afterwards he handed the government and his wife to his brother Dom Pedro (1667–83).

Dom Pedro II (1683–1706) convened a *Cortes* in 1698: the discovery of gold at Mato Grosso in Brazil secured the king's financial independence (and stunted domestic manufacture; only the colonies generated wealth, which was spent on imported goods). In 1703 the **Methuen treaty** implemented a defensive alliance with England and Holland; the subsequent commercial treaty generated favourable terms for Portuguese wine in Britain, and for British cloth in Portugal. The latter terms were the more significant, being the death sentence of the Portuguese textile trade. In the same year, Philip V invaded Portugal, but Spanish and French troops returned to Madrid in 1706.

The wealth created by Brazilian gold was compounded by that of **diamonds**, discovered there in 1728. Although the Crown did not always receive its one-fifth share, **Dom João V** (1706–50) reaped an estimated 107 million cruzados over a period of 44 years. However, the money did little to benefit Portugal. The king modelled himself on Louis XIV of France, lavishing much of his fortune on ostentatious building projects and the aggrandizement of his standing in the Catholic world. When he died, there was not enough money left in the royal treasury to pay for his funeral.

His featherbrained son, Dom José (1750–77), was dominated by the tyrannical minister later entitled **Marquês de Pombal**. This 'hairy-hearted' autocrat was made chief minister shortly after the earthquake of 1755, which devastated Lisbon and the Algarve. He presided over the rebuilding of Lisbon and the Algarve's Vila Real de Santo António in a remarkably short time, using straight grid-patterned streets in both programmes. He destroyed his enemies, the Jesuits, and the entrenched aristocracy, and implemented a policy of state-aided capitalism to reduce the foreign deficit and erode Portugal's stultifying network of privileges. The benefits of Pombal's rule were temporary, limited, and overshadowed by the cruelty of his reign.

Pombal had no regrets: 'The prisons and the cells were the only means I found to tame this blind and ignorant nation.'

As soon as she acceded to the throne, **Dona Maria I** (1777–92) banished Pombal to his estates. Many of his trading ventures were scuppered, and political prisoners were released. When the queen went screaming mad, her son Dom João (later João VI) governed.

The Napoleonic Wars

Napoleon put Portugal back on the European map—if only to decide how best to apportion the country. The French threatened to invade unless Portugal supported their naval blockade of Britain; Portugal refused to commit economic suicide, and **Junot** marched into Lisbon in 1807, stationing most of his French army in the Alentejo during the occupation. The British had provided a fleet to whisk the royal family to Brazil, out of harm's way; they were to remain there until 1821. The British generals **Wellesley** and **Beresford** were left to secure the defence of Portugal. Twice the invaders were driven out. They returned, but recalled their final garrison in 1811. Two fishermen set sail from Olhão, in the Algarve, to take the news to the royal family in Brazil. The British, for their part, were granted free access to Brazilian ports—enabling them to trade without depending on Portugal as an intermediary. Thus the Portuguese lost a vital source of profit. Their commerce was wrecked and their treasury in debt.

Liberals vs. Miguelites and the War of the Two Brothers

Dom João VI (1792–1826) remained in Brazil, and Beresford continued as marshal of the Portuguese army. When he temporarily left the country, an army-backed revolution took place in Oporto. An unofficial *Cortes* was summoned, which devised a sweeping constitution: the *Cortes* was to be a single-chamber parliament elected by universal male suffrage; feudal and clerical rights were to be abolished.

The timid king returned from Brazil in 1821 and agreed to abide by this constitution, though it fettered his power. He died in 1826 and his eldest son and heir, **Dom Pedro IV** (1826–8), acceded to the throne. Things were not straightforward; he had already become Emperor of the newly independent Brazil, and was living there. His solution was to abdicate the throne of Portugal in favour of his young daughter, Dona Maria da Glória—on condition that she marry his brother Dom Miguel, and that Dom Miguel accept a **Constitutional Charter**. The betrothal took place, but Dom Miguel (1828–34) reneged on the agreement. He was declared king with absolute powers, and there followed a purge of liberals. His brother, Dom Pedro, returned from Brazil to fight for the Portuguese throne, a bloody task in which he was assisted by excellent generals and British support for the liberal cause. Dom Miguel finally capitulated at Évora-Monte in 1834, and was exiled to Austria.

Liberalism

The state was not only war-weary but bankrupt. The liberals sought wealth by dissolving the country's monasteries and convents in 1834—nearly a quarter of the cultivated land in Portugal changed hands. Dom Pedro died soon after his victory, leaving the throne to his teenage daughter, **Dona Maria II** (1834–53). Governments came and went rather rapidly: some backed the Constitutional Charter of 1826; others supported the constitution of 1822. Neither was prepared to strike at the roots of the country's financial crisis: the unproductive economy, which relied on foreign investment and loans, and directionless governance. Governments became more stable after 1852, when the Duke of Saldanha introduced modifications to the charter, and a new electoral law had been applied.

During the brief reign of Dom Pedro V (1855–61), Fontes Pereira de Melo set up a **Ministry of Public Works**. Roads and railways were built; agricultural production increased accordingly. However, Portugal's balance of payments took a drastic downturn; the country lacked industrial raw materials, skilled labour (in 1870 there were 150 qualified engineers in Portugal) and investment capital.

Nadir of the Monarchy

When **Dom Carlos** (1889–1908) acceded to the throne, he inherited a country bewildered by the succession of governments in power since 1871. Portugal had sunk into a mire of high unemployment, strikes and public demonstrations. In 1890, Portugal's hopes of gaining control of the territory linking her colonies of Angola and Mozambique were thwarted by an ultimatum from Britain. This rattled the belief that the British Alliance was a guarantee of security, and tipped Portugal into crisis.

The king was the butt of his nation's dishonour, and made matters worse by placing a dictator, João Franco, in charge of the government. Amidst growing discontent, the king and his eldest son Prince Dom Luís Felipe were shot dead in Lisbon in 1908. The king was succeeded briefly by his younger son, Dom Manuel II (1908–10).

The monarchy was finally snuffed out in 1910; the king fled to Britain after an uprising by Republican revolutionaries and their supporters in the navy. This freak victory led to the **proclamation of the Republic** on 5 October 1910 and gave rise to many a new road name.

The Republic

The Republicans gained the support of the Church, the British and rural Portugal—but were never democratic. They limited freedom of speech, and muzzled the Press. Popular discontent was swelled by Portugal's (limited) involvement in the First World War after 1916, on the side of the Allies. The war exaggerated the weaknesses of Portugal's economy, prompting a series of strikes. In 1917 a military revolt gained popular support, inaugurating seven years of chaos: there were 45 governments between 1910 and 1926. By 1923 the escudo had fallen to one-twentieth of the value it registered against the pound in 1917. Faced with this intolerable instability, the army overthrew the 'democratic' regime in 1926.

The New State

Out of the morass emerged **Dr António de Oliveira Salazar**, an economics professor at Coimbra University, who was made Minister of Finance in 1928. With total control of revenue and expenditure, he turned a 330 million escudo deficit into a budgetary surplus—in his first year of office (and his regime continued to balance the budget until it was overthrown in 1974). In 1932, Salazar became prime minister, an office he retained until 1968. His *Estado Novo* ('New State') stressed nationalism, and Salazar secured the trappings of dictatorship: political parties, unions, and strikes were abolished; censorship was enforced; and the hated political police (the PIDE) thrived. Some 100,000 informers supplied the police with details of their friends, families or associates.

Portugal remained neutral during the Second World War and, in the postwar period, communications were extended and modernized. The construction of dams brought hydro-electric power. This enabled Portuguese industry to grow at a rate of 9 per cent per year in the 1950s and 1960s.

The colonies ('overseas provinces') formed an integral part of the *Estado Novo*. Local independence movements in Angola (1961), Guinea-Bissau (1963) and Mozambique (1964) ushered in dirty wars that were to sap Portugal's meagre resources. By 1968, more than 100,000 Portuguese troops were fighting in Africa.

Democracy

The unpopularity of the wars in Africa and discontent with the oppressive regime crystalized into the Movement of the Armed Forces (**MFA**), which toppled the *Estado Novo* in a bloodless coup on 25 April 1974, called the Carnation Revolution because the soldiers carried the flowers as a symbol of their peaceful intentions.

The African territories were granted their independence, and Portugal accommodated three-quarters of a million *retornados* from there. The revolution had a real effect on people's lives: the secret police were dispersed; censorship was lifted; industry, banks and insurance companies were nationalized; and nearly 4 million acres of land, especially the large *latifundia* of the Alentejo, was expropriated. In fact the landless rural workers of the Alentejo were the sinews of civilian support for the revolution. In October 1975, *latifundia* around Beja were occupied by workers. Roughly 900 cooperatives were established—and are currently being dismantled or falling apart due to lack of initiative and governmental back-up. Today much of the nationalization process is being reversed, as the government pushes through a series of privatization programmes in a rush to meet EU deadlines.

The country came close to civil war in November 1975, when a counter-coup attempted to prevent a communist takeover. In 1976 a new constitution was drawn up, under which the prime minister and cabinet were responsible to the popularly elected president and to the Assembly of the Republic, which was elected by proportional representation.

Portugal Today

Recent Portuguese politics have been muddled, and nobody is more aware of that than the man in the *tasca*, who sends the whole business to the devil and leaves someone else to sort it out. The roots of his passivity go back a long way: the 18th and 19th centuries lacked a strong liberal tradition, so the population remained ignorant of the powers and limitations of democracy. In the absence of a middle class clamouring for a true parliamentary system, the landed élite dominated politics in Portugal. Salazar's aim to stunt the awakening of political consciousness compounded the situation.

Forty-eight years of dictatorship and two years of revolutionary chaos left a legacy of over-centralized economic structures, flimsy infrastructure, a skeletal education system and inadequate social welfare and housing.

But things have changed rapidly and are still changing. Portugal joined the then EEC in 1986, and the Union is now pumping billions of dollars into the country to help modernize the economy. Portugal is one of the EU's poorest countries, with 3 per cent of the EU's population and about 1.5 per cent of its economy, but it receives more than 10 per cent of regional and structural funds—though EU support will trail off in 2006. Resources are flooding into communications, transport, education and professional training. The tax and financial systems are being reformed, as are agrarian law and labour practices. In the larger cities, construction is booming.

The middle classes have never had it so good. The gap in income compared with EU partners is steadily closing, having leapt from 54 per cent of the per-capita average to about 74 per cent today. In a country where 40 years ago fewer than half of homes had electricity, motorists now have motorway tolls docked electronically from their bank accounts as they zoom past toll-gates. But there are still pockets of poverty, as any visitor to the Alentejo will see, and Portugal has the EU's highest adult illiteracy. The health service, the public administration and the justice system are in desperate need of reform, and centre-left Socialist Prime Minister António Guterres was re-elected pledging to do just that.

Portugal was the last European power to dismantle its empire, an era which ended in December 1999 when Portugal returned Macao to Chinese rule after 442 years. Now the emphasis is on building up co-operation within the Community of Portuguese Speaking Countries (CPLP), which incorporates 200 million people. Portugal's fearful relationship with Spain is changing as economic interdependence grows. Its neighbour is now its second biggest client, after Germany.

As Portugal's obsession with football is catalyses preparations to host the 2004 European soccer championships, the country's economic prospects are looking good. The rate of inflation is 'acceptable' and the country is considered close to technical full employment with a jobless rate below 5 per cent. And the sun's still shining.

Topics

The charm of the Algarvians is one of the most compelling reasons for travelling here. People tend to be gentle and friendly, while retaining great dignity. A genial pessimism pervades much of life, though it's often backed by quiet pride. All Portuguese are unfailingly tolerant of foreigners, as George Borrow discovered in 1835: 'I said repeatedly that the Pope...was the head minister of Satan here on earth...I have been frequently surprised that I experienced no insult and ill-treatment from the people.' Their capacity for acceptance and fatalism is said to be inherited from the Moors; certainly, the people of the Algarve more than any other Portuguese are capable of just throwing up their shoulders and plodding into the next day with a muttered *não faz mal* (never mind).

Sometimes tolerance is occasioned by passivity. In 1726 Brockwell wrote: 'Be their Business ever so urgent, or the Rains ever so violent, they never hasten their Pace...and seem to number each step they take.' Then again, it could just be pure indolence; an Algarvian friend once equated being Portuguese with being terminally lazy, adding that this is very much a coastal malaise.

But the Algarvians can be firm of purpose when they set their minds to it, and highly adaptable. The latter quality is not always apparent: there's a deep-rooted resistance to change. If you are travelling on a bus and open a window, someone will close it; but if you get on the bus before anyone else and open a window, it will remain open throughout the journey—as the other passengers see it, the window has always been open, so it should stay open. On the other hand, 'progress' is sometimes employed for its own sake, as the revamp of various historical buildings attests (*see* 'The Fortress' in Sagres, p.142).

Algarvian women age early, another fact that did not escape Brockwell's attention: 'No sooner are they in their Perfection than they suddenly decay... Thirty once turn'd, they become as justly despicable, as before they were admirable.' Young, stylish Marias keep their arms firmly around the necks of lucky Antónios, Manuels or Josés—then suddenly they are clad in black and gossiping around a crate of lettuces. If not with everlasting youth, however, they are blessed with a perpetual lightness of spirit and a readiness to toil alongside and laugh with their men.

Politeness is elevated to elaborate courtesy: envelopes are commonly addressed to *excelentíssimo* (most excellent) so-and-so. It was Dom João V who first entitled his secretary of state 'Excellency'. The nobles were disgusted, but found it expedient to use that address for any chance acquaintance, and the custom caught on. Otherwise, Algarvians don't stand on ceremony much, though they religiously greet each other with *bom dia*, *boa tarde* and *boa noite* according to the time of day. Men shake hands and women peck on both cheeks and no one, aside from fresh youngsters (*see* 'Resort Life', p.46), reveals any expanse of flesh.

Algarvians speak fast and furiously; even at the best of times Portuguese sounds more like Russian than a Romance language, though if you have some Spanish, Latin or French you should be able to read a bit. English has been taught in schools since the Revolution of 1974, so if you're in difficulties, grab someone under the age of 40. Language won't be a problem in coastal resorts, but if you plan a trip inland be prepared to communicate by gesticulation.

The more fanciful side of the Portuguese temperament is shaped at an early age; children are told the bizarre but tragic tale of *Carochinha* (Cockroach), an ugly insect who receives numerous proposals of marriage after she discovers a crock of gold. The only sincere candidate is a mouse, who falls into boiling water and dies.

Light and Colour

If you hail from a polluted urban metropolis you are bound to be impressed by the Algarvian sky. It seems infinitely higher, wider and more astounding in its array of vibrant colours than seems entirely fitting for such a small region. Layers of clouds race across each other and when it rains you see the storm approach from a distance before it briefly showers you and then moves on. Almost never does the whole sky cloud over with dull uniform grey.

The colours of the Algarve are intense: primary blue sky, bright white buildings, russet soil and the fluid greens of the sea deepening to velvety blue further out. And in between, a salad of shades. There is very little air pollution in the Algarve, giving the light a clarity that can initially dazzle. It is this rare quality that is attracting so many artists to the region, that and the fiery shades of the sunsets. Algarvian sunsets have always been special; the Moors called it the Sunset Land. All over the province the sun bids its daily farewell, running the gamut of pinks, reds and oranges (and, in the case of Cape St Vincent, sometimes even a green flash, *see* p.146).

Sebastianismo

After the disastrous battle of Alcácer-Quivir in 1578 (*see* p.37), the body of Dom Sebastian could not be found. A whirlwind of rumours proclaimed the return of the king, and speculation gained momentum after Portugal was annexed to Spain in 1580. Dom Sebastian was cast as a hero who would throw off the Spanish yoke and restore the glory of the Portuguese; he became the focus of a messianic cult that was enthusiastically embraced by the New Christians—ostensibly converted Jews—who feared increased persecution under Spanish rule.

The popularity of Dom Sebastian has far outlasted the four pretenders (youth, hermit, pastry cook and Italian) who popped up before 1600. In essence, *Sebastianismo* is akin to *saudade* (*see* below), and it continues to revive in times of national despair. One such revival occurred when Prince Dom Miguel returned from Brazil in 1828, and possibly when Salazar—then Minister of Finance—turned around the budgetary deficit in 1928–9 (*see* pp.40–41).

Saudade and Fado

Saudade is a state of mind that characterizes the Portuguese temperament. There's no literal translation: 'longing' or 'yearning' come closest. It is a passive desire for something out of reach, either in the future or in the past. It pricks with an almost religious constancy and can be seen hovering in the depths of those large, sad, brown Portuguese eyes.

The musical equivalent of *saudade* is that melancholic, gut-wrenching song called *fado* (fate). The hard, untrained voice of the *fadista* is accompanied by a guitar; together they revel in tragedy, or assume a torpid resignation towards it. There's something very Arabic in the catches and sweeping undulations of a *fado* melody.

The words of the *fado* are not too important; *fadistas* often improvise. However, some *fados* tell the story of Maria Severa, a great *fadista*, whose mother was known as *A Barbuda* (the Bearded Lady). Maria used to let rip in Lisbon's Mouraria, next to the Alfama, where she conducted a stormy romance with a bull-fighting nobleman, the Conde de Vimioso. What the *fados* fail to mention is that Maria died at the age of 26 not from a broken heart, but from a surfeit of roast pigeon and red wine. Today's diva is Amália Rodrigues. Even she was banished from the airwaves during the initial confusion of the 1974 revolution, when it was illegal to broadcast *fado* on the radio—on the grounds that it encouraged listlessness and fatalism, and was therefore harmful to social progress.

Resort Life

Life in the Algarve coastal resorts has little in common with that in the rest of Portugal. Attitudes are more relaxed but activity is more frenetic. The annual influx of tourists brings an open-mindedness and absorption of different cultures that makes the locals pleasantly easygoing, while unfortunately eroding the more interesting aspects of Portuguese life and ritual. Catholicism does not exert the same stranglehold on people here as in the rest of the country. Late marriage and remarriage are common; a seemingly endless procession of middle-aged couples with grown-up children whip off on sunny days to get wed, occasioning much hooting of car horns by joyous friends.

Young Algarvians grow up on the beach, at ease with nature and the power of the sea, though they have few qualms about littering clifftops and beaches. Here rests the paradox: on the coast there's so much natural beauty that few people are concerned with preserving it. Yet life is not just about sun, sea and fun. Most Algarvians depend on tourists for their livelihood and consequently work constantly for 4 or 6 months while resigning themselves to an enforced break for the rest of the year. It is not unusual to see the landlady of your perfect little room driving a taxi or working in a restaurant kitchen by day. With social life also booming in the summer, the months between May and September are lived intensely.

Young Algarvians often speak passable versions of several languages and like to emulate their northern European cousins; they wear the same clothes, watch the same films, listen to the same music and smoke the same hash—there is really no gap in experience between the younger generations. This enables an easy exchange between the young Algarvians and the tourists, ideal for the lazy days and busy nights of the resorts.

Moorish Influences

The blood and customs of the Algarve have been much dominated by the Moors, who occupied the region from the early 8th century to the mid-13th century. Few Moorish buildings survive but their architectural legacy is evident in the whitewashed cuboid houses with shuttered balconies, roof terraces, inner patios and slim chimneys patterned like sugar cellars, through which smoke percolates. Physically, the people of the Algarve have inherited darker complexions than their northern counterparts, and tend to be more garrulous and agitated in temperament.

The Moors' most important and lasting contribution was the management of water; they introduced bucket wheel wells (called '*nora*') for raising it, which can now be seen lying disused throughout the countryside, although a mule-powered version was used until recently. They taught the Portuguese all they knew about irrigation and how to cultivate sloping land by cutting terraces into the hillsides. They introduced the abundant orange, lemon, peach and loquat groves and the means by which they could flourish. As for the wealth of distinctive almond trees, a popular story tells of how a legendary Moorish king married a Scandinavian beauty and brought her to his capital at Silves. He offered her his all, but she was unhappy; she missed her country's snow. So the king planted thousands of almond trees, known ever since as 'Algarvian snow'.

Azulejos

Portugal's tiles are one of the most exuberant and irrepressible facets of her artistic heritage. They are not peculiar to the country but in Portugal tiles are used more widely and for a greater variety of purposes than anywhere else. *Azulejos* date back to Moorish times; the term itself may be a corruption of two Arabic words, *azraq* (azure) and *zalayja* (a small polished stone). The Portuguese have as much trouble pronouncing the word as foreigners.

In the late 15th century, tiles with geometric designs were imported into Portugal from Seville. To prevent their tin-glazed colours from blending with one another in the furnace, they were separated by channels filled with linseed oil, or by ridges in the clay paste.

In the 16th century, the Italians introduced the majolica technique, by which the clay was covered with white enamel; this could then be painted directly. Andalucían craftsmen brought vitality to Portugal's *azulejos* when she was yoked to Spain (1580–1640), and it was during this period that the Portuguese developed their enthusiasm for the tiles.

Early 17th-century tiles were either solid blocks of dark blue or green arranged in simple geometric patterns, or more commonly *azulejos de tapete* (carpet tiles). The latter imitate Moorish rugs, in yellow and blue. Tiled altar fronts were made to look like textiles, and in the second half of the century *azulejos* were first used in narrative sequences. Both Portuguese and Dutch tiles of the period were exclusively blue and white, influenced by the Ming porcelain popular in Europe at the time.

The early 18th century saw the introduction of the Dutch-style independent *azulejo*, each displaying a single non-narrative motif. These cost a fraction of the price of traditional tiles, and during their 40-year vogue a succession of flower, ship, donkey, castle and bird *azulejos* appeared around the country. Large tile panels depicting religious scenes mark the apogee of the *azulejo* at this period.

Baroque tiles teem with thick acanthus foliage, scrolls of stone, cherubs and urns sprouting frilled Dutch tulips, and in the 1730s in particular *azulejo* scenes depicted the pleasures of an idle life, after artists such as Watteau and Boucher. Tones of olive green and burgundy supplemented the blue and yellow, particularly in border garlands and swathes of vegetation.

The majority of the Algarve's *azulejos* date from the 16th to 18th centuries; the most impressive are in the Church of São Lourenço in the town of Almansil (*see* p.89). They date from 1730 and are the finest work of Policarpo de Oliveira Bernardes. Faro's cathedral (*see* p.53) displays 18th-century tiles, as does Lagos' Chapel of Santo António (*see* p.128). Tiny churches in little-visited villages are often cooled by blue and white *azulejos*; the churches at Vila do Bispo (*see* p.146) and Alte (*see* p.122) are good examples.

Manueline Portals

The Manueline style is Portugal's own contribution to the world's architecture; its ebullient forms encapsulate the thrill of the Age of Discoveries, and its treatment of space belongs to generations of horizon-gazers. It developed out of the late Gothic style, and reached its peak between 1490 and 1521, during the reign of Dom Manuel, from whom it takes its name. The Manueline is an unique style, with substyles derived from the Spanish Plateresque (finely detailed motifs in low relief), the Moorish revival called *mudéjar*, and a concoction of fantastic maritime motifs.

This was Portugal's great age, when wealth from trade with the East generated numerous new artistic ventures, which attracted foreign craftsmen to Portugal. Flemish, Spanish, French and *mudéjar* craftsmen wielded the most influential chisels in Portugal. Manueline architecture required a feast of sculptural embellishment and thus serves as the finest showcase of Manueline sculpture. In the Algarve the best examples of Manueline style are seen around church doors: ropes twist around columns, as do rigging, anchors and exotic fruits. Look out for the parish churches of Monchique (*see* p.115), Alcantarilha (*see* p.103), São Bartolomeu de Messines (*see* p.121) and the portal of Alvor's sandstone church (*see* p.111), in which decoration springs out from a giant octopus tentacle. Loulé's hospital door is also buoyantly Manueline.

Henry the Navigator

No other historical figure dominates the Algarve quite as pervasively as Henry the Navigator. Sagres is still sometimes known as Vila do Infante (Prince's Town), and the new highway that will span the province is called the Via do Infante. The Algarvians have few national heroes and monuments but are still captivated by the image of Prince Henry.

Prince Henry, the fourth son of Dom João I, was born in 1394. He was brought up in a court which was shedding its rough manners to take up the ideals of the chivalric code, under the moral influence of his English mother, Philippa of Lancaster. Henry was an intriguing personality; despite being the driving force behind Portugal's voyages of discovery, he never went on the expeditions himself since, acutely aware of his rank as a royal prince, he could not contemplate the prospect of spending many months at close quarters with his men. At the turn of the 14th century, the medieval world was already showing symptoms of the Renaissance, and throughout his life Henry displayed character-istics typical of both ages: he was a brave and honourable medieval knight, always eager to fight the holy war, while also being a driven and curious explorer and staunch empiricist.

Henry's indomitable will and ability to lead men through sheer determination first became apparent when, aged 18, he and his brothers proposed an expedition against the Infidel in Moorish Ceuta. Henry was dispatched to the north to raise troops and build ships. He motivated the whole city of Oporto to abstain from meat for a year in order to save it for the trip. They ate offal instead; to this day they are known as *tripeiros* (eaters of tripe).

Later, when Gil Eanes returned utterly dejected from an unsuccessful trip to round Cape Bojador in 1433, Henry strongly urged him to go back, firing his imagination and renewing his zeal. Gil was successful this time, disproving the widely held belief that the world ended here, complete with scaly monsters and boiling water.

Henry's military career was not one of unmitigated success. At Tangier he had to leave his brother Prince Ferdinand as a hostage of the Moors. Ferdinand died after five years in captivity. Henry, whose natural countenance was austere, was said to have rarely smiled after this time; Azurara, the 15th-century court chronicler, describes an expression that 'at first sight inspired fear in those unaccustomed to him.'

Throughout his life, Henry showed the type of religious zeal highly praised in the Middle Ages: he conquered lands held by the Moors and saw an opportunity to spread the word by discovering what lay beyond the known world. Extending the boundaries of Christendom was his justification for his obsession with the African interior and the sea route to the Indies, with all its gold and potential for trade. However, Henry sometimes took religious justifications to self-delusional levels; he was responsible for Europe's first slave market (*see* 'Lagos', p.128) in 1444 but, instead of being struck by the essentially un-Christian act he was overseeing, he was pleased to be converting heathens and Mohammedans to Christianity. In reality, his keen sense of ecomonics probably had more to do with his support of the slave trade; his fervour for exploration was growing all the time and he knew that his captains needed financial incentives to undertake hazardous journeys into the unknown. Henry's own tastes were simple: he led a life of abstinence, always wearing a horse-hair shirt under his clothes and spending hours contemplating the ocean and the stars.

The year 1443, in which his brother Ferdinand died, saw Henry throwing his energies into building the settlement at Sagres, spending more time there away from a world in which his chivalric values were becoming increasingly defunct. From this time on Sagres came to symbolize the Renaissance Henry, the man who claimed 'knowledge is that from which all good arises'. Historians disagree over whether Henry's fabled school of navigation was a formal academy; there is little evidence to support this. But certainly major studies were undertaken in shipbuilding, navigation and cartography, and breakthroughs were made in each field. Henry gathered the nautical experts of his age at Sagres, and the first caravels were built here. He cast medieval superstitions to the wind in his studies of navigation and cartography, adopting a scientific attitude to the study of the stars and drawing up maps based on factual accounts rather than myths. He became an active Protector of the University of Lisbon; his ascetic overtones can be heard in the proclamation that 'no student shall keep in his quarters a horse, donkey, falcon or, on a permanent basis, a woman of loose morals'.

He died in 1460. Diogo Gomes, a devoted squire, summed it up with: 'My Lord the Infante had remained a virgin till his death, and what and how many good things he had done in his life it would be a long story for me to relate.' Henry's legacy to Portugal was one of seafaring triumphs and growth of trade. He died in considerable debt since he had been a generous man, providing pensions to the families of his seamen and rewarding his captains well; his only expense was his thirst for discovery. Ultimately he had fulfilled his medieval desire for glory by pursuing his Renaissance quest for knowledge of the unknown.

Talha Dourada

The discovery of gold and diamonds in Portugal's colony of Brazil brought a flood of wealth to a monarch who sought glorification through his monumental building works; Dom João V's liberality attracted foreign craftsmen to Portugal, and the arts of Portugal were shaken into vibrant life.

The most exciting sculpture of the age was *talha dourada* (gilt-painted carving), which the Portuguese used with peculiar enthusiasm. The gilt made with Brazilian gold leaf produced a theatrical effect well suited to Baroque tastes; during its vogue in the 18th century, it spilled from the apse to the pulpits, *azulejos* and picture frames in the nave. In the Algarve it was most commonly used around altars, often in small parish churches, surprising the present-day visitor and giving the impression that the church is showered in gold. Good examples are the Chapel of Santo António in Lagos (*see* p.128) and the tiny church at Vila do Bispo (*see* p.146).

Faro and Inland

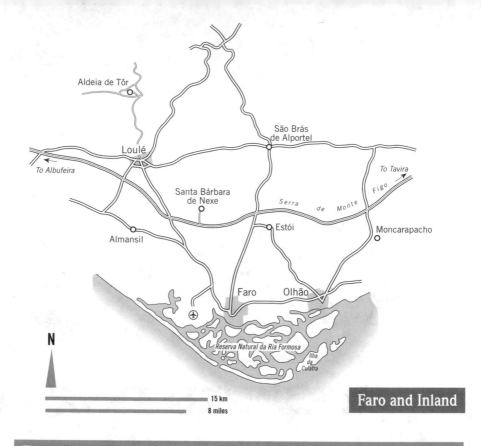

Faro and Inland

Faro

Faro, the capital of the Algarve, is built around an attractive harbour at the edge of a wide lagoon. Some 297km from Lisbon and 53km from the Spanish border at Vila Real de Santo António, it is a pleasant town, studded with squares where you can linger under shady carob and pink-flowering oleander trees, or sit under the palms of central Jardim Manuel Bivar and watch the sun glinting on the water of the harbour. It's a gentle place with white, shambling houses and interesting monuments, as well as a string of designer shops along its pedestrianized shopping streets, where people sip coffee and shoot the breeze. Faro feels different from the other coastal resorts because it is home to many businesses and industries; smart locals rub shoulders with sunburnt tourists while the students of the university bring a bit of fizz to the place.

Nothing has been quite the same since the airport was built; Faro is now the destination of hundreds of charter flights. A few passengers remain rooted here, soaking up sun and beer, but the majority head straight for the resorts, so the town's tourist scene is particularly transient.

History

Dom Afonso III captured Faro from the Moors in 1249 and rebuilt the town walls. In the 15th century these encircled a group of Jewish residents who set up a press to print Hebraic texts. The bishopric of the Algarve was transferred from Silves to Faro in 1580; Elizabth I's favourite, the Earl of Essex, may have been the bishop's first English visitor. In 1596, after sacking and burning Cadiz, he landed at Faro beach with Lord Howard of Effingham, Sir Walter Raleigh and 3,000 troops. Portugal was ruled by England's enemy Philip II of Spain at this period and hence was a fair target. The city was deserted, and Essex installed himself in the bishop's palace—in which he found 200 black leather volumes tooled in gilt. (Two years later he presented the clerical collection to his friend Sir Thomas Bodley, who had recently founded a library at Oxford. The first Bodleian librarian complained that 'diverse sentences' had been censored by the Inquisition.) The English 'removed' the books, set Faro on fire and departed. Parts of the city were destroyed by earthquakes in 1722 and 1755.

Getting Around

Six kilometres out of town, **Faro airport**, ✆ 289 808 800, copes with over 5 million visitors per year. From mid-May through October, every day except Tuesdays, on the hour 8–8, air travellers get a free ride into Faro on the Aerobus— just show your plane ticket. Buses 16 or 18 take 20mins into town and cost around 160$00. A taxi to the centre of town will cost about 1,500$00—agree on the price first if the meter is not being used. Airport buses depart from a stop opposite the tourist office and one facing the bus station.

From the **railway station**, walk down the Avenida da República, past the **bus station**, to get to the harbour. If you feel impelled to go to Faro beach, bus nos.16 and 17 leave every half-hour from opposite the tourist office.

Tourist Information

Expect a queue in the **tourist office**, 8 Rua da Misericórdia next to the Arco da Vila, ✆ 289 803 604 (*open daily during summer 9.30am–7pm*). For English-language information on buses, call ✆ 289 803 792; for details of trains, call ✆ 289 801 726. The **post office** is in the Largo do Carmo. The daily **market** is in the Largo Mercado off the Rua Dr Justino Crimano. The region's main hospital can be reached on ✆ 289 803 411 at Rua Leão Peredo. If you would like a free **guided tour** of historic Faro, call the Town Hall on ✆ 289 803 711.

The Old Town

The old part of town rests secure behind fortified walls. Enter through the 18th-century Italianate **Arco da Vila**, a gate with a niche for St Thomas Aquinas, who was invoked to save the city from a plague in the 17th century.

The pretty, cobbled Rua do Município opens on to a square edged with orange trees, in which stands the Renaissance **cathedral (Sé)** (*open Mon–Sat, 10–5 for visitors, 6 for masses*). It has appropriated the tower of its Gothic predecessor and the building has a wide nave flanked by 18th-century *azulejos*, and a wild, dovecote-like Baroque reliquary.

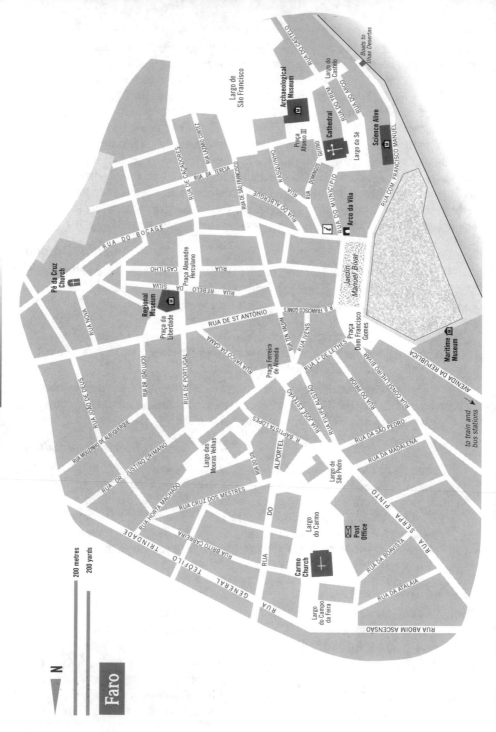

Faro

N

200 metres
200 yards

Pé da Cruz Church
RUA NOVA
RUA DO BOCAGE
RUA DE CAÇADORES
RUA DA TERESA
RUA LÁZARO CORTEZ
Largo de São Francisco
Archaeological Museum
RUA DO CASTELO
Largo do Castelo
Boats to Ilhas Desertas
RUA DO TREM
RUA DO ARCO
Cathedral
Praça Afonso III
RUA RASQUINHO
RUA DE SÃO FRANCISCO
RUA DO ALBERGUE
RUA DOMINGOS GUI
Largo da Sé
Science Alive
RUA COM. FRANCISCO MANUEL
Regional Museum
Praça da Liberdade
Praça Alexandre Herculano
RUA REBELO DA SILVA
CASTILHO
RUA
RUA DE ST ANTÓNIO
R. D. FRANCISCO GOMES
RUA DO MUNICÍPIO
Arco da Vila
Jardim Manuel Bivar
RUA DR JOÃO LÚCIO
RUA JOÃO DE DEUS
RUA DE PORTUGAL
RUA VASCO DA GAMA
Praça Ferreira de Almeida
RUA TEN. VALDOM
RUA IVENS
RUA 1º DE LETHES
RUA FILIPE ALISTÃO
Praça Dom Francisco Gomes
Maritime Museum
AVENIDA DA REPUBLICA
RUA MOUZINHO DE ALBUQUERQUE
RUA DR. JUSTINO CIRIANO
Largo das Mouras Velhas
RUA DO SOL
R. BAPTISTA LOPES
ALPORTEL
RUA DOS ESTÃO
RUA DO PRIOR
RUA CONSELHEIRO BIVAR
RUA DA SÃO PEDRO
to train and bus stations
RUA HORTA MACHADO
RUA CRUZ DOS MESTRES
RUA BRITO CABREIRA
RUA DO
Largo de São Pedro
RUA DA MADALENA
RUA SERPA PINTO
GENERAL TEÓFILO TRINDADE
RUA
Largo do Carmo
Post Office
RUA DA BOAVISTA
Carmo Church
Largo do Campo da Feira
RUA DA ATALAIA
RUA ABOIM ASCENSÃO

54

The quirky chinoiserie organ was painted in 1751, and looks like an elaborate version of something a monkey would grind. Ask the friendly custodian for a guided tour. Just outside the side entrance, note the remains of a **capela dos ossos** (Bone Chapel), a taster for the main event at the Carmo Church (*see* p.56). For a more uplifting experience take the 68 narrow winding steps to the top of the tower for a wonderful view over the Old Town rooftops and the lagoon. Watch the international flights from the nearby airport, and the domestic flights from the top of the old Bishop's Palace and the Arco da Vila where two pairs of storks have nested.

Behind the cathedral, the Convento de Nossa Senhora da Assunção now houses the **Archaeological Museum** (*open Mon–Fri 10–6.30, Sat 10–1; closed Sun and holidays*), whose illuminating collection was retrieved locally. Part of it is displayed in the stunning two-storey cloister of 1543, with beady-eyed gargoyles and a peaked and lichenous terra-cotta roof. The convent was built by Dona Leonor, third wife of Dom Manuel; her blazon ornaments the portico, complete with shrimping net. The two 1st-century busts of Hadrian and Agrippina, wife of Emperor Claudius, were discovered at nearby Milreu (*see* p.59)— circle Agrippina to see her elaborate hairstyle—while the excellent 3rd-century mosaic detailing half of Neptune's face, surrounded by two of the four winds, was found close to the railway station. A cabinet near the mosaic displays Roman *lachrymae*, tiny vessels intended to hold tears. Upstairs there is a recently opened exhibition of Islamic finds.

Take time to explore the lovely quiet cobbled streets of the Old Town. Tucked away in a peaceful corner is the **Galeria do Trem**, which opens periodically to stage exhibitions of Portuguese art. Pick up a copy of *Agenda* from the tourist office for opening times.

Outside the Old Town

Just outside the Old Town on the edge of the marina is Faro's newest attraction, **Ciência Viva** (Science Alive), a hands-on centre which attempts to explain various scientific princi-ples with lively interactive exhibits (*open mid-Sept–June Tues–Fri 10–5, weekends and holidays 3–7; July–mid-Sept Tues–Sun and holidays 4–11pm; adm half-price on Wed*). Aimed more at locals than foreign visitors (most captions and explanatory notes are in Portuguese only), it is nonetheless staffed by friendly helpers who will cheerfully demon-strate how the hands-on stations work. In the evenings star-gazers can visit the observatory.

Two of Faro's other museums are worth a visit. On the dock past the Hotel Eva, the **Maritime Museum** (*open Mon–Fri 9.30–12, 2.30–5; closed Sat, Sun and holidays*) contains models of fishing boats from the past and present, helpfully labelled in English.

Algarvian handicrafts, photos of typical houses and peasants in traditional dress, and re-constructions of interiors are on display at the **Regional Museum** (*open Mon–Fri 9–12.30 and 2–5; closed weekends and holidays*). Go to the end of the Rua António de Santo and it is on the corner of the Praça da Liberdade. From here, veer right into the Rua do Pé da Cruz, at the end of which stands the small 17th-century **Church of Pé da Cruz**. Knock on the door for entry (*enquire at the turismo about opening times*). The church may have been built by New Christians—Jews forced to convert to Christianity in the 16th century—and contains fascinating visionary frescoes reminiscent of the work of William Blake. Painted by an unknown artist fond of yellow and black, the panels include *God Creating the Sun and Stars*, and the *Creation of the Animals*. The chancel contains two very strange compositions of blue and white *azulejos* depicting an unpeopled Calvary, surrounded by frescoes of the ladder and cross. (A duplicate image hangs in the Jerónimos Monastery at Belém.) Another uncommon feature is the outdoor chapel of Nosso Senhor dos Aflitos (Our Lord of the Distressed).

Tower blocks loom behind the **Carmo Church** in the Largo do Carmo, wrecking the effect of its grand façade of 1713. Lovesick angels support the richly gilded retable; to the right, a door leads to the panelled sacristy, and thence to the macabre **Capela dos Ossos** (Bone Chapel; *open Mon–Fri 10–1 and 3–5, Sat 10–1*). The walls of this simple and ghoulish chamber are entirely lined with some 1250 skulls and other monks' bones, extracted from graves around the church in 1816.

Beaches

There are some excellent **beaches** within easy striking distance of Faro—just hop on a ferry (*departs regularly from just outside the Old Town*) for a 40-minute ride to the **Ilhas Desertas**. Here you will find some 6km of Robinson Crusoe-like beaches in the warm lagoon waters of the protected Ria Formosa Parque Natural. Despite the name, mod cons include waterskiing and windsurfing. Another option is to take the bus back towards the airport to **Faro Beach**, which offers the choice of the cool Atlantic or the warm lagoon waters but is jam-packed in high season.

Where to Stay

expensive

****Hotel Eva**, Avenida da República, ✆ 289 803 354, ✉ 289 802 304, is far and away Faro's best hotel. The spacious rooms have large balconies with wonderful views of the harbour and the old town walls; the service is well-meaning and the management thoughtful. Rooms with sea views cost more. Competition threatens to arrive in the shape of the ****Faro Hotel**, though whenever it opens it will not have the marvellous views of the Eva.

The other major player in town is the ***Hotel Dom Bernardo**, Rua General Teófilio da Trinidade, ✆ 289 806 806, ✉ 289 806 800. It's modern and comfortable, but bland, and on a busy road towards the top of town. You'd be better off in a good *pensão*.

moderate

Probably the best choice in this category is the very friendly ***Residencial Algarve**, 52 Rua Infante Dom Henrique, ✆ 289 895 7001/2, ✆ 289 895 703. Rebuilt in 1999 in the exact architectural style of the late 19th-century original, it has a nice breakfast area and all rooms have cable TV and air-conditioning plus spanking-new bathrooms.

Just outside the Old Town is the **★★Residencial Samé**, 66 Rua do Bocage, ℂ 289 824 375, ✉ 289 804 166, unprepossessing from the outside but typically Portuguese inside with pleasant public rooms, clean, tidy tiled bedrooms and friendly staff. All rooms have TV and air-conditioning. Close to the railway station, **★★★Pensão Afonso III**, 64 Rua Dr Miguel Bombarda, ℂ 289 803 542, is popular with small groups. Rooms are a fair size, but the whole is nondescript. **★★★Pensão Iorque**, 37 Rua de Berlim, ℂ 289 823 973, is a comparatively quiet retreat on the edge of town, where rooms have TVs and fridges.

inexpensive–cheap

Most of the cheaper places to stay are in or around the Rua Conselheiro Bivar, off Praça Dom Francisco Gomes, or its extension, Rua Infante Dom Henrique, where there are also several grocery stores. Friendly **★★★Residencial Madalena**, 109 Rua Conselheiro Bivar, ℂ 289 805 806, ✉ 289 805 007, has clean basic rooms and dark corridors. For a bit of real Portugal, the distinctive and very friendly **Casa de Hóspedes Adelaide**, 9 Rua Cruz dos Mestres, ℂ/✉ 289 802 383, has some decent and very cheap large rooms to let. There is a communal kitchen and Adelaide is a colourful and chirpy landlady.

If all else fails (as it may well do in high season), there is a **youth hostel**, ℂ 289 801 970, ✉ 289 801 413, on the Rua do Matadouro, near the police station. Faro's **campsite** is on the sand spit, ℂ 289 817 876.

Eating Out

expensive

Restaurante O Gargalo, 30 Largo do Pé da Cruz, ℂ 289 827 305, is set in a pretty square with a small blue and white church at its mouth and a spouting fountain in its middle. There are tables outside, but the cool, calm interior is a treat. The multi-domed ceiling canopies, heavy wooden furniture and stained-glass windows add an ecclesiastical note. The food is excellent—this may be the place to experiment with *bacalhau.*

moderate

In the Old Town the best place to eat (indeed the only place to eat a proper meal within the old walls) is the classy **Mesa dos Mouros**, Largo da Sé, ℂ 289 878 873, which occupies a sturdy ancient stone house and a classy terrace right by the cathedral. Stylish and modern, it's a good place for fish and *tapas.*

Cidade Velha, just the other side of the cathedral is a very pleasant little snack bar, which also sprawls out on to the cobbled pavement. **Taverna do Sé**, just behind the church, is also worth seeking out for its mellow atmosphere (jazz or classical music often wafts through its windows), coffee and cakes or a cool glass of beer. In the centre of town, just off the pedestrianized streets, the **Adega Dois Irmãos**, Lago do Terreiro do Bispo, ℂ 289 823 337 (*expensive– moderate*) has been satisfying local palates and countless visitors since 1926 with perhaps the best fish and seafood in town. If you fancy a more informal meal try its sister restaurant, **Sol e Jardim** (*moderate*) two doors away, or pop your head into its neighbour, the **Adega Nortenha**. This is actually four eateries in one, each with a separate entrance: a basic locals' *tapas* bar, a formal restaurant, a crêperie and a *pastelaria*. Be promiscuous and have a different course in each place. For fresh fish, pick your own from the tank at **Vasco da Gama**, 49a Rua Vasco da Gama, ✆ 289 821 666. Beady eyes are the fishes' only defence.

cheap

Just outside the Old Town walls, **Adega Rocha**, 51 Rua da Misericórdia (no phone) is a thoroughly local experience. Sit down at a table and a plate of whatever is on the barbecue will be plonked down in front of you with a speed that would make McDonald's blush. Typically it's a plate of mixed fish with the usual potatoes and salad accompaniment. Another memorable place for a great local meal is the **Tasca O Chalaver**, 120 Rua Infante Dom Henrique, ✆ 289 822 455. You choose your dinner from a large fish- and meat-covered slab, then it is transferred to a huge open grill which smokes away under a black hood. The white walls are satisfyingly soot-marked, and covered by gnarled vines which squiggle across the sloping, corrugated-iron ceiling.

Just around the corner at **Adega Nova**, 24 Rua Francisco Barreto (no phone), there is a similar atmosphere of local bonhomie and good helpings of cheap but good-quality no-nonsense food in a beer-hall atmosphere.

Pay a visit to little **A Tasca**, 38 Rua do Alportel, ✆ 289 824 739, a joy of a restaurant. Locals sit at solid wooden tables, selecting large portions of excellent food from a small and very traditional menu. The sprightly owner serves each dish with a well-justified 'yum, yum'. Try *xarém com conquilhas*, a sort of thick maize broth cooked with garlic, herbs, sausages and cockles presented in a deep clay pot and easily enough for two. Right on the seafront is the **Café Aliança**, a venerable Faro institution. This old rambling place serves everything from full meals to a cup of coffee. It's atmospheric when full but rather depressing and down-at-heel in the cold light of day with just a few customers spread around.

While doing the shopping on Rua de Santo António, look out for the mouth-watering treats at the **Gardy** *pastelaria–croissanteria* at No.33. It is the takeaway offshoot of its famous namesake café opposite.

Entertainment and Nightlife

Faro's **nightlife** is fun and funky, concentrated around Rua do Prior, off Rua do 1 de Maio. After midnight, crowds of street-smart Portuguese and hip tourists head to bars such as the **Kingburger**, **Metropolitan** and **Adega dos Arcos**. A tiny road crosses Rua do Comprimisso and hosts a university hall of residence. The student bar, announced by a Heineken sign, is very lively during term times before everyone spills into the clubs such as **24 Julho** at about 2 to dance until dawn.

Estói and Milreu

Estói Palace

Open Tues–Sat 9–12.30 and 2–5.30. Frequent buses run to Estói from Faro (15mins).

The Algarve's only *palácio* is decaying 9km north of Faro at **Estói**. The late 18th-century building itself is closed to the public, undergoing conversion into a *pousada*, but the fanciful façade and garden, mashing together styles from the neoclassical to Art Nouveau, can be viewed. The weathervane is in the shape of a horse, perhaps indicating an equestrian streak in the Counts of Carvalhos, who lived here.

A short drive to the west, along roads bordered with arum lilies, lie the **Roman ruins** at **Milreu**, once a patrician's villa. Little is left standing above ground, and the site lacks atmosphere, but there are some witty fish mosaics in the baths next to the residential area. The entrance was remodelled in the 4th century, becoming a small vestibule with two semicircular fountains on either side. The temple consecrated to water deities is another 4th-century building. The agricultural quarters, to the southeast, are divided into small rooms for farm labourers. You will find a useful English-language guide on sale at the entrance.

Moncarapacho

Ten kilometres east of Estói lies a quietly sunny village arranged around the Gothic **Church of Santo Cristo** at its centre. Outside, the sculptural decoration of the clean Renaissance portal depicts Jesus bound and flanked by his captors. A brazenly gilt baroque altar lights up the interior of this well-cared-for church; the scent of fresh flowers is intoxicating. The pillars and underside of the arches were once painted with an intricate flower design in red and black, which is fading fast. Next door is a small **museum** (*open Mon, Wed and Fri 11am–3pm*), which houses the collection of the local priest who's now in his late 80s. The gem of this whimsical accumulation of sacred art is an 18th-century Neapolitan nativity scene made up of 42 delicate pieces, rescued by the priest from a Faro convent many years since. The church square is shaded by purple-flowering jacaranda trees, and carob and palm leaves rustle above the locals who sit framed by a mustard-coloured house and watch life crawl by.

Where to Stay

★★★★**Estalagem Monte do Casal**, Cerro do Lobo, ✆ 289 891 503, ✉ 289 891 341 (*expensive*) is reached from Estói by taking the road to Moncarapacho. It's a pleasantly converted 18th-century farmhouse, set in lush, fragrant grounds with a rustic restaurant and well-shaded pool. This haven of tranquillity offers a number of suites with large rooms but these can become booked up by tour operators, so be sure to make your reservations early. The restaurant (*expensive*) serves carefully prepared regional food, proffered by polite staff, most of whom seem to be English.

Two kilometres north of São Brás de Alportel, 16km north of Faro, a grassy driveway curves up a gentle hill planted with olive trees to the low-key **Pousada de São Brás**, ✆ 289 842 305, ✉ 289 841 726, central reservations ✆ 218 442 001, ✉ 218 442 085, or book through Caravela, ✆ (020) 7630 9223. The main reason for coming here is its peace and quiet; rooms are a reasonable size and pleasantly decorated in an elegant and tasteful modern-meets-traditional style. They are air-conditioned though there is no television or radio. Grounds include a swimming pool and a tennis court. However, the food is very disappointing and the atmosphere in the dining room is that of a 1960s Grand Hotel in a British seaside resort, over-formal and stultifying.

Loulé

Twenty kilometres northwest of Estói is the Algarve's largest inland town, set in countryside alive with orange and lemon groves. Loulé is aesthetically undistinguished; its main attraction is as a market town and handicraft centre, with crafts workers always busy in their open workshops. The artisans, many of Moorish origin, have been practising basket weaving, lacemaking, pottery and copper work since Loulé's recapture from the Moors in 1249.

Getting There

Frequent buses make the half-hour journey from Faro. The **bus station** is on Rua Dr F. da Silva, off Avenida José da Costa Mealha, which turns into the central Praça da República.

Tourist Information

The **tourist office**, ✆ 289 463 900, is off the bottom of Praça da República in the castle forecourt.

The **post office** is on Rua Dom Paio, Peres Correia, Ed. Castelo.

Loulé's **market**, on Praça da República, is a curious building with an arabesque dome topped by the crescent moon of the Muslims. It bubbles with trade every morning, reaching a peak of activity on Saturdays.

A weekly **country market** also visits the town on Saturdays, drawing an assortment of bargain-hungry tourists who flood Loulé until after lunch. The market is wise to its powers of attraction and a genuine bargain is rare.

The country around here is ideal to explore on **horseback** and the garrulous proprietor of Quinta do Azinheiro at Aldeia de Tôr, some 8km north of Loulé, ✆ 289 415 991, has a large stable of fine horses for hire at very reasonable rates.

Loulé takes its festivals more seriously than the rest of the Algarve, which is generally half-hearted in its pre-Lent celebrations. Loulé's **carnival** around February is charming. Mamas photograph their daughters dressed as fairies, and their sons dressed as gangsters—who wave when they remember—on floats pulled by tractors, for five full days of merriment.

The Easter festival of the Sovereign Mother is a more solemn occasion: on Easter Sunday, a 16th-century image of the Virgin is carried into the town from a nearby shrine and returned through crowd-lined streets two weeks later.

A few walls of the Moorish **castle** still remain and the restored walkway incorporates the **municipal museum**, which displays the signatures of some of the medieval masons who worked on the castle.

Loulé's most outlandish building perches on a hilltop some 2km west of town, visible from the town centre. The pure white dome of a modern church looks like a UFO, or transport for an angel born without wings. It appears to be abandoned.

In front stands the tiny 16th-century **Chapel of Nossa Senhora da Piedade**, crumbling quietly. The stained-glass window behind the carved and painted altar casts deep-coloured light on the tiled walls. Large plaster panels depict the last days of Christ; some have blackened to obscurity. On a little table by the altar there appears to be an accumulation of stray human bits. Don't be alarmed: these wax *ex votos* are an odd but touching feature of many churches. The limbs, heads, chests, breasts, stomachs, hands, babies and pigs are intended to attract divine cures for their respective ailments. They are often heaped on altars in a promiscuous jumble, or hung from strings.

Shopping

Head for Rua das Bicas Velhas to watch potters at work in the small shop signed 'Artesanaria Pottery'; a couple sit to the side of their display, he in front of the wheel shaping the pots while she paints dry ones. Round the corner at 19 Rua Dom Paio Peres Correia, just before the castle, is the more pricey **Casa Louart**, where you can have ceramics hand-painted to your own specifications. It takes three to four days to process a commission for anything from an ashtray upwards. **Casa O Arco** on Rua dos Almadas (underneath an arch off Praca Dom Afonso III) has some nice plates, pottery and hand-painted *azulejos*.

Rua da Barbaça behind the castle is full of craft workshops: **Caldeiraria Louletana** sells all manner of things copper. Its speciality, a large hand-beaten *cataplana*, costs 9,000$00 and will last forever. A few doors away, **Correaria Louletana** specializes in equestrian leatherware.

Slightly out of the way but still very central is the **Casa Alenterjana**, on Rua Condestável Nuno Alvares Pereira (just off Largo Afonso III behind the castle). This mouthwatering delicatessen is devoted to the produce of the Alentejo, stocked principally with hams, cheeses and regional wines.

The understated ★★★**Loulé Jardim Hotel**, Largo Manuel de Arriga, ✆ 289 413 094 (*moderate*) is the town's only hotel. It occupies the corner of a lovely square fanned by the hazy purple blooms of jacaranda trees. Modern and well-designed, the rooms are built around a small and sunny quadrangle. All around are plants and flowery sofas, enhancing the cool and fresh feeling of the public rooms.

If you prefer self-catering, the hills around Loulé are dotted with some lovely villas. Four particularly beautiful retreats, all created from traditional houses and farmsteads, are: **Quintassential**, a two-bedroom cottage and two one-bedroom cottages; the **Garden Cottages** at Boliqueime, two cottages for two people (no children); **Quinta das Figueiras**, which accommodates up to six people; and **A Quinta**, which can take up to eight. The latter two have private swimming pools, the former have shared pools. For details call Simply Portugal in the UK on ✆ (020) 8541 2207.

Eating Out

Loule's best-known and most acclaimed restaurant, serving first-class regional food, is **Bica Velha**, at 17 Martim Moniz, behind the castle. However, it is only open in the evenings (*Mon–Sat*), which is inconvenient if you are visiting Loulé for the morning markets. In this case, try its neighbour at No.41, **A Muralha**, ✆ 289 412 629. Set in a lovely bougainvillea-decked rustic garden, this *churrasqueira* includes among its specialities *cataplanas*, *feijoada de mariscos* (beans and shellfish) and of course grilled fish and *espetada* (kebabs), all at moderate prices. Also in the centre of town, on Rua Sà de Miranda, are **Casa dos Arcos**, ✆ 289 416 713, and **Paralelo 38** (*no telephone bookings*). Both are highly rated for their cheap–moderate-priced traditional food, though neither enjoys a very inspired dining room.

A more interesting dining experience, as long as you have your own transport, is to be had at one of the many excellent rustic restaurants (*moderate*) just outside Loulé. **A Carruagem**, ✆ 289 412 775, on the road to Quarteira, **Moinho do Ti Casa**, ✆ 289 438 108, on the road to Querença, and particularly **O Paixanito**, ✆ 289 412 775, also on the Querença road, are favourites with locals and ex-pats. All are family-owned and have unpredictable hours so you will have to book ahead to make sure of a meal.

Tavira and the Eastern Coast

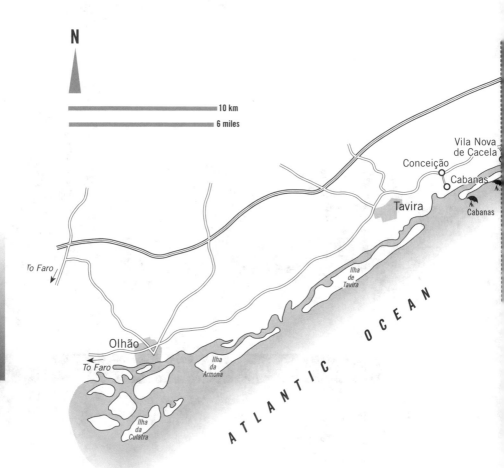

Head east of Faro for beautiful, baking beaches sheltered by islets and for the Rio Formosa nature reserve. Development is oozing towards the border with Spain, but there are no high-rise hotels outside the crowded package resort of Monte Gordo. There, groomed gamblers roll the dice at the beachfront casino. A few kilometres away, in peaceful hamlets almost too tiny for the name, chickens flee visitors with a rush of feathers.

The *sotavento* (leeward) shore offers long beaches lapped by calm, warm water, as opposed to the *barlavento* (windward) beaches with their

beefier waves. Tiny crabs scuttle off thorugh the sand as ferries dock on the jetties. Penetrate a little inland and wander through orange, lemon, peach and apricot groves divided by ancient walls crumbling in the heat of the sun.

Visitors to Tavira and Olhão will find the locals friendly and relaxed, with none of the hard-nosed hard-sell tourist tactics common in the larger resorts, partly because both towns host their own small industries. Everyone finds time to sit around throwing back the *bicas* and nattering humorously, in a perpetual post-prandial lethargy. A balm for the weary.

Olhão

Eight kilometres east of Faro, the fishing town of Olhão is sheltered from the open sea by a series of offshore islands, which comprise part of the Rio Formosa Estuary and nature reserve. Ferries run from Olhão to the two flat islands of Armona and Culatra, hidden from view, which are fringed with uncrowded white-sand beaches.

Olhão's cubic houses with their flat roofs and external staircases were inspired by trade with North Africa, and brought a modest fame—they owe nothing to the Moors, as the town was founded in the 16th century. Its moment of glory came in 1811, when two local fishermen sailed to Rio de Janeiro in a caique without navigational charts, to tell the fugitive King Dom João VI that Napoleon's troops had left Portugal. As a reward the king granted Olhão the status of a town, and renamed it Olhão da Restauração (a cognomen that was dropped as it brought back unpleasant memories of the subsequent War of Restoration).

Getting There and Around

Frequent **buses and trains** take 15mins from Faro. For bus information, ring © 289 702 157. Inexpensive **ferries to the islands** depart from the quay, a short walk from the tourist office. Buy your ticket at the kiosk before boarding. Ferries make the 15-minute trip to **Ilha da Armona** every 60 or 90 minutes June–Sept. (They run three times daily in May and Oct, and twice daily at other times.) Ferries to the **Ilha da Culatra** depart seven times daily June–Sept, and four times daily for the rest of the year.

The helpful **tourist office** (*open Mon–Fri 9–12 and 2.30–5, Sat 9–12; June–Sept daily 9.30–7*) is in the Largo Sebastião Martins Mestre, ✆ 289 713 936. Just walk up the Rua Olhanense and it is on the left.

Olhão's huge **market** (*Mon–Fri*) occupies two large halls overlooking the harbour with silver domes at each corner. You'll see more variety of fish and shellfish than Noah did. On Saturdays there is also a general open-air market outside.

Olhão celebrates the fertility of the sea by staging a large seafood festival in August. The streets are awash with masticating crowds, jostling each other around long trestle tables.

The town is decaying sleepily; all the action happens at the restaurant-edged harbour. The jumble of old streets has overflowed into a dull grid pattern, and many of the residents are rickety, though always neatly coiffed; there is a superfluity of barber shops in Olhão. At the centre of town stand two churches roofed with terracotta. An angel with a bell skirt serves as a weathervane for the **Igreja Matriz**, built in 1698. At the rear of the church, the **Capela dos Aflitos** (Chapel of the Suffering) is always open, for the wives of fishermen to pray during storms. To see what the seagulls see, climb to the top of the church tower (*usually open Tues–Sun 9.30–12 and 3–6, or try knocking on the adjacent door for the key*).

olhão

Beaches

On **Ilha da Armona**, passengers disembark at Armona's single settlement, facing the mainland, where there are a couple of laid-back restaurants, and swimmers enjoying the warm water. Follow the main path for 20 minutes, past interminable prefabricated beach huts, to the smooth, fine beach, which has a friendly atmosphere and is long enough to offer escape from other people. For accommodation on Armona try the **campsite**, ✆ 289 714 173, or Orbitur, ✆ 289 714 173, who have inexpensive bungalows.

Along the sand spit called **Ilha da Culatra**, several rundown fishing villages face the mainland, mixing uncomfortably with a rash of huts. The ferry's first stop is **Culatra**, a grim settlement—it's better to stay on board and go to **Farol**, ¾hr from Olhão, a village of beach huts flanked by sand beaches, where the **Hotel Bar Tropical** offers the only accommodation.

Ria Formosa Nature Reserve

The reserve was established to protect the rich variety of water birds—especially various herons—and marine life that finds a hoime on the sand islets between Faro and Manta Rota. Even if you haven't brought your binoculars there's a good source of information, a little of it in English, about the district's wildlife a kilometre east of Olhão at **Quinta de Marim** (*open weekdays 9–12.30 and 2–5*). The 60-hectare environmental education centre features displays, examples of eco-systems and a mill powered by the tides.

The region's most curious creature is the famed Portuguese water dog, a sort of large unkempt poodle with webbed feet. Algarvians claim that these dogs can be trained to dive several metres to chase shoals of fish into nets and, more plausibly, that they retrieve drifting tackle and nets. Very few still work in the Algarve; more often they just procreate in the reserves. Although there are fears for the breed's future in Portugal, a substantial number of water dogs are found in England and America.

Where to Stay

 Olhão's accommodation is cheap and low-key. The four-storey **★★Hotel Ria Sol**, 37 Rua General Humberto Delgado, ✆ 289 705 267 (*moderate–inexpensive*), occupies a convenient spot near the centre of town. The hotel is relatively upmarket: all rooms have their own bathrooms and some have balconies. The service is eager.

★★Pensão Bicuar, 5 Rua Vasco da Gama, ✆ 289 714 816 (*cheap*) has decent rooms with colourful bedspreads, while **★★Pensão Boémia**, Rua Dr Estevão, near Largo da Liberdade, ✆ 289 721 122 (*cheap*) is probably the nicest *pensão* in town, with a very friendly owner, and clean modern rooms with cable TV; some have balconies with picture-postcard views over the Olhão rooftops and alleyways. **★★★Pensão Bela Vista**, 65–67 Rua Dr Teófilo Braga, ✆ 289 702 538 (*cheap*) is small, clean and decent, and the rooms are a good size; Granny sits by the balcony at the end of the corridor, knitting.

Olhão's **campsite** is 2km east, ✆ 289 700 300.

Eating Out

Restaurants are elbow to elbow on Avenida do 5 Outobro, opposite the harbour, offering very fresh fish. **Pescador 2** (*cheap*) is full of diminutive fishermen tucking into the catch of the day. **O Aquário**, on Rua Dr João Lúcio (*moderate*), serves a nicely spicy prawn curry to diners sitting beneath a mural of a mermaid. There is nothing touristy about **Vai e Volta**, Largo do Grémio (*cheap*), which occupies the corner of a peeling square. Everything is grilled over charcoal outside and second helpings are always on offer. The Portuguese clientele bubbles with laughter. Another fish option, this time with a view of the sea and distant beaches, is the simple **Snack Bar Ria Formosa** (*low moderate*) in the gardens just before the fish market (coming from Faro direction).

If you fancy a change from fish, try **Doca's Pizza**, Avenida 5 de Outubro, ✆ 289 713 118 (*moderate*), a smart Italian restaurant hidden behind smoked glass windows; they have a good range of pastas, pizzas and salads. One to try on the islands is the **Restaurant St Antoine** on Ilha da Armona, ✆ 289 706 549, where Didier and Ilse bring a touch of Belgian cooking to Algarve fish dishes.

For delicious *bolos* and marzipan sweets created by genial bakers, visit the **Pastelaria e Confeitaria Contreiras e Almeida** on pedestrianized Rua Dr João Lúcio, which fills with a sweet-scented cloud.

Luz de Tavira

Twelve kilometres east of Olhão, it's worth pausing at this village to visit its small **church**, which stands starkly white against the azure sky, with a large Renaissance portal rippling out in many tiers. The dome above is flanked by a pair of fishtails; the side door is a Manueline flourish of twisting grapes and vine leaves.

Tavira

Thirty kilometres northeast of Faro and 23km southwest of Vila Real de Santo António, the most beautiful town in the Algarve has hardly been affected by its moderate flow of visitors; the only tide to sweep through it is that of the Gilão River, whose banks are lined with both grand and humble houses, and which is crossed by a bridge originally built by the Romans.

Founded by the Turduli *c.* 2000 BC or by the Greeks *c.* 400 BC, Tavira's fortune was based on tuna fishing. Shoals of the fish used to be harpooned off Faro from the end of April to the end of June, as they swam eastwards to spawn in the Mediterranean, and off Tavira, when the fish returned westwards, thinner, in July and August. Tuna are now only found on the high seas, but the Tavirans have retained a taste for the firm grey meat.

Tavira's gentle hillslopes, castle battlements and 25 churches create a lovely roofline of peaked and weathered terracotta. There are wonderful beaches nearby.

Getting There

Frequent buses and trains run from Faro (both ¾hr). The **bus terminus** is on Rua dos Pelames, ✆ 281 322 546, from which you turn left and walk two minutes to reach the tourist office, while the **railway station** is 1km away, along the Rua da Liberdade.

Tourist Information

The **tourist office**, ✆ 281 322 511, is situated at 9 Rua de Galeria.

The **Caixa Geral bank** on Rua José Pires Padinha opposite the garden has an **automatic exchange machine**, though facilities can become stretched on summer weekends.

The **post office** is a two-minute walk up the Rua da Liberdade; there is a good **bakery** (*padaria*) closer to the main square.

Tavira's **SOS clinic**, © 281 381 750, where English is spoken, is on Avenida Dr Mateus Teixeira de Azevedo.

Guided walking tours of the town are on offer daily from the prosaically named **Historical Itineraries of Tavira** for a small charge. Either ask at the helpful tourist office or call © 281 321 946 for details.

Around the Town

Tavira's ruined castle walls still top the town and give spectacular views. Immediately below, the **churches of Santa Maria and Santiago** are a beautiful, Moorish ensemble, heralded by Santa Maria's cockerel weathervane. The **Misericórdia**, near the tourist office, has an attractive Renaissance portal, built between 1541 and 1551, with Saints Peter and Paul at its corners. There is a fine pair of 18th-century bench seats in the **Carmo church** (cross the river and go through the Largo de São Braz; collect its huge key from No.22 opposite).

Tavira has in recent years become a centre for local artists and writers; the men gather in Tavira's bars at night and impress American girls with their creativity. There are regular exhibitions of local art at **Galeria Municipal**, part of the town hall on Praça da República, and **Casa das Artes** on Rua João Vaz Corte Real. The conversion of the **Old Market** is due for completion in summer 2000, and will provide another cultural and commercial centre.

The **Ilha de Tavira** is a dazzling offshore sandbank stretching 11km west from Tavira, lapped by the Algarve's warmest jade-green waters. Get there by taking the bus marked Quatro Águas (*June–Sept frequent service*) from the stop next to the cinema. The 10-minute ride connects with a ferry (*crossings 8am–11pm*). During the summer there is a direct ferry which leaves from near the market. The quay is on the eastern tip of the island, surrounded by beach huts. A brief walk will remove you from the crowds. A handful of restaurants and bars have sprung up on the Ilha, directed at the population of the **campsite** (© 281 324 555), which harbours a varied crowd, from families to young travellers sprouting dreadlocks. **The Sunshine Bar** is a fun place with a youthful feel, run by a jolly Anglo-Irish couple.

The area around Tavira is blessed with many species of wild flower. The 6km walk to Tavira's **National Forest** ('Mata Nacional') follows a path through orange groves, farmland and small communities; the road is edged with carob, almond and fig trees. At their feet, small poppies, irises and pink and scarlet pimpernels burst into bloom. The forest of eucalyptus trees is not as grand or lush as it sounds, but the air is fresh with its cool scent and birds trill happily. Take the highway east out of Tavira and turn left after the Eurotel; a small sign shyly announces 'Mata Nacional da Conceição'.

In 2000, Benamor (*see* p.18) became the first new **golf course** to open in the Algarve east of Faro.

Tavira

Rio Séqua

ESTRADA DE ASSECA

RUA JOÃO VAZ CORTE REAL

RUA DA BORDA ÁGUA DA ASSE

ESTRADA DA BELAFRIA

RUA DOS PELAMES

Bus
Station

RUA DETRAZ DOS MUROS

Church of
Misericórdia

RUA DA GALERIA

RUA D
GALER

Tourist
Office

Church of Santa
Maria do Castelo

Castle
(ruins)

RUA DA LIBERDAD

RUA ANTÓNIO VIEGAS

Post Office

SOS
Clinic

RUA DR MIGUEL BOMBARDA

AVENIDA DR MATEUS TEIXEIRA DE AZEVEDO

RUA TENENTE COUTE

To train
station

N

200 metres
200 yards

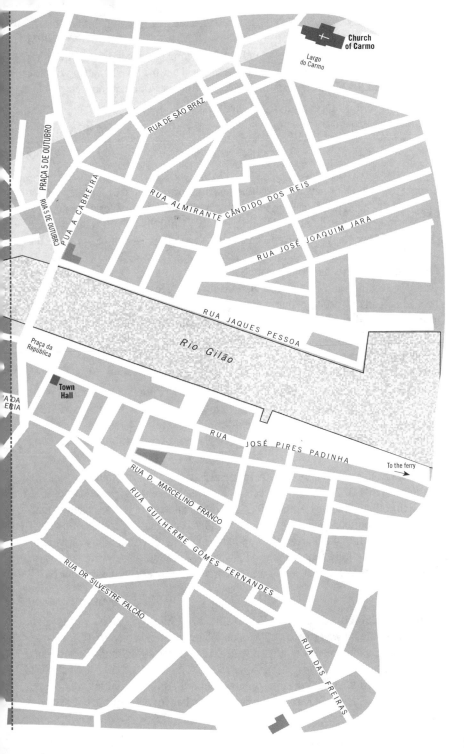

Church
of Carmo

Largo
do Carmo

RUA DE SÃO BRAZ

PRAÇA 5 DE OUTUBRO

RUA 5 DE OUTUBRO

RUA A CABREIRA

RUA ALMIRANTE CÂNDIDO DOS REIS

RUA JOSÉ JOAQUIM JARA

RUA JAQUES PESSOA

Rio Gilão

Praça da
República

Town
Hall

A DA
ERIA

RUA   JOSÉ   PIRES   PADINHA

To the ferry
→

RUA D. MARCELINO FRANCO

RUA GUILHERME GOMES FERNANDES

RUA DR SILVESTRE FALCÃO

RUA DAS FREIRAS

Shopping

Considering its elegant appearance and the discerning crowds it draws, Tavira has always been disappointingly short of good shops. That may well change with the long-awaited **Old Market**, open (hopefully) in summer 2000 (*see* above).

Next to the tourist office, on Rua da Galeria, **Al Arte** has some nice hand-painted ceramics and *azulejos*.

Where to Stay

hotels

 A major new luxury hotel, the **Albacora**, with 161 rooms, an indoor pool, health club and two restaurants, all set in extensive grounds, is scheduled to open in summer 2001. Until then if you want to stay at a hotel you'll have to go a couple of kilometres east of Tavira, to the ★★★**Eurotel**, Quinta das Oliveiras, ✆ 281 324 324, ✆ 281 325 571 (*expensive*) with its adjoining villa complex of Quinta das Oliveiras. There are plenty of facilities and lovely grounds inhabited by geese, but the place is often booked up early by package-tour operators.

The best *pensão/residencial* in Tavira is **Residencial Marés**, 134–40 Rua José Pires Padinha, ✆ 281 325 815, ✆ 281 325 819 (*expensive–moderate*), just along the front past the converted market. Though pricey, it's extremely comfortable, with river views.

Spruce ★★**Residencial Princesa do Gilão**, 10–12 Rua Borda de Água de Aguiar, ✆ 281 325 171 (*inexpensive–cheap*), overlooks the river, with very good views towards the main part of town. ★**Residencial Castelo**, 4 Rua da Liberdade, ✆ 281 323 942 (*inexpensive–cheap*), is a warren of rooms, with self-catering options.

The best cheap place to stay is ★★**Residencial Lagôas**, 24 Rua Almirante Cândido dos Reis, ✆ 281 322 252 (*cheap*), across the river from the Praça da República—turn right off the Praça Dr António Padinha. Small and clean, it is arranged around two levels of rooftops. There are communal fridges, and laundry facilities on one of the roofs, which make a great place to look at the stars with a bottle of wine or two. The wonderfully good-humoured landlady Maria jokes in several languages, and runs the excellent **Bica** restaurant downstairs (*see* overleaf, 'Eating Out').

Solares de Portugal

Quinta do Caracol, ✆ 281 322 475, ✆ 281 323 175 (*expensive*), on the landward side of the railway station, is a wonderful 200-year-old converted farmhouse, whitewashed and draped with bougainvillea. Each of the seven homey apartments includes a basic kitchenette and a shower room; some overlook the raised circular pool, once used for washing laundry, now painted and intended for wallowing. Other facilities include a hard tennis court and a bar frequented by the resident owners and their family. The railway track is nearby, but trains are infrequent. There is one 2-person apartment and six 4–5-person apartments. Bookings can also be made through Simply Portugal, ✆ (020) 8541 2207.

The **Convento do São Antonio**, 56 Atalaia, ✆ 281 325 632 (*luxury–expensive*), behind the army barracks, is a 17th-century monastery, lovingly converted and filled with antiques. It's been in the family of the charming Isabel for two centuries, and is patently her passion. The six bedrooms retain the peaceful aura of monks' cells. If luxury is more your line, opt for the suite. Bathed in Tavira sunshine, the watchtower overlooks the salt marshes, and the circular swimming pool is flanked by an ancient bucket-mill well. Guests are free to eat or linger in the central courtyard. Excellent value for the warmest of welcomes.

Quinta da Fonte do Bispo, 270 Estrada Nacional Santa Catarina, ✆/✉ 281 971 484 (*inexpensive*), is a *Solares de Portugal* property about 11km northwest of Tavira on the road to São Brás. This converted farmhouse lounges in six hectares of wooded land, which includes a swimming pool and tennis courts. The six self-catering apartments are stone-floored and wood-beamed, with a bedroom, kitchenette and a sitting room with sofa-beds for the kids. They are as rustic as the bar and breakfast room which opens on to a flower-draped patio. Sandra Gomes oversees the smooth running of the farm while chatting away in good English mysteriously tinged with a slight cockney accent.

villa rentals

Simply Portugal (✆ (020) 8541 2207) are agents for the splendid **Moinho do Sol**, a converted windmill at Estorninhos some 15km from town. Its hilltop perch offers a panoramic 360° view of the surrounding countryside and in addition to the conventional double bedroom there is a special 'siesta gallery' where you can snooze and watch shooting stars. Another characterful, comfortable and well-run property just outside Tavira is **O Pequeno Castelo**, run by a friendly young German family. Simply Portugal handle booking for its apartment, which sleeps four people (though you can also go direct), and the 'little castle' also does bed and breakfast (*inexpensive*) and evening meals on request. It is located at Santo Estevão 6km from Tavira, ✆/✉ 281 961 692.

For excellent tourist villages with communal facilities, try **Pedras d'el Rei**, ✆ 281 325 354, ✉ 281 324 020, or **Pedras d'el Rainha**, ✆ 281 320 182, ✉ 281 320 282 (*both moderate*), located at Santa Luzia, 3km west of Tavira, and at Cabanas, 5km east of Tavira. Both are well designed and close to undeveloped beaches. The villas' wooden-trellised windows overlook shared lawns, so the sites feel spacious and private, while the interiors are simply furnished in cool local materials. Both villages incorporate a swimming pool, restaurant, post and telephone facilities, babysitter and a well-stocked supermarket, which sells firewood for chilly winter evenings. The beach is a short walk away. Villas range in size from 2–10 beds. For other villa rentals ask at the tourist office.

expensive

The **Quatro Águas**, © 281 325 329, on the harbour where the ferry departs for the Ilha, is a cool, elegant restaurant with a fish tank of beady-eyed crustaceans. An army of rooftops lays siege to the **O Patio Restaurante**, 30 Rua António Cabreira, © 281 323 008, a boisterous-looking place with a rarefied atmosphere. The extensive selection of seafood is of the highest quality and the portions huge.

moderate

A little closer to the centre of town, **Imperial**, 22 Rua José Pires Padinha, © 281 322 234, is always bustling and is renowned for its fish. *Closed Wed.* If *cataplana* is your thing then Imperial do it very well, but you will get the widest possible selection further along the quayside at **O Caneção**, 162 Rua José Pires Padinha, © 281 325 260, who modestly boast of producing the world's best. What is for sure is that they wok up some unusual varieties, including lamb. *Closed Thurs.*

Ameijoas na Cataplana

The Algarve's signature dish is basically clams in a pan. If you don't have a *cataplana* pan, use a heavy-based pan or wok with a lid; the tighter the lid, the more the flavours will be locked in.

Ingredients (*serves 4–6*)

> *2kg clams, washed, scrubbed and soaked (change the water once or twice and discard any which are open)*
> *1tbsp olive oil*
> *2 onions, sliced*
> *4 garlic cloves, crushed*
> *100g smoked bacon*
> *150g chouriço/chorizo style sausage*
> *2 medium tomatoes, skinned and chopped*
> *1 green pepper, thinly sliced*
> *2 cups white wine*
> *half tsp paprika*
> *few drops piri-piri sauce (see p.118) or tabasco if not available*
> *1 bay leaf*
> *salt and pepper to taste*
> *1 tbsp parsley, chopped*

Heat the oil in your chosen pan and fry the onion and garlic, chop up the bacon and sausage and toss it in, together with the tomatoes, green pepper and white wine. Simmer for a few minutes, season with salt, pepper, paprika, piri-piri and add the bay leaf. Add the clams, stir gently, put the lid on and cook for 10–15 minutes on a moderate heat. Sprinkle with parsley and serve with crusty bread.

Aquasul, 11–13 Rua Dr Augusto da Silva Carvalho, is a cosy restaurant on the north side of the river with sassy staff. It's the place to go if your stomach is rebelling against fresh fish; good pizzas and starters provide variety.

cheap

For a good cheap fish meal aim for the down-to-earth **Carmina**, 96 Rua José Pires Padhina, ✆ 281 322 236. It's festooned with fishing paraphernalia, with more stories than captain Ahab, full of salty old sea dogs and right opposite the fish auction. *Closed Sun.*

Petisqueira Belmar, 16 Rua Almirante Cândido dos Reis, ✆ 281 324 995, is a small and busy restaurant with a sloping ceiling. Popular with tourists at lunchtime, the atmosphere is friendly. Go for the half-portions, which are quite big enough and delightfully cheap; the succulent swordfish steak comes with a butter and herb sauce. On the same street, **Bica**, on the ground floor of the Residencial Lagôas, ✆ 281 322 252, is very plain but serves the most delicious fresh tuna steaks, cooked with onions in butter, and a range of beautifully prepared food. The massive portions are very good value and the house wine is very drinkable.

Entertainment and Nightlife

Tavira's **nightlife** is played out along the river front with young Portuguese threading their way through Tavira's smiling tourists. **Arco Bar**, 67 Rua Almirante Cândido dos Reis, is popular with a gay and straight crowd. The atmosphere is mellow, with low tables and a friendly Dutch owner. A metallic hangar on the outskirts of town houses Tavira's best disco, **UBI**, a popular venue which hosts different party nights. Keep an eye out for posters around town advertising the infamous *espuma* (foam) nights, an import from Ibiza. To get there follow Rua Almirante Cândido dos Reis to the edge of town; the disco is in a large warehouse on the right. It's open from 11pm to very late, though you can get there earlier and get in the mood with a beer or three at its **Bubi Bar**. A hot newcomer in 2000 was the **Ref' Café**, Rua Gonçalo Velho (south of the river almost on the front to the left of the Roman Bridge). They open from 9pm until 3am, playing drum'n'bass, acid jazz, jungle and other dance beats..

From Tavira to Vila Real

A short walk from Conceição, 5km east of Tavira, **Cabanas** is a simple fishing village sheltered from the sea by a sandbank, with many restaurants on its promenade. The last one, **A Roda** (*moderate*), has a lovely terrace draped with bougainvillea. Squelch out to the sandspit at low tide, when the locals are digging for shellfish with trowels, and when fossils can be found on the beach at the end of the coast road. The beach is one of the friendliest in the Algarve, popular with families, but not exclusively so. The mainland sandy beach is backed by grassy dunes and a ruined fort.

If anywhere in the Algarve deserves the epithet 'unspoilt', it's the hamlet of **Cacela Velha**, on the coast 3km east of Cabanas. Surrounded by ploughed fields, the settlement clusters around a whitewashed church and a little 18th-century fortress perched atop a cliff. Most of the mainland beach has been colonized by silvery bushes, but there are sheltered spots amongst them where you can sunbathe and picnic, or you could try to persuade someone to row you over to the sand spit that shelters Cacela from the sea (at low tide you can even walk across). This is a great place to watch the sun go down to the sound of tinkling goat bells, and afterwards sit outside at the hamlet's only restaurant, **Casa Velha** (*cheap*).

The sole reason for going to **Vila Nova de Cacela**, 2km further east, is to eat huge portions of wonderfully fresh grilled fish at low prices at **A Camponesa**, ✆ 281 951 351 (*moderate*), off the main road. The surroundings are about as simple as you can get: concrete floor, corrugated-iron roof, Formica tables, paper placemats, and no walls. It's a popular restaurant full of people delighted to have found the Real Thing. There is a **campsite** 2km inland from Vila Nova at Caliço, ✆ 281 951 195.

Some 2km east of Vila Nova de Cacela is the small and unremarkable modern resort of **Manta Rota**, with its handful of restaurants and bars on the beach. The development is low-key and low-rise, mainly consisting of holiday homes and villa complexes. The wide white and fine-sanded beach is mostly frequented by families. **Praia da Alagoa** is another fine family beach languishing beneath the tall gaze of the Altura Hotel. About 6km further east of Manta Rota, **Praia Verde** is the most unspoilt stretch of beach east of Tavira, completely undeveloped, with no facilities bar the **Pézinhos n'Areia** restaurant (*moderate*). A tourist village, ironically called 'Real Village', is under construction in the heart of the pine woods. Get there before it is completed.

Monte Gordo

A little farther on, 4km west of Vila Real de Santo António, the joyless modern resort of Monte Gordo has little to recommend it. Grid-patterned streets of no-frills houses with gardens are being elbowed out by lofty hotels and large restaurants, which vie for space overlooking the very wide white beach popular with the British and Dutch. Monte Gordo is awash with signs advertising hotels and restaurants, and pointing the way to various places. The most helpful one is '*saída*'—'way out'.

Tourist Information

There is a **tourist office,** ✆ 281 544 495 (*open summer 9.30–7; shorter hours in winter*), on the beachfront just before the casino, which is usually filled with tourists demanding bus and train timetables for excursions to 'anywhere'. **Bicycles** may be hired at 23 Rua Pedro Álvares Cabral, near the pharmacy.

Boat Trips

Boat trips up the River Guadiana are run by Riosul, Rua Tristão Vaz Teixeira 15, ✆ 281 510 200. They also do Jeep safaris alongside the river or you can combine the two into a 'Super Safari'.

Where to Stay

If you must stay for a few nights, all is not lost; the very pleasant low-rise ★★★★**Hotel Casablanca**, Rua 7, ✆ 281 511 444, ✉ 281 511 999 (*expensive*) is set back from the beach and is equipped with small indoor and outdoor swimming pools, a poolside snack bar and a walled sun area. Bedrooms are cool and attractive. The ★★★**Hotel Baia de Monte Gordo**, Rua Diogo Cão, ✆ 281 510 500, ✉ 281 510 509 (*moderate*) is clean and functional.

The modern ★★**Pensão Monte Gordo**, Avenida Infante Dom Henrique, ✆ 281 542 570 (*moderate*) is favoured for its spot on the seafront. Monte Gordo's **campsite** is on the road to Vila Real, ✆ 281 542 588.

Eating Out

Copacabana, Avenida Infante Dom Henrique, ✆ 281 541 536 (*expensive*) serves reliable Portuguese food on a fragrant terrace surrounded by flowers.

If you can brave the brief walk along the town's soulless main thoroughfare, Rua Pedro Alvares Cabral, right at the end, on the left, at No.37, is the **Adega Tipica do Swiss Bar Restaurant**, ✆ 281 544 360 (*moderate–cheap*). Their down-to-earth menu might include such old favourites as *feijoadas a transmontana* (beans and meat), and *arroz de polvo* (octopus with rice) at remarkably low prices. Or you could go for their 'Swiss' specials, *fondue bourguignonne* or *fondue chinoise*. Turn left at the end of the street to find **O Tapas**, 24 Rua Pedro Vaz Caminha, ✆ 281 541 847 (*moderate–cheap*), which still packs in the locals and serves them large portions of good fish and seafood. The meat selection is limited. *Closed Mon.* **Mota**, ✆ 281 542 650 (*cheap*), is a spacious hamburger grill on the beach, with seats outside.

The bakery on the opposite corner, **Padaria Pani Ficadora Jovem**, ✆ 281 544 428, sells aromatic fresh bread, moist cakes and neat marzipan fruit.

Entertainment and Nightlife

The **casino** on Avenida Infante Dom Henrique, ✆ 281 512 224, opens at 6pm and will invite you to roll the dice till 4am. The restaurant and bar close earlier, perhaps to protect innocent diners from the sight of gamblers losing their shirts. Remember to take your passport.

Vila Real de Santo António

At the eastern tip of the Algarve, the frontier town and tuna-processing port of Vila Real de Santo António vegetates at the mouth of the River Guadiana. A bridge crosses to Ayamonte in Spain.

When Dom José ascended to the throne in 1750, the Portuguese bank of the Guadiana was deserted south of Castro Marim. The Marquês de Pombal ordered the town to be built in five months in 1774, on the site of a settlement flushed away by a tidal wave *c.* 1600. This was to be the headquarters of the pilchard- and tuna-fishing industry; to ensure the success of his venture, Pombal ordered Monte Gordo to be burnt flat. The layout resembles that adopted by Pombal in the reconstruction of Lisbon (wide streets cut into squares) but has none of Lisbon's elegance.

Getting There and Around

Buses and trains run frequently to and from all major stations in the Algarve. For information on buses, ring © 281 541 395.

Tourist Information

The tourist office is in the Centro Cultural, Rua Téofilio Braga, © 281 281 142.

Boat Trips

The gently winding Guadiana, smooth and banked with rich greenery, is navigable as far as Mértola (*see* p.177). Book a trip with Turismar in Monte Gordo, © 281 513 504; they depart Vila Real most days in high season at 9.30am, going upstream as far as Alcoutim (*see* p.83).

Since the construction of the new road bridge, Vila Real has lost most of its ferry traffic, which previously landed just a few yards from the centre of town, and suffered a commercial decline. Recently however, the town seems to have spruced itself up, most noticeably in the conversion of the splendid old Moorish-style market building topped by bright yellow domes to become the **Centro Cultural**, with regular exhibitions of art and music. You'll find it just off the main square along the pedestrianized Rua Teofilio Braga.

The fascinating little **Manuel Cabanas Museum** features some remarkable woodcut art. It was expected to remain somewhere on the small main square and if you can spot it it is worth a few minutes of your time. The main square, **Praça Marquês de Pombal**, is furnished with a church, an obelisk, dragons' tooth paving and a border of trimmed orange trees—a pleasant place for a coffee at one of the many cafés.

Where to Stay and Eating Out

★★★**Hotel Guadiana**, Avenida da República, © 281 511 482 (*expensive-moderate*) is a hotel in the grand style with several national flags flapping outside and a sweeping staircase within. The large air-conditioned rooms are good value, tastefully furnished and thoroughly modern, with a television in every room. The manager is a friendly soul, who gently regrets the building of the bridge to Spain. ★★**Hotel Apolo**, Avenida dos Bombeiros Portugueses, © 281 544 448 (*moderate*), on the edge of town towards Faro, is basic with fun, kitsch trimmings. In high season, it is expensive for what you get. A cheap option is the town's modern **youth hostel**, 40 Rua Dr Sousa Martins, ©/@ 281 544 565.

There are several restaurants on the bank of the Guadiana, unremarkable except for the renowned **Caves do Guadiana**, 90 Avenida da República (*expensive-moderate*), which serves superlative seafood.

Up the River Guadiana and Inland

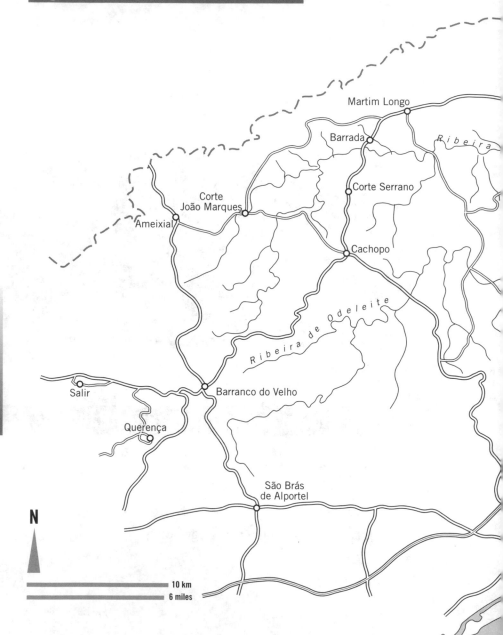

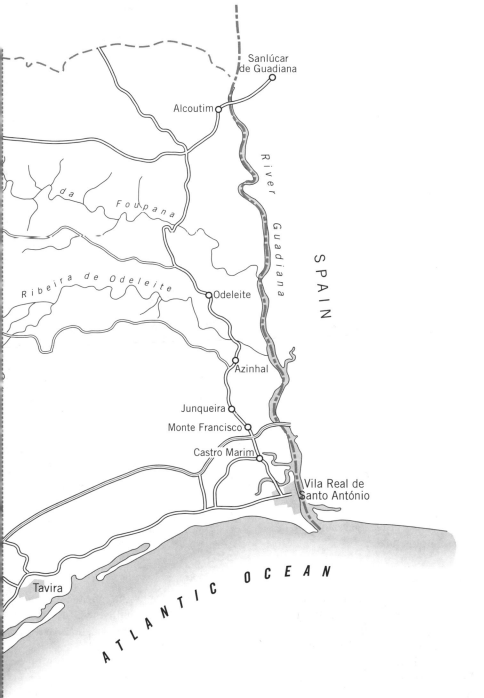

This is the Algarve that tourists haven't yet discovered. The stunningly beautiful River Guadiana winds its way from the Serra do Caldeirão, through fertile, cultivated valleys lined wiht wild arum lilies and explosions of orange-topped cacti. The landscape has changed little through the ages and neither have some of the faming methods. The Barrocal locals are positively jaunty, but they bear a heavy burden of poverty. The couples labouring in the fields may appear picturesque, but spare a thought for their backache and arthristis.

If the Guadiana's still, clean waters sound appealing, you may be able to charter a boat at Vilamoura and sail the river. If you're not a sailor, the best way to explore this area is by car. A four-wheel-drive vehicle is best suited to negotiating some of the secondary roads, which are little more than dirt tracks. Buses are infrequent, so it's common to see pairs of women laden with baskets of herbs hitching by the roadside. Few speak English, so you may need to communicate with smiles and gestures. In return, you might be invited home.

Spring is the most glorious time to visit; amidst the cork oaks, pines and eucalyptus, rock roses bloom from a multicoloured carpet of wild flowers. Accommodation is scarce, but it may be possible to find a room in someone's house in one of the larger villages such as Cachopo or Barranco do Velho; just ask in cafés and flash a wide smile—the Algarvians like an open face.

Castro Marim

Sheep wade through the marshes 4km north of Vila Real de Santo António, and emerge with dirty underbellies. Their shepherds hail from Castro Marim, a little town set in the lee of a hill topped by a semi-circular **fortress**, built by Dom João IV on foundations laid by Dom Afonso III in the 13th century. Dom João IV was also responsible for the construction of the **Fortress of São Sebastião** on a hill opposite. Inside, the small 14th-century **Igreja de Santiago** is another church distinguished solely by its association with Henry the Navigator, who worshipped there when he visited Castro Marim. Dom Dinis granted

Castro Marim to the Order of Christ, recently founded to replace the disgraced Knights Templar. The town served as their headquarters until their removal to Tomar in 1334.

Castro Marim is more impressive from a distance than close to; the only feature of interest is the **Reserva do Sapal** nature reserve (*open daily dawn to dusk*), whose headquarters are in the former fortress, and who publish maps of a marshy 7km walk past fenland and commercial salt pans. Keep an eye out for waterbirds such as the flamingo and avocet picking their long-legged way through the shallow-water feeding grounds.

The **tourist information office** on Praça 1 de Maio, ✆ 281 531 232 may be able to help you find accommodation in private houses.

A rewarding drive 40km north to Alcoutim takes in fabulous countryside and passes through the tiny villages of **Monte Francisco, Junqueira** and **Azinhal**. If Castro Marim is small and sleepy, these villages are tiny and comatose.

Odeleite

A splendid road winds 26km north from Castro Marim, hugging the hills and offering glimpses of the Guadiana. Odeleite is a small settlement on the river, built in a gully so the houses are piled on top of one another. Red and pink bougainvillaea cascades down the white house fronts, and low stone walls crumble slowly. Solitary mules rest on large tracts of riverside land. Shepherds wear cheery red caps. Fat cacti bloom papery orange flowers. The road follows the river for 14km to Alcoutim.

Alcoutim

The village of Alcoutim rests on the bank of the River Guadiana, mirrored across the water by the Spanish village of Sanlúcar de Guadiana, close enough to hear the braying of a Spanish donkey and the chiming of Spanish church bells, one hour ahead of Portugal's. The dogs of Alcoutim do not tire of barking at foreigners; its chickens do not cease from pecking between the cobblestones set unevenly and steeply between houses edged with red geraniums.

By 1688, Alcoutim had long been a centre for smuggling tobacco and snuff into Portugal from Spain. When the superintendent of the Junta do Tabaco discovered a hoard of the stuff, 'the whole population rose in arms'; the superintendent and his cronies were chased from the village by a crowd which included its governing officials.

One corner of the otherwise plain 14th-century ruined **castle**, at the highest point in the village, is planted with daisies and set with trestle tables; it makes a lovely place to picnic, overlooking a poultry yard and the river.

A 17th-century low relief of John the Baptist is set into the corner of the **Igreja Matriz** by the river. Next door, the plain restaurant, **O Soeiro** (*cheap*), doubles as Alcoutim's only *pensão* in summer. If you want to stay in the village earlier in the year, to see the spring flowers, ask around for a room or enquire at the often shut **tourist office**, Praça da República, ✆ 281 546 179 (*officially open 9.30–5.30*), just up the road from the church. The tourist office staff can give you details of daily **boat trips** on the river. The boat winds south to Foz de Odeleite, or cruises north to Mértola and sometimes Spain. The journeys in either direction are hazily beautiful; the cost is around 4,500$00 per person, if all eight passenger places are filled.

One of the Algarve's best **youth hostels**, ✆/✉ 281 546 004, is just out of the village. It is set in a lovely position overlooking the river, and bicycles and canoes can be rented here.

Inland from Alcoutim to the Barrocal

The Barrocal region, named after the limestone that underlies most of the northeastern Algarve, makes up about a quarter of the province, but is sparsely populated and little visited. It is bounded by Alcoutim and Ameixial in the north, and by Castro Marim and São Brás de Alportel in the south. Very little happens in between to dilute rural life, far removed from the busy, bright and beer-soaked resorts of Albufeira or Quarteira. The limestone mountains of the Serra do Caldeirão reach just half the height of Monchique's peaks, but their inhabitants are locked in a stronger timewarp. Small white hamlets are scattered irregularly in the valleys, surrounded by sloping farmland which defies the use of tractors or other modern machinery. Crops are planted and harvested by hand, by men and women with deeply lined faces.

The N124 road between **Alcoutim** and the small village of **Cachopo** passes through some stunning countryside. Fields of dull gold stretch into the distance, divided by ancient rough walls quietly shedding the odd stone. The menthol scent of eucalyptus fills the air. The only sounds are those of sheep bleating and stealthy iguanas scuttling across the road. Fields of wheat sway above rusty soil, and time stands still. Just before **Martin Longo** (25km west of Alcoutim) lies the roadside restaurant **O Monte Branco** (*cheap*), with a large colourful terrace commanding good views. There's a sandpitted playground with a slide, swing and treehouse to keep the kids entertained. Should you suddenly have a hankering for pub games, a games room provides a pool table, dartboard and table football. Most importantly, it serves a perfect milky *galão* (caffè latte).

Continuing from Alcoutim, turn south just before you reach Martin Longo on to the 506 to Vaqueiros to visit the ancient copper mine at **Foupana Ecological Park**, also known as the Cova dos Mouros Parque Mineiro. The site dates back to a Chalcolithic settlement around 2300 BC, of which there's a reconstruction. Well-informed guides conduct tours of the surface workings, including the crumbling miners' accommodation and shafts, run by the British from the mid-19th century until the mine closed in the 1930s. Underground tours may be offered in the future, and a safari park is planned.

A few kilometres southwest of Martin Longo, just past **Barrada**, feast on the view of the Foupana River as it weaves through brown hills dappled with trees and squat bushes, and striped with terraced crops. the best way to enjoy the view is to walk the 10km to **Corte Serrano**.

The road to the tiny snoozing village of **Cachopo** to Tavira is one of the most scenic in the Algarve. For the first couple fo kilometres it runs along a mountain ridge with a sheer drop on either side, plunging into deep valleys and rising on to rounded slopes thick with pine.

A little farther west, **Barranco do Velho** is noteworthy only for being the meeting place for the roads from Loulé (15km) and São Brás de Aportel (13km). From here a scenic but pot-holed road winds 32km north through rich-soiled mountains and whitewashed settlements to Ameixial, near the Alentejan border.

Ameixial

Here locals are as likely to lope around in mule-drawn carts as cars. A few hasty tourists pass through but they barely fluster village life: men in caps sit on stone benches discussing football, straw-hatted women weave baskets or gather behind a van to inspect the day's fish, fresh from the coast. They are friendly souls, bidding strangers a smiling *bom dia* after a quick inspection.

A **neolithic burial site**, the *Anta da Pedra do Alagar,* is a couple of kilometres away off the road to Martin Longo, signposted from the village. Believed to be 6,000 years old, the smoothly weathered dolmens don't betray their great age; the atmosphere here is charged with benign spirits.

If you're feeling cramped by the crowds, and you're looking for somewhere to picnic that's literally off the map, try the tiny settlement of **Vermelhos** some 8km southwest of Ameixial. The residents can't resist leaving their houses at the sound of unfamiliar voices. They are indulgently amused by tourists marvelling at the beauty of surroundings they see every day. A stream trickles beside the settlement, shaded by cork oaks, and butterflies ride smooth air unruffled by passing cars.

To get to Vermelhos, drive west from Ameixial on a road surfaced as far as Corgas (spot the advert for home-brewed, belly-burning *medronho*). Continue through green countryside heavy with lazy bees. When the road forks, carry straight on, cross the bridge and wind your way past rotund cacti until the road forks again. Take the left turning marked Salir, and continue on to Vermelhos.

You can continue a few kilometres southwest to Salir, if your navigational skills are up to it. At each fork in the road, turn left until you come to a junction of sorts, with a house on the left and a sign to Ribeira da Cima. Turn right uphill and take the next left. At the junction with Freixo Seco, turn right on to a surfaced road and into the 21st century.

Salir

Straggling down the hill beneath its castle ruins 14km north of Loulé, Salir is much vaunted as a 'typical' and unspoilt village. *Típico*, in Portuguese, doesn't quite mean 'typical' in the sense of 'representative'; it's more akin to 'quintessential', and ferreting out anything *típico* is a national pastime. Thus Coimbra University is described as a typical university, or Fernando Pessoa a typical poet. Restaurants advertise themselves as *típico* to suggest that they embody something peculiarly Portuguese. The cult of the *típico* was fostered by Salazar's nationalism, and still remains a Portuguese passion.

Salir lives up to this label, composed as it is of crumbling whitewashed bricks amid citrus, almond and fig trees. Brazenly bright-coloured climbing flowers seem to bind the low cottages together. In mid-afternoon, as you wind through the steep streets, only the sounds of daytime soap operas filter through the open doors and their beaded curtains. At the top of the village, inside the castle walls, are stone benches and tables for picnics; the middle altitude fosters greener countryside and the views are particularly splendid here.

Almansil to Albufeira

The most intensively developed stretch of the coast takes its holiday trade seriously. Unfavourable publicity beset the Algarve in the 1980s, reflecting badly on rapidly expanding resorts such as Albufeira. Things are more pleasant in reality than reports suggest: the hotels are tall, but the water is calm and clearly clean. East of Albufeira at Falésia the coastline changes from dune-backed golden expanses of sand to precarious burnt-orange cliffs peppered with fantastic rock formations overhanging the sand and shallow water. These long beaches lure those who prefer to relax in the sun, crowds drawing crowds, and more active sorts will be attracted by the watersports on offer, especially at Vilamoura; but although people flock to the popular strands, lurking among the cliffs there are still quiet coves. And with many of the Algarve's golf courses squeezed into this stretch of coast, it's also a good base for a golfing holiday. The *raison d'être* of resorts such as Quarteira, Albufeira, Quinta do Lago, Vale do Lobo and Vilamoura is to provide the best possible ingredients for a holiday; how you put them together is up to you.

Almansil is nowadays no more than a dusty traffic-choked feeder town for the major golfing resorts nearby, and sprawls between two horribly busy main roads. Just between the two roads, however, tucked away in its own little hamlet, is the much-visited **Church of São Lourenço**. It is covered with astonishingly beautiful *azulejos* depicting the life of the saint, dated 1730 and signed by Policarpo de Oliveira Bernardes. This is unquestionably his finest work, which elsewhere does not live up to the masterful craft of his father, António, in Évora, Barcelos and Viana do Castelo. The tiles have been designed to complement the architectural features of the church, and the best examples are found in the *trompe l'œil* cupola.

One of the Algarve's hidden gems goes by the name of the **Centro Cultural de São Lourenço**, ℰ 289 395 475 (*open Tues–Sun 10–7*), which occupies the little house next to the church. it hosts a permanent exhibition of the work of local artists, but the real treat is the delightful sculpture garden, which is full of witty surprises. Young children in particular will enjoy the giant insects and animals ingeniously fashioned from scrap metal.

A few metres downhill, almost right alongside the thundering EN125, **A Tralha Antiguidades** is a small antique shop well worth a look if your idea of souvenirs inclines more towards antique telescopes and Louis XIV chairs than hideous pottery cockerels. There are bigger branches in Albufeira and Portimão.

Vale do Lobo and Quinta do Lago

Vale do Lobo and Quinta do Lago are what the brochures call 'Sportugal'—purpose-built luxury resorts dedicated primarily to golf, though there are many other first-class sporting options (the tennis school at Vale do Lobo, for instance, is run by the former English tennis star Roger Taylor). The sprinklers are always at work to keep the lawns green, and the emphasis is on low-rise whitewashed 'village' complexes elaborated from the local style of architecture, with a liberal dose of lattice-work chimneys. Serious money bankrolls these resorts, keeping the roads wide, the bushes trimmed and the vast villas hidden behind pines and careful landscaping. Shops are cosmopolitan chic, discos spangly and many-tiered, and pricy restaurants provide food from around the world. Golf buggies ferry expensively coiffured women across the fairways. These two resorts boast the lowest population per hectare on the Algarve coast; one must have room to breathe, after all.

There are four major **golf courses** in the area: Pinheiros Altos, Quinta do Lago, San Lorenzo and Vale do Lobo. Detailed descriptions and prices can be found on pp.18–19.

Where to Stay

Some of the finest five-star hotels in the Algarve are located here. The ★★★★★**Hotel Quinta do Lago**, ✆ 289 396 666, ✉ 289 396 393 (*luxury*) surrounds itself with 1,700 acres of pine forests and has its own private beach. The Quinta do Lago golf course is adjacent and there is a health club, watersports and tennis facilities.

★★★★★**Le Meridien Dona Filipa**, ✆ 289 394 141, ✉ 289 94 288 (*luxury*) is Vale do Lobo's flagship hotel, with beautifully furnished and superbly equipped rooms, an award-winning children's club (in high season) and access to San Lorenzo golf course (*see* above).

Both of these hotels can be booked through Caravela, ✆ (020) 7630 9223.

Eating Out

Several good international restaurants serving well-heeled golfers' appetites can be found in and around Almancil. For top quality beachside drinks and dining go to **Julia's 1**, at Praia Garrao, ✆ 289 396 512, or **Julia's 2** (also known as Barca Velha), at Vale do Lobotel, ✆ 289 393 939 (*both expensive–moderate*). Choose seafood and the African rice.

Quarteira

Quarteira, on the coast just east of Vilamoura, 6km from the east–west highway, is a jungle of apartment-hotels overlooking a very long, sandy stretch of beach. The unadventurous sizzle on the sand in front of the hotels, which look like a child's experiment with Lego. The beach stretches all the way to Faro, whence frequent buses make the 30-minute journey. However, for all its aesthetic failings Quarteira, unlike its posh neighbour Vilamoura, still has a Portuguese heart. You'll find it near the fish market where grizzled old salts mill around and where a clutch of small, cheap fish restaurants offer excellent value.

Quarteira is famous for its **Gypsy Market**, the largest in the Algarve, drawing coachloads from far and near. It used to take place by the fishermen's quarter but has now moved to a less atmospheric location across the dual carriageway. If you are in town on a Wednesday morning—and it is worthwhile for the hullabaloo and crowds, if not the merchandise, then you can't miss it.

On the main EN125 between Imancil and the Vilamoura turn-off is the smallest of the Algarve's three main waterparks, Atlantic Park (*open April–September*, ✆ 800 204 767).

Nearby at Alto do Semino is the Vila Sol Club **golf course** (*see* p.20 for detailed description and prices).

Quinta dos Rochas, ✆ 289 393 165, 🖷 289 399 198 (*expensive*), is 2km out of Quarteira on the way to Almansil. It is quietly situated with cool rooms and friendly staff, though an outdoor swimming pool could shatter your peace. It's not bad for this area, though on the expensive side and somewhat indifferently furnished.

There is a **campsite** 5mins from the beach, 1km east from the centre, ✆ 289 302 821, with good facilities.

Vilamoura

Roughly 22km northwest of Faro, and close to Quarteira beach, Vilamoura is the largest touristic development in Portugal. Although it is now 25 years old, building is still in progress—but that's not uncommon in the Algarve. High-rise hotels vie with one another for air space, though there is no heart to the settlement. Confusing collections of signs point to sports centres, golf courses and holiday villages, and it can take a little time to find your way to the **marina**, the main attraction of this resort, with anchorage for 1,000 yachts. It is flanked by luxury hotels and restaurants from which you can watch the rich as they hop off their boats and straight into the **casino** (*see* below).

Any of the seven kiosks at the far corner of the marina (walk right around from the Marinotel) should be able to satisfy your **watersport** whims. They also offer barbecue cruises and grotto tours. There is no permanent **tourist information** office here, but in summer a booth is erected on a corner of the marina.

Keep an eye out for poorly signposted steps leading to the **Cerro da Vila Museum** (*✆ 289 312 173; open daily 10am–1pm and 3–8pm; adm*), where Roman ruins add a touch of history to this ultra-modern resort. A smart new museum has been built to house the finds and, while it probably won't make any converts, it is well captioned and certainly offers a few minutes' diversion from yacht-watching. If you have children in tow, the **Roma Golf Park** next door is an entertaining little crazy-golf course picking up the Roman theme.

There are two **beaches** within walking distance of the marina (though few people do actually walk in this resort). Behind the giant Marinotel is the predictably named **Praia da Marina**, divided from the sands of Quarteira by just a few metres of rocky shore. More attractive is **Praia da Falésia**, an immaculately groomed glorious long golden sweep. It is reached across a footbridge spanning an inlet of the sea and picturesque meadows and dunes, which is presumably how all this coast appeared before the developers arrived.

On the way to the Praia da Falésia you cannot help but notice the Algarve's latest attraction, **Vistarama**, a tethered balloon ride located by the beach car park. The balloon, which works by a winch and helium, takes you slowly and quietly to a height of 500ft/152m. Views stretch from Faro in the east to Carvoeiro in the west and it's also a good way to make sense of the confusing jumble that Vilamoura seems to be when you are down at ground level. The cage is completely secure so children are very welcome, and it even claims to be suitable for people who suffer from fear of heights. At around 3,000$00 it's not cheap by Algarve standards—but by ballooning standards it's a snip. And if you want a second ride, perhaps to see the illuminated marina illuminated by night, there is a 20 per cent discount.

Vilamoura has four **golf courses**; as well as the Sheraton Pine Cliffs at Praia da Falésia. For details and prices *see* pp.19–20.

Shopping

The Marina features many of the well-known European and US high street retail names but for local stuff at very reasonable prices try **Casa Caravela** near the Marinotel. It's good for gifts, particularly tableware and ceramics.

Where to Stay

The sumptuously neutral 1990s ★★★★★**Marinotel**, ✆ 289 389 988, ✉ 289 389 869 (*luxury*) offers state-of-the-art design. It is equipped with all the trimmings plus fabulous views of the marina and the sea. The fat-cat clientele can rest assured that the presidential suite has bullet-proof doors. Other similarly luxurious hotels include ★★★★**Hotel Dom Pedro**, ✆ 289 389 650, ✉ 289 315 482, and ★★★★★**Hotel Atlantis**, ✆ 289 389 977, ✉ 289 338 996.

Eating Out

Pricey but not out of reach, **Akavit**, ✆ 289 380 712 (*expensive*) serves some of the best food in the Marina. It puts a modern European spin on old Portuguese favourites and also offers several Swedish specials too. Its classy nautical paraphernalia spills on to the dockside.

More than a hint of Gallic flavour pervades **Normandia**, ✆ 289 313 686 (*moderate–cheap*), which boasts over 80 different types of beer and 40 whiskies. Their stock in trade is crêpes but the *spécialité de la maison* is French-style grilled chicken.

Tucked away behind the marina, in the Pateo Marina shopping centre, is **Don Afonso** ✆ 289 212 688 (*moderate*), where you will get a good Portuguese meal in a smart traditional dining room. *Open evenings only.*

Entertainment and Nightlife

The **Casino de Vilamoura**, behind the Marinotel, ✆ 219 316 080, where the yachties go to be seen in the small hours. As well as gaming it stages spectacular floor shows and has recently added the Blackjack Disco Club, which opens nightly from June through September and Thursday to Sunday from October through May. An alternative with more street-cred, is **Kadoc**, one of the Algarve's longest-established clubs, pumping out high-volume Euro-thump to a young crowd. If you're over 30 and fancy a dance, but have no taste for techno, try Kadoc's more mellow club-within-a-club, **Kadoclube**, open Friday and Saturday nights. You'll find it on the Estrada de Vilamoura between Vilamoura and Albufeira close to the EN125. A quieter after-dark option is the **Vilamoura Jazz Club** at Praça do Cinema, which touts live jazz most nights from 10.30pm onwards. Call ℭ 289 316 272 to see what's on.

Falésia

At Falésia, 8km to the east of Albufeira, the coastline metamorphoses from an uninterrupted expanse of sand into coves backed by smooth cream and ochre cliffs, liable to subside should you get too close to the edge. The irresistible smell of pine woods wafts across the clifftop paths. The nearest accommodation, at **Aldeia das Açoteias** holiday village one or two kilometres inland, consists of concrete hutches with access to good training facilities and is only recommended for the athletes at whom it is aimed. To get to Falésia by public transport, take a regular bus from Albufeira to Aldeia das Açoteias, then catch the beach-bound shuttle from there.

Albufeira

Some 39km northwest of Faro and 50km east of Lagos, the pretty, hilly seaside village of Albufeira has become Portugal's most popular package resort. Part of the settlement was submerged by a tidal wave following the earthquake of 1755; in the summer months, Albufeira is submerged by a different kind of tidal wave—one that takes longer to subside. The whitewashed pedestrian streets seethe with sun-lovers, who are supplied with cheap beer and saucy postcards. Touts in the main square sell time-share apartments.

Albufeira's **old town** to the west of this spreading resort still has a distinctive character, even if every other building is a restaurant or bar. The east is completely suburban, with hotels and apartments filling in every inch of space. It reaches its nadir in Montechoro, an unappealing strip of burger joints and English-style pubs.

Getting There

Frequent trains and RN buses run from Faro (1hr) and from Lagos (1¼hrs), stopping at each stage along the way.

Tourist Information

The patient **tourist office** is in the Rua 5 de Outubro, ℭ 289 585 279, on the way to the beach tunnel. The **post office** is next door. It's a 5-minute walk from the **bus station**, ℭ 289 589 755, to the centre of town; to get to the tourist office, walk along the Av da Liberdade, turn right at the tip of the gardened Largo Eng. Duarte Pacheco, then turn left into the Rua 5 de Outubro.

The **train station**, ℭ 289 571 616, is 6km north of town at Ferreiras, with connecting buses marked *Estação*.

The daily **market** sells the usual fish, fruit and veg every morning except Mondays on Rua do Mercado. The **gypsy market** comes to the north of the town, by the municipal market, on the first and third Tuesday of the month.

There are two **medical centres** in Albufeira, dealing with the usual sun- and drink-related ailments: one on Areia de São João to the east of the old town, ✆ 289 587 326; the other, *Clioura*, has a doctor on call 24 hours, ✆ 289 587 000.

For **books**, The Algarve Book Centre, 6 Rua Igreja Nova, will buy, sell or exchange English, French, Dutch or German books. The quality of reading material depends on the latest holiday book trends.

Just to prove that Albufeira is not the culture-free zone that a cursory glance might suggest, a **Museum of Archaeology** has recently opened a few steps up from the Sol e Mar hotel (*open Oct–May Tues–Sun 10.30am–5pm, and 2.30–8pm in high season*). There are free guided walks around Old Albufeira from February to June at 10.30 every Wed–Fri. However, you must book your place through the tourist office, not the Albufeira one but perversely the town hall *turismo* in nearby Santa Eulália. Ask at the Albufeira tourist office to see if you can short-circuit the system.

Beaches

The beaches of Albufeira's eastern resorts, **Santa Eulália**, **Praia da Oura** and **Olhos de Água**, all signposted from the centre, are dotted with red rocks rising out of the sand like pop-up picture-book monsters. The development is perfectly pleasant, mostly comprising apartments; it's just not terribly Portuguese.

From the town a tunnel hewn out of rocks leads sun-hungry tourists past begging gypsies directly to **Praia da Albufeira**, a longish beach solid with bodies in the summer. The mornings are marginally the quieter part of the day; young tourists indulge in Albufeira's nocturnal delights till dawn and so rarely rise before lunch (*see* p.97). To the left is the Fisherman's Beach, peppered with vivid fishing boats and a varied set of restaurants ranged along the coastline. To the west a conical rock pierces the sky; a path cut into the cliffs enables you to walk round the headland, through caves and wide chambers above tunnels in which the sea sighs. With benches cut into the cliff, the path turns into something of a Lovers' Lane at night.

Shopping

Albufeira is chock-a-block with tourist tat, and it can be hilarious looking at the illuminated stalls which line the streets in the centre on warm summer evenings. For rugs, shawls and other items head for the **Santa Casa da Misericordia** on Rua 5 de Outubro. Profits support orphaned, disabled or elderly Albufeirans.

Just off the same street, almost opposite the tourist office on Rua Joao de Deus, is the dusty **A Tralha Antiguidades**, a fascinating collection of Portuguese and Algarvian antiquities, most of them far too large to fit in your suitcase.

The most civilized place to buy your booze is **Garrafeira Soares** in the square. It has an excellent selection at keen prices and a tapas bar upstairs where you can taste a wide range of wines, ports, *aguardentes* and Portuguese liqueurs. A glass of 40-year-old port will set you back around 2,000$00, just about the price of a large plate of five sorts of *enchido* (*charcuterie*) to accompany it.

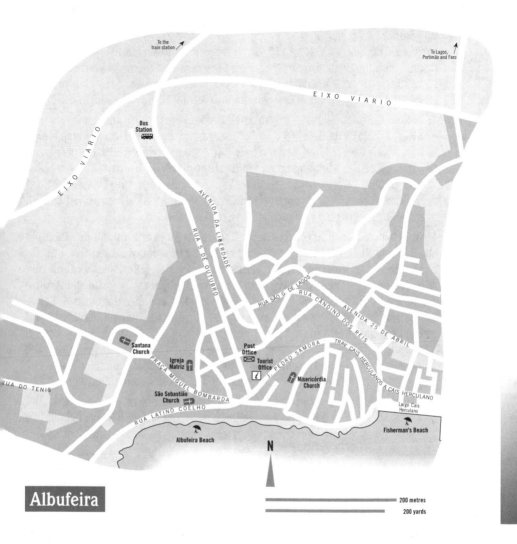

Albufeira

200 metres
200 yards

Shops selling multi-cultural ethnic art and jewellery, mostly from North Africa, are common here, as in much of the Algarve. **Tribu**, at No.13, on the lower part of Montechoro's hideous Avenida Sá Carneiro (otherwise known as 'The Strip'), stands out from the dross surrounding it.

Where to Stay

★★★**Hotel Rocamar**, Largo Jacinto D'Ayet, © 289 586 990, © 289 586 998 (*expensive*) is along the road from the Church of Sant'Ana and provides standard, airy rooms, with private balconies overlooking the beach. On the quieter west side of Albufeira, ★★★★**Boa Vista**,

Rua Samora Barros, ☎ 289 589 175, ✉ 289 589 180 (*expensive*; *bookings also through Caravela*, ☎ *(020) 7630 9223*) is splendidly located in a peaceful place just five minutes' walk from the beach and the centre of town. The restaurant and swimming pool terrace have stunning views. Rooms are a good size, but old-fashioned, and some fall short of four-star quality. Ask for one overlooking the sea.

The Rua Coronel Águas leads to the Avenida do Ténis; they meet at the ★★★**Residencial Vila Bela**, 15 Rua Coronel Águas, ☎ 512101 (*moderate*), which is attractively layered and beflowered, with bright rooms and balconies overlooking the small swimming pool. ★★★**Residencial Vila Branca**, Rua do Ténis, ☎ 289 586 804 (*inexpensive*)—just inland of the Largo Jacinto D'Ayet provides very smart rooms with air-conditioning and TV, and a nicely furnished bar, all overseen by the friendly receptionist. Breakfast is provided.

Most of Albufeira's cheaper accommodation is located in and around Rua Cândido dos Reis and Rua São Gonçalo de Lagos, which is fine if you want to party, but less conducive to an early night, i.e. before 4am. So avoid **Pensões Polana** and **Albufeirense**. ★★**Pensão Silva**, Travessa André Rebelo, opposite the Atrium restaurant, ☎ 289 512 669 (*cheap*)—down an alley opposite the tourist office— offers six pleasant rooms in an old building with flaking ceilings, and ★★**Residencial Frentomar**, Rua Latino Coelho, ☎ 289 512 005 (*inexpensive*) is a modern, quiet option west of the Old Town. Its sea-view rooms overlook the whole of Albufeira's beachfront. Rooms are fairly basic (no air-conditioning or TV) but bright and airy, and there is a TV room and a snooker room downstairs.

A **campsite** is located about 1½ kilometres north of Albufeira at Alpouvar, ☎ 289 587 630, ✉ 289 587 633. It's very well equipped, boasting the highest grading of four stars, with restaurant and snack bar, a swimming pool and tennis courts.

Eating Out

Overlooking the beach, near the fish market, **A Ruina**, Largo Cais Herculano, ☎ 289 512 094 (*expensive; reservations advisable*), is a fun place to eat delicious seafood. The lower part is more atmospheric: it features dripping candles, turtle shells, stone-studded walls, tree-trunk tables and the menu on a blackboard. Some diners choose to sit in a cordoned-off area right on the beach. For a cheaper taste of good local food, with less of an emphasis on fish, go next door to **Tasca do Viegas**, 2 Rua Cais Herculano, ☎ 289 514 087 (*moderate*). Their *arroz de tamboril* (monkfish rice) is delicious and reasonably priced for two people to share.

Directly overlooking A Ruina, with good views over the beach, **Anna's**, 7 Rua Nova, ☎ 289 513 558 (*expensive*), is highly recommended for its excellent international food.

A short walk away on the other side of the hill, **Atrium**, at 20 Rua 5 de Outubro, ☎ 289 515 755, occupies the glitzy ballroom of an old theatre. The food isn't great, but there are regular performances of *fado* and folk music. On the other side of the street and up some steps, the main attraction at **Casa da Fonte**, ℗ 289 514 578 (*moderate*), is the secluded open-air patio, where you can dine beneath lemon trees and grape vines. The food is fairly standard, though. There's a nice bar, too.

There's a good selection of restaurants on the clifftop immediately west of the Old Town. First of all you come to cosy **O Dias**, 2 Praça Miguel Bombarda, ℗ 289 515 246 (*expensive*) where you can sit on the sunny little balcony and watch your meal sizzle on the grill and your compatriots sizzle on the beach. Next door, Michelin-listed **O Cabaz da Praia** (*expensive*) is a romantic treat. The name means beach basket, but this is no picnic. The chef and owner are French, and the food is a superb marriage of Gallic and Portuguese cuisine. It's expensive for the Algarve, but worth it. *Closed Thurs and lunchtime Sat.*

Continue along the cliffs past Bizarro's (*see* below) to **O Penedo**, Rua Latino Coelho, ℗ 289 587 429 (*moderate*) by the Residencial Frentomar. The beautiful little terrace takes advantage of the curve of the cliff to offer unbeatable views along the beach. The food is interesting and very tasty, the prices are very reasonable given the location, and the staff are friendly, young and cosmopolitan.

Entertainment and Nightlife

After dark head for Rua Cândido dos Reis and Rua São Gonçalo de Lagos, which are composed almost entirely of bars and restaurants that stay up late. Walk down here in the height of summer and every few steps offers a fresh assault on the senses: one thumping tune drowns out another as people dance on your feet and neon dazzles your vision. Beer-fuelled fun lasts until about 4, then everyone goes to **Kiss** disco on Areia de São João until 7am.

Another hot venue just out of the centre is **Locomia** at Santa Eulália. If you want to stay in town there is the alternative attraction of 'Music Street' (one block back from Fisherman's Beach) featuring Albufeira's main disco, **7½**, and the grungey delights of **Snoopy's Bar** almost next door.

For less ear-splitting sounds head along the clifftop west to **Bizarro's**, a bar where the Woodstock generation will feel right at home. The charming long-haired laidback owner has been here for 22 years and invites a Brazilian guitarist along every Tuesday. The perfect place to sip a caiparinha cocktail and watch the sun set.

Around Albufeira

Just west of Albufeira lie some stunning rugged beaches, all with fine sand bounded by sparkling green water, scattered with stray rocks from the vivid amber cliffs. These are slightly quieter, attracting a hire-car crowd; Albufeira's loud young hipsters don't often make it out this far. A bus from Albufeira drops you off on the highway a long walk from the coast. The development at **São Rafael** (4km west of Albufeira) is low-key but chock-a-block with villas. It is popular with German and Swiss couples of more mature years, and young families yearning for quiet.

Beaches

Praia do São Rafael is a small beach with rock formations jutting out of the sea, gently lapped by shallow clear water, making it a good exploring ground for children. It's one of the most picturesque beaches along this stretch of coast. A snack-bar serves simple meals. Farther along the road, a left turn leads you along a narrow and pot-holed road to a clearing by a tennis court. Park here and take the right-hand path through pine-covered ground to a small cove bracketed by pock-marked, sandstone cliffs. To the west they reach out into the sea in a series of weird formations. This is **Praia da Coelha**, a popular family beach.

When the tide's out, another small beach can be reached to the right, but be careful not to get trapped. **Praia do Castelo** is easily crowded because of its size; if you feel cramped, hire a boat to explore the caves and grottoes. A restaurant perches on stilts and a lifeguard snoozes beneath; parents can relax with a beer while watching the tinies on the beach. The long **Praia da Galé** at Vale de Parra, 7km west of Albufeira, stretches all the way to Armação de Pêra—to escape the crowds just walk west beyond the Henry Moore rocks. Backed by a dune high enough to obscure the buildings, this beach is popular with a variety of visitors, from families to young couples. Pink-shouldered tourists tuck into prawns and sardines at the large snack-bar.

Near Galé beach is the links-style 18-hole Salgados **golf course** (*see* p.19).

Where to Stay and Eating Out

A good place to stay is **Pensão Maritim**, ℂ 289 591 005 (*moderate*), which has nice rooms leading off a dark corridor. The friendly owner welcomes independent travellers and provides local information. The third-floor restaurant offers good views to the beach and a menu whose prices veer wildly from dish to dish. A minibus from here runs guests into Albufeira twice a day, or you can walk there over the cliffs in about 30 minutes.

To Portimão and Monchique

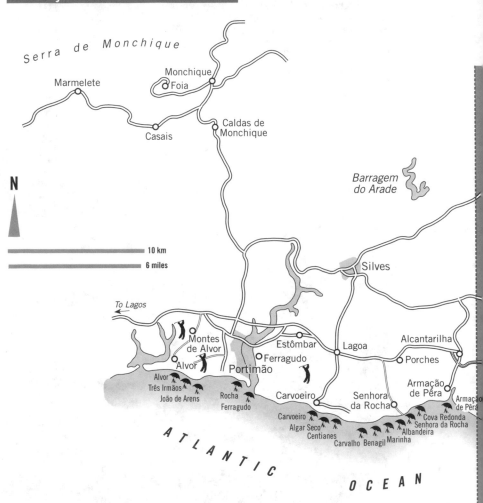

The beaches along the coast from Albufeira to Alvor are long enough to offer plenty of opportunities to escape from the crowds, if you are prepared to stride out beyond the recumbent bodies. If you feel a tad oppressed by the large-scale development, head for a deserted clifftop and contemplate the gentle foam-fringed waves and elementally inspired rock formations.

Resorts such as Armação de Pêra and Carvoeiro are geared towards self-catering and package tourists and have little to offer the independent traveller. However, larger towns such as Portimão have a heartbeat independent of the tourist trade. Here you can eat fresh sardines grilled on charcoal barbecues beside your table, take a boat to explore the nearby red grottoes and coves, then move on to visit the ghoulish chamber made from human bones in Alcantarilha's tiny parish church.

Inland from Portimão you enter a different, wooded world. If ever you worry that the Algarve has been spoilt, just head into the Monchique mountains, and villages such as Marmelete and Casais: the refreshing mountain air, broad views and pure spring water are guaranteed to restore jaded spirits. This is a realm of remote farmhouses and cottages, where beaded curtains drape the doorways and rickety outdoor tables serve as stalls selling hand-made woollen rugs or home-produced fruit and honey. If you're feeling brave, try a shot of *medronho*, the local firewater distilled from arbutus berries.

São Bartolomeu de Messines

Alte

Algoz

To Faro

Albufeira

Armação de Pêra

Eight kilometres west of Albufeira the high-rises of Armação de Pêra jostle each other for air. Giant machines dig foundations for more space-efficient accommodation, throwing up clouds of dust and gravel. The vestiges of the old village, including an 18th-century fortress with a small chapel overlooking the fisherman's beach, lie towards the east of the resort, but the narrow streets have been swamped by new buildings.

Tourist Information

There is a tourist information office on the front, ℰ 282 312 145.

Beaches

All the beaches named have at least one restaurant or snack bar where you can eat a full meal or just buy a bottle of water. Armação de Pêra claims to have the longest beach on the coast so you can usually find some personal space in which to recline. In high summer it seethes with small tots screeching around reclining bodies of all ages. At **Cova Redonda** more children build castles on a large, curving beach above which tower sandstone cliffs. It's linked by a tunnel to **Praia da Senhora da Rocha**, a lovely beach set against over-hanging sea-scarred cliffs and bisected at high tide by giant rocks. The western part is nicer and good for diving. Children dig trenches on the smaller eastern cove, but here it's too late to stave off the developers: a series of long, low-rise buildings dot the clifftops. The chapel of Nossa Senhora da Rocha watches over all; it's a curious hexagonal building with a pyramidal roof on which a gull perches. From here there are glorious views of the coastline and the ocean. Amateur fishermen hang long rods from the cliff, ever hopeful for the elusive bite.

Head west along cliffs topped with rosemary and cistus until you come to an indistinct dirt track that leads to a narrow stretch of unpopulated sand. Next is **Albandeira** beach, consisting of two tiny coves. At high tide these are separated by rocks stoically bearing their battering by the waves, and Portuguese families scuttle into the cliffs like crabs. The long and sandy **Praia da Marinha** is scattered with rock bridges and free-standing shelves rising out of the sea; its image adorns many a holiday brochure. It attracts a younger and sexier crowd of travellers, and tends to be busy all year round. A long flight of stairs leads down to the small cove of **Benagil**, where bright fishing boats provide shelter on the beach for the few without umbrellas. There are two snack bars squeezed on to the beach. Albandeira, Marinha and Benagil beaches can all be reached from the main highway by going south on the road almost opposite the International School. From Benagil, a long and winding dirt road leads to **Carvalho** beach, fittingly known as Smuggler's Cove; the overhanging cliffs have formed lots of grottoes and walkways which now harbour mischievous children.

Where to Stay

 If you must stay here, surrounded by concrete as it is, do it in style at the ★★★★**Hotel Garbe**, ✆ 282 315 187, ✉ 282 315 087, *www.nexus-pt.com/hotelgarbe* (*luxury, can book through Caravela,* ✆ *(020) 7630 9223 to avoid paying the inflated rack rate*). The grand old lady of the resort, the Garbe caters almost exclusively to package tourists but its bedrooms, public areas and facilities are of a high standard and it enjoys the perfect beachside location. To escape the crowds head just west out of town to the promontory of Nossa Senhora da Rocha and the pleasant ★★★★**Albergaria Nossa Senhora da Rocha**, above the beach, ✆ 282 315 752, ✉ 282 315 754 (*expensive*). The rooms are modern and the staff very friendly. The upstairs rooms have balconies and a view of the sea beyond the busy car park.

There are two three-star **campsites**, one just outside town on the road to Alcantarilha, ✆ 282 312 260, and the other at Canelas, about a kilometre from Alcantarilha, ✆ 282 312 612.

Eating Out

A fun place to eat is **Zé Leiteiro**, Rua Portas do Mar, ✆ 282 314 551 (*cheap*), on a road leading up from Armação's beach. It's a simple and bustling restaurant with long green tables outside and long checked tables inside. Ignore the few meat dishes on the menu and choose the fish of the day. Plates are refilled *ad infinitum.* On the same street is the more upmarket **Serol**, 2 Rua Portas do Mar, ✆ 282 312 146 (*moderate*), another of the town's most highly regarded fish restaurants. It's nothing special to look at but the crowds of locals and Portuguese holidaymakers speak for themselves. *Closed Wed.*

Just above the Praia da Nossa Senhora da Rocha, tucked away around the corner from the Viking Hotel, is **Casa d'Italia**, © 282 314 761 (*moderate*). This quiet, friendly little *hacienda*-style Italian restaurant is a real find, with a beautiful, small round pool and grassy garden for a post-prandial loll.

Porches

Four kilometres northwest of Armação de Pêra, the village of Porches has managed to stay aloof from the surrounding resorts, and its heart, around the church, remains tranquil, charged with the spirits of the past.

Shopping

Porches is famous for its pottery with its working kilns and produces beautifully crafted, hand-painted ceramics. Visit **Olaria Pequena** (*open Mon–Sat 10–1 and 3–6*) on the N125 opposite the sign to Porches, a small blue-edged cottage selling prettily painted ceramics and pots. A few yards west across the road is the much bigger **Porches Pottery** (*open daily 9–9*). It stocks a huge range of pottery and ceramics as well as cork work and tiles in some unusual colours and designs. Tiny, handmade Algarvian houses start at 400$00 but large hand-painted panels of *azulejos* can cost an arm and a leg.

Eating Out

The splendid French-inspired restaurant, **O Leão de Porches**, © 281 381 384 (*expensive*), occupies a 17th-century farmhouse in the centre of the village near the church. The voluptuous scent of roses permeates the cobbled courtyard. The menu is delicious—try the rabbit braised in the oven with red wine, mushrooms, onions and herbs. Book ahead. *Closed Wed.*

Alcantarilha

A sleepy village snoozing about 9km west of Albufeira and 3km inland from Armação de Pêra, Alcantarilha consists of a maze of steep narrow streets. The local **church** is remarkable not only for the Manueline coils around its front portal but for its small side-chamber set with over a thousand skulls and femurs of past parishioners. The **Capela dos Ossos** is eerily cool, with a crucifix hanging in the middle. From the sublime to the ridiculous, on the N125 between Alcantarilha and Lagoa looms the waterslide park **The Big One**, © (free) 800 204 014 or © 282 322 827 (*open May–Sept*), which is big on thrills though smaller than its rival Slide and Splash near Lagoa (*see* below). The new Banzai slide is the highest in Portugal, an almost sheer drop of 23m, while at 92m its Kamikaze ride claims to be the longest in the Algarve.

About 4km east of Alcantarilha, on the N125 near Guia, is **Zoomarine**, © 289 560 300, a Florida-inspired marine park for children where various sea creatures perform diverse manoeuvres for their delight. There are funfair rides and a collection of brightly arrayed parrots. Puzzling.

Lagoa

Lying 18km west of Albufeira and 10km east of Portimão, Lagoa is the Algarve's most prominent wine-producing centre. A solidly provincial town with delicate purple jacaranda trees shading the church square, it hosts the region's biggest trade fair, *Fatacil*, in August. Lagoa really comes to life at the end of September and the beginning of October, when the grapes are harvested and pressed. If you want to purchase wine, head for the **Lagoa Cooperative**, ✆ 281 381 557 (*open Mon–Fri 9.30–11.30 and 2–5.30*), the largest of the *adegas*, incorporating over 300 grape producers. A litre of the youngest wine sells for around 250$00, and prices rise with age.

On the road to Lagoa stands the biggest and best of the region's waterslide parks, **Slide and Splash**, ✆ 282 341 685, clearly signposted from the main road, containing the usual spaghetti network of giant slides.

Carvoeiro

Carvoeiro (about 5km south of Lagoa) lost most of its charm years ago, though the ghost of the original village can be seen cutting into the cliffs. There is a plague of supermarkets for the package-tour holiday-makers from the self-catering apartments that make up the majority of this unappealing resort. A confusion of bars and restaurants spill tables on to the streets and in high season the central square is solid with cars and tourists.

Carvoeiro Pestana Golf Club, ✆ 282 340 900, offers two 18-hole courses. A couple of kilometres east of Carvoeiro is Vale de Milho **golf course**.

Beaches

The main **beach**, although very picturesque, is quickly packed and not the best option locally. Take the road going left (east) from the square to get to **Algar Seco**, a tide-and-wind formation of orange rocks which rise on each side of a cluster of café umbrellas. Children happily spend hours exploring all the rock chambers and the water here makes for an interesting snorkel. A little farther east is **Praia das Centianes**, a popular cliff-edged beach at the bottom of a long flight of steps. Continue east to the beautiful coves of Praia da Carvalho, Benagil and Marinha (*see* p.102) , though beware that in season these too may well be very busy.

Portimão

Seventeen kilometres east of Lagos and 28km west of Albufeira, Portimão fumes on the western bank of the River Arade, a couple of kilometres from the coast. An impressive new bridge straddles the river, the twin of the bridge over the Guadiana (*see* p.77). This built-up town with a population of 50,000 is a major port and sardine-canning centre. It has little to recommend it for an overnight stay, though a quick visit to its famous fish and sardine restaurants, and a brisk walk around the town, is worthwhile.

Standing at the mouth of the River Arade, Portimão was settled by the Carthaginians and maintained by the Romans. The town has mushroomed since the 1920s, when the Arade silted up and Portimão became a busy port and fishing centre.

Sardines

Sardines are at their best during the summer months, when the fish have reached maturity, although constant demand requires that they be served throughout the year. the skin of a raw sardine should feel slightly loose when pinched; the skin of a grilled sardine should peel off easily in a strip. The fish are usually grilled and served whole, with rocks of sea salt. eat them as the Portuguese do, allowing the juices to seep into a hunk of bread but avoiding the bones, head and guts.

Getting There and Around

The **train station** is to the north of the town on Largo Ferra Prado, from where its about a 15-minute walk straight down to the pedestrianized shopping street, Rua do Comércio. Frequent trains from Faro take anywhere between one hour and almost two. Frequent trains from Lagos take half an hour.

Frequent EVA **buses** take an hour to travel from Albufeira, 30 minutes from Lagos and about two hours from Faro. Buses, ✆ 282 418 120, come and go from two streets parallel to one another: Avenida Afonso Henriques and Avenida Guarané, a short walk east of the sardine dock. An express bus that runs the length of the coast from Vila Real to Lagos stops at Portimão, taking about 3hrs from Vila Real, 2hrs 20mins from Tavira and 1½hrs from Faro.

Tourist Information

The **tourist office** is inconveniently located a 5- to 10-minute walk from the centre of town by the sports stadium on Avenida Zeca Afonso, ✆ 282 419 131.

For **medical assistance** use the Clínica da Rocha in Praia da Rocha, ✆ 282 414 500.

The most central **post office** is on the main square in front of the harbour, Rua Serpa Pinto. Nearby is the **British Consulate**, at 7 Largo Francisco A Mauricio near Largo da Barca, ✆ 282 417 800.

The 14th-century **Igreja Matriz** stands at the highest part of the town. It was rebuilt after the 1755 earthquake, renovated in the 19th century and now retains only the original portal. Inside, 19th-century *azulejos* line the walls and an impressive *talha dourada* altar glints with several layers of gilding. From the church make your way along Rua Dr Ernest Cabrito heading towards the quayside. Pause awhile at **Largo 1 de Dezembro**, a lovely square with solid benches covered in panels of *azulejos* depicting significant events in Portuguese history. Even the flower beds are edged with blue and yellow tiles.

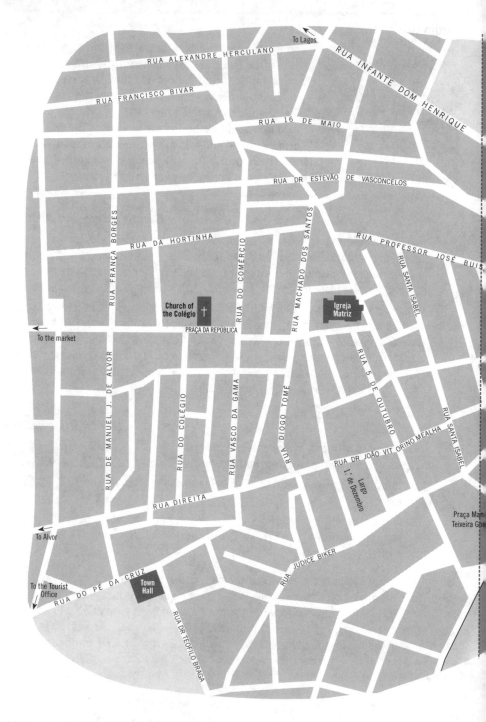

To Portimão and Monchique

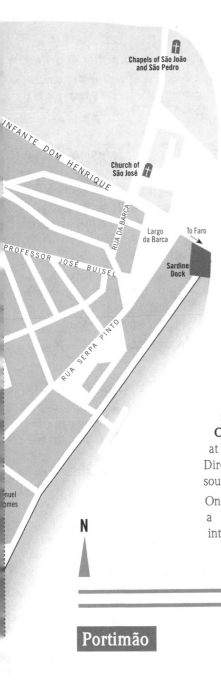

Chapels of São João
and São Pedro

Church of
São José

INFANTE DOM HENRIQUE

PROFESSOR JOSÉ BUISEL

RUA DA BARCA

Largo
da Barca

To Faro

Sardine
Dock

RUA SERPA PINTO

nuel
>mes

N

150 metres

150 yards

Portimão

Head along the southernmost part of the Largo 1 de Dezembro, Rua Judice Biker, to the garden squares by the water and the famous '**sardine dock**'. A rash of seafood restaurants clusters round the harbour by the old bridge, serving the sardines demanded by tourists. This used to be a lively place to watch the activity on the river: the sardine boats setting off in the mornings and returning in the afternoons to unload basketfuls of the small silver fish amid much bustle and noise. But the new wharf has moved these shenanigans to the other side of the river, away from curious eyes. Be prepared for some building work on and around the sardine dock. Preparations are under way to move all the cheap sardine restaurants to the other side of the bridge. This is part of a larger plan to pedestrianize and gentrify the whole of the dockside, which will be happening over the next few years.

Shopping

Portimão has a reputation as a shopping town but there is not a great deal of variety for visitors to get excited about aside from the usual tourist fripperies and a good number of leather and shoe shops (look on and around Rua Santa Isabel).

O Aquário is a popular place, with three large shops at Rua Vasco da Gama, Praça da Republica and Rua Direita, selling crystal, porcelain, copper items and souvenirs/gifts.

On Rua Judice Biker, opposite Largo 1 de Dezembro, is a branch of **A Tralha Antiguidades** with an intriguing collection of antiques.

Regular exhibitions at **Galeria Portimão**, 5 Rua Santa Isabel (*open Mon, Wed, Fri 10.30–1 and 3–7; Sat 10.30–1*) on a street leading up from Praça Manuel Teixeira Gomes, the main square beside the harbour, showcase the work of local artists.

A five-minute walk from the centre, along Av São João de Deus, will take you to the busy fish, fruit and vegetable **market**. The huge **gypsy market** materialises on the first and third Monday of each month.

Sports and Activities

Fishing and boat trips along the coast or up the river to Silves depart from the quayside. If you want to pit your wits against a shark, try **Cepemar Algarve's Big Game Fishing Centre**, ✆ 282 425 866/✆ 282 425 341, which has a good safety reputation.

Where to Stay

★★Residencial O Pátio, 3 Rua Dr João Vitorino Mealha, ✆ 282 424 288 (*inexpensive–cheap*), bursts with character, thanks mostly to the cheerful hand-painted Alentejan furniture: delicate flowers and twisting leaves climb high headboards. Try for a room that opens on to the patio and roof garden, or one that has 17th-century decorated tiles. The cheaper rooms have showers instead of baths,

★★★Residencial Arabi, 13 Praça Manuel Teixeira Gomes, ✆ 282 426 006, ✆ 282 426 007 (*inexpensive*) overlooks the square and the harbour beyond. The wide marble staircase is graced with plants and pictures with a Moorish theme. The rooms are pleasant enough, although those overlooking the square can be noisy.

Portimão's **campsite** is some 4km out of town on the Monchique road, ✆ 282 491 012.

Eating Out

You can have a cheap sardine feast at any one of half a dozen basic establishments at the sardine dock (*see* above). Happy diners fill long wooden tables along the quayside, supplied by smoky barbecues with a constant stream of sardines and other fish. In character and quality the eateries are all much the same, though the first in the line, **Taverna do Maré**, and the last, **Casa Bica**, are recommended.

If you want to set your sights and your budget higher, head through the arches to the vivid Largo da Barca and Rua Vasco Pires, where the garrulous clientele is mainly Portuguese and the square is filled with the smell of fish sizzling on the charcoal grills. Long tables and benches line the square; deep pink flowers tumble down the walls. These are counted among some of the Algarve's best fish restaurants). **Dona Barca**, ✆ 282 484 189, usually draws the plaudits, though its neighbours, **Forte & Feio**, ✆ 282 418 894, and **O Barril** on Rua Vasco Pires (immediately off the square), ✆ 282 413 257, are also excellent. All have similar wide-ranging fish- and seafood-based menus and are in the *expensive–moderate* price range.

Portimão sprawls a couple of kilometres towards the mouth of the River Arade, which is guarded by the **Fortaleza de Santa Catarina**. The courtyard of the fortress is open (*free*) and is worth a trip for its great views. Below it a new marina has recently been completed. The fortress on the opposite side of the river is privately owned.

Praia da Rocha, at the river mouth, is a beautifully flat, sandy beach backed by 70m cliffs in earthy shades. It must have been idyllic, once. Now it is packed with monster hotels and crowded with bodies, bars and restaurants. It's only worth visiting if you're interested in early designs for tourist developments, as this was one of the first on the coast. There are a couple of vantage points equipped with telescopes, presumably to help the punters find a space on the beach.

Praia da Rocha is completely independent of Portimão, with its own **tourist office** at Avenida Tomás Cabreira, ℰ 282 419 132, and a variety of international restaurants along the main beach strip. It's very lively at night, with a **casino**, ℰ 282 415 001, based at the Hotel Algarve on Avda Tomás Cabreira, that puts on the usual floorshows. September brings a treat for unsuspecting tourists when the **Algarve Folk Music and Dance Festival** draws traditionally dressed groups from all over Portugal, with a competition ending on the beach.

On the eastern bank of the River Arade, **Ferragudo** stands opposite Portimão like an echo from the past. The village has retained much of its charm, at least around the riverfront, where there's a buoyant morning market: fishing boats bob in the lagoon, contentedly sniffing the fruits of their catch being charcoal-grilled at the few waterside restaurants. Fishing nets drape the pavement and beaded curtains stir in the open doorways of flaking, whitewashed houses. The settlement straggles uphill, but it's best not to stray too far from the bridge as modern development soon takes over. The main beach, **Praia Grande**, is quite large and within the Arade's breakwaters, but the view of skyscrapers at Portimão's and Praia da Rocha is a turnoffk. A couple of smaller beaches nearer the point are more attractive.

The steep little village of **Estômbar**, 5km east of Portimão, is uncompromisingly Portuguese, which is remarkable considering its location on this stretch of coast. The white cottages are edged with burnt pink or vivid blue and a crumbling **church**'s obligatory Manueline portal and Baroque belfries are festooned with lights. At **Sitio de Fontes** a rickety wooden bridge sways across the water and happy picnickers splash about in the stream.

Where to Stay and Eating Out

There are numerous hotels for all budgets. ★★★★**Hotel Apartamento Oriental**, Avda Tomás Cabreira, Praia da Rocha, ✆ 282 413 000, ✉ 282 413 413 (*luxury*) is an exotic, Xanadu-type affair with many minarets, set in lovely grounds with 85 luxurious studios. At the other end of the price spectrum, though with a situation that is every bit as good, the ★★**Pensao Residencial Solar Penguin**, Avda António Feu (off Avda Tomás Cabreira), ✆ 282 424 308 (*cheap*) is a haven in this brash noisy resort. It is run by Dorothy Boulter, a wonderful old English lady who was one of the original Praia da Rocha 'settlers' in the 1960s. It's frayed at the edges and it won't be everyone's cup of tea, but you won't find a more charming place in all the Algarve.

Another refuge from the package crowds is the **Albergaria Vila Lido**, Avda Tomás Cabreira, ✆ 282 424 127, ✉ 282 424 246 (*expensive*), at the quiet end of the resort towards the Fortaleza de Santa Catarina. This too has a nice old-world air, though it is very smart, very Portuguese and with all mod cons.

First impressions of tacky tourist eating places may not be promising but there are some very good restaurants here. In the centre of the resort, find peace at **The Penguin Terrace** (O Teraço de Pinguim), on the steps leading down to the beach by its parent the Pensão Residencial Solar Penguin,, ✆ 282 483 623. It's a delightful laid-back place with a great beach view and inventive twists on old Portuguese favourites plus excellent salads.

Just below here, on the beach, **Casalinho** (*moderate*) may look no more than your average beach restaurant but is highly rated by the locals for its fish and other Portuguese specials. Be flash and go for one of its flambées.

Alvor

Frequent buses make the short journey from Portimão to Alvor; it takes about 15 minutes. The higgledy-piggledy port at the mouth of the Alvor Estuary had escaped tourist development until relatively recently; now it almost merges with the sprawl that is Praia da Rocha. Eighteen kilometres east of Lagos and 4km west of Portimão, Alvor (not to be confused with Montes de Alvor) was known to the Romans as *Portus Hannibalis*, before the Moors named it *Albur*. Alvor was captured and recaptured several times during the 12th century, until in 1250 the Moors were finally driven out. In 1495, the 40-year-old Dom João II and 25 *fidalgos* billeted themselves on the *castellan* of Alvor, Alvaro de Ataide, after the king caught a chill in Monchique (*see* p.115). Physicians drugged him into a stupor. The chronicler Garçia de Resende takes up the tale: Dom João begged those around him 'for the love of God to wake him up and not let him die like a beast'. They tried. Dom Diogo de Almeida seized the monarch's beard and shouted, 'Senhor, wake up.' He woke, saying, 'Prior, that hand could with more decorum be placed elsewhere, for there are feet!' Shortly afterwards, the Bishop of Tangier was closing Dom João's eyes and mouth, when the king murmured, 'Bishop, it is not yet time.' With that he died. The Lisbon city council commiserated by forbidding all barbers to shave a beard or cut any hair for six months. Alvor shone for a moment in 1975 when the agreement for Angolan independence was made there.

The wetlands of **Alvor Estuary** have been at the centre of mild controversy for a number of years; the area is a rich breeding and feeding ground for water birds, enabling ornithologists to carry out useful studies of the various waders found. Environmentalists campaigned for the area to be declared a nature reserve in order to impose a tighter control on rampaging development. Alas, as is so often the case in the Algarve, the developers have won the day and in 2000 yet another Algarve marina began construction. The man in the *turismo* smiles ruefully and shrugs, 'It is progress.'

Tourist Information

There is a tourist office at the top of the hill leading down to the main street on Rua Dr Afonso Costa, ✆ 282 457 523.

In the old part of town the narrow streets, of almost unsullied whiteness, lead up a low hill to the yellow-bordered 16th-century **Igreja Matriz**. Its fascinating Manueline portal is carved in reddish stone; the concentric arches depict sea flowers, dragons, lions and musicians, all wrapped by a giant octopus tentacle. Inside are some fine *azulejos*.

Five kilometres west of Portimão at Montes de Alvor lies the famous **Penina Golf Club**. **Alto Golf**, Quinta do Alto do Poço, Alvor, forms part of the Alto Club tourist development but is open to all. *See* p.18 for details and prices.

Beaches

The long **beach** is a little way off, backed by low dunes. It attracts some beautiful young people, but it's overlooked by a clutch of horrid Lego-like hotels. Towards Portimão stretch a couple of smaller beaches. The first one at the eastern end of Alvor beach is **Três Irmãos**, a small cove always thronged by a large number of families. **Praia do João de Arens** is a kilometre or so to the east and quite secluded, the rocks forming caves and grottoes; the steep climb down from the cliffs doesn't deter many people. **Praia do Vau** can be reached from the coast road from Praia da Rocha and is marginally quieter than the main beaches. Access is easy, making the beach well-suited to young children. The views from these clifftops are stunning and blow-holes pepper the coast—be watchful as some are unfenced.

Overlooking the Três Irmãos beach, **✶✶✶✶✶Hotel Alvor Praia**, ✆ 282 458 900, ✉ 282 458 999 (*luxury; book through Caravela,* ✆ *(020) 7630 9223*), is more attractive than some of the surrounding monstrosities, being only six floors high. It has all the facilities you'd expect, plus a range of accompanying sporting activities. You need to book well ahead. On the main EN125 between Alvor and Lagos stands the **✶✶✶✶✶Le Meridien Penina** (*luxury; book through Caravela,* ✆ *(020) 7630 9223*). Set in a 360-acre estate which incorporates three golf courses, including the famous Penina (*see* p.18) this is heaven for both golfers and their widows seeking a luxurious retreat. the hotel boasts superb rooms, all five-star facilities, private beach club and an excellent children's club.

Alvor's **campsite** is on the outskirts of the village, ✆ 282 458 002.

Alvor is well stocked with good fish restaurants, mostly on or just off the main street, Rua Dr Frederico R. Mendes, which plunges straight down to the harbour. At the very bottom down by the river quay, **Os Pescadores** (*cheap*) serves good, honest food in a pleasant setting. Plastic chairs are arranged under umbrellas, from which diners watch their fresh fish being lovingly grilled. Fish is priced by the kilo and served with salad and unskinned potatoes.

Directly behind and overlooking Os Pescadores is **Hellman's**, ✆ 282 458 208 (*moderate; open evenings only*), which puts a modern international spin on local cooking as well as offering several of its own inventive dishes. The views from its top terrace are superb.

Vagabondo, Rua Dr Frederico R. Mendes, ✆ 282 458 726 (*moderate*) is under the same management and offers the same blend of friendly lively young staff and innovative modern cooking, and with a patio of orange and almond trees on which to sprawl. *Open evenings only.* For a traditional Portuguese restaurant, set in a one-storey house at the top of the hill, make your way to **Tasca Morais**, Rua Dr António José de Almeida, ✆ 282 459 392 (*cheap*). The food is simple—go for the *cataplana*—and the service is very friendly. *Evenings only; closed Wed.*

Inland: The Serra de Monchique

Beginning 23km inland from Portimão, the breathtaking Monchique hills form a barrier between the Algarve and the Alentejo. The highest points are at Foia (902m) and Picota (744m), sufficient to shelter the Algarve from northerly winds and trap the rain blown inland from the coast, giving the western end of the range the highest rainfall in the Algarve, most of which falls between the end of November and the beginning of May. Steep streams bubble out of the schist, making it easier to irrigate terraced plots of land. There are several places on the road to Foia from where, on a clear day, you can see the whole of the west coast as well as a large chunk of the south coast.

The hills are thickly wooded with eucalyptus, cork oaks like cheerleaders' pom-poms, and every shade of pine tree. When the commercially grown eucalyptus is cut—usually in February—the small leafy branches are lopped off and left to rot *in situ*, thus making a slippery surface on which to slide the trunks down. These Australian invaders gained a foothold in the area about a hundred years ago and quickly took over. Because they grow quickly, they are useful for the ever greedy paper industry, but they deplete subterranean water sources and disrupt the natural ecological food chain.

The roads are flanked by yellow-flowered mimosa. Peonies and pale purple rhododendrons bloom before the end of April, while small arbutus trees flourish throughout the range— keep an eye out for their large, dark green, toothed leaves, and globular, warty, red fruits. Better still, try the flavourful *medronho* brandy distilled from the berries. It's not the brandy but the flat light that makes the hills appear to be superimposed on one another.

Medronho

If you thought moonshine was something that happened when the sun went down, you're in for a shock. The Algarve's distinctive firewater is distilled from arbutus berries and can be purchased from shops under a variety of labels, but the best stuff is home-made. it's also illegal, but that doesn't seem to prevent most households in the mountains keeping a little hidden away somewhere.

In October and November, mountain folk take to the slopes to pick ripe berries. After a couple of weeks' fermentation, the mash is left for up to four months before it is distilled. The end product is an elixir that defies description. Some say it tastes like paraffin, others that it's merely an acquired taste. For most, *medronho* is a joyful tipple to be thrown back in a shot.

As for checking quality, many methods are mooted. Some suggest shaking a little and observing the size of the bubbles: the bigger, the better. Others advocate rubbing a drop on the back of the hand—a figgy smell indicates mass production. Either way, you should feel it burn in your stomach, not in your throat.

So make friends with someone local, and hope you're invited home. Or you could take an empty litre bottle into one of the small brown bars in the narrow side streets of Monchique. the proprietor will often sell you some from a jar of home-made hidden behind the counter. But be careful: sometimes this stuff's over 70% proof—so make sure you know the way home.

Caldas de Monchique

North of Portimão, houses quickly give way to beds of tall reeds and carpets of little yellow flowers. The good tarmac road rises to Caldas de Monchique, 21km from Portimão, 25km northwest of Silves. The tiny spa town is set in a niche in the Serra de Monchique, 250m above the beachy plains and lulled to sleep by a tide of trees. The climate is refreshing and the air clear, but alas, the heart has been knocked out of Caldas de Monchique. Its old buildings—peeling, rustic and charming—have been demolished to make way for a flurry of spanking new hotels due to open in summer 2001.

Hopefully the developers won't find a way of messing up the delightful walks through the woods. Amble up the main path and turn left by the three trees that form a triangle. Cross the little bridge and drink the pure spring water that surfaces here.

Caldas de Monchique was popular with the Spanish bourgeoisie in the 19th century. They left a casino, which until recently housed an expensive **handicraft market**. It may return with the redevelopment.

The grim buildings just below the settlement are the water-bottling factory and the Termas de Monchique **spa** (*open 1 June–15 Nov*), which is particularly good for rheumatism and respiratory disorders. Water emerges from the ground at 32.1°C. The facilities of the spa have also been upgraded to cope with the boom in demand that the new accommodation at Caldas is expected to bring. For details of treatments call © 282 910 910.

Where to Stay

 With the redevelopment of Caldas de Monchique comes a wide choice of brand-new accommodation, the ★★★**Hotel Termal**, the ★★★**Pensão Central**, the ★★**Hotel Ecarnação**, the ★★★★**Estalagem Dom João II** and *apartamento turísticos*.

Just off the central square, and thankfully untouched amid all the kerfuffle, is the small, compact and pretty ★★★★**Albergaria do Lageado**, © 282 912 616 (*inexpensive*), which offers basic but very pleasant bedrooms in the summer season only; its charm begins with the trellised patio off the dining room, from which a path leads up through a rock garden to a lovely family-sized swimming pool (*open to non-residents*). Guests lie on deckchairs surrounded on three sides by tree-covered slopes and birdsong. The restaurant serves simple dishes.

Monchique and Around

The road winds 7km north from Caldas de Monchique, climbing 200m to Monchique, a little town of 10,000 souls. The views of the coastal plain are fabulous, as are the camellia trees. The lush countryside and its climate, always slightly cooler than the coast thanks to its elevation, is perfect for trekking (*see* 'Activities and Walks', p.116). You will see more walkers in and around Monchique than anywhere else in the Algarve.

Having designated Dom Manuel as his successor, Dom João II visited Monchique in 1495. He saw one of his courtiers victorious in a wrestling match against the locals one chilly Sunday morning and, although his doctors advised that it was too cold to swim, the king bathed twice. He also insisted on following the hounds when they found boars in the woods. This activity rendered the king gravely ill. Later, having decamped with his retainers to Alvor, the king died.

The tourist office, © 282 911 189 (*open Mon–Fri 10am–4.30pm, Sat 10am– noon; closed Sun*) can be found in Monchique's cheerful lower central square, Largo dos Chorões, with a fountain and a clever modern twist on the traditional Algarvian *nora*, or well. The café, shaded by a palm tree, is a nice place to sit awhile and rest.

Amongst a jumble of unsightly modern houses, a cobbled street leads up from the main square to the **Igreja Matriz**, which has an odd Manueline portal from which five carved knots radiate. Above the town are the flower-clad ruins of the Franciscan monastery of **Nossa Senhora do Destêrro**, founded in 1632 by Dom Pero da Silva, later Viceroy of India. Some of the locals make their living as shoemakers, potters and basket-makers, who pollard their willow trees to produce flexible shoots. These are then tied in bundles and weighted down at the bottom of irrigation tanks until they are used for basketry in the summer.

West of Monchique, the road climbs past stacks of logs, and eucalyptus trees. Recalcitrant cows are led along the road, which suddenly enters a land of heather and scrub. The exhilarating peak of the range is **Foia**, 8km from Monchique and forested with innumerable broadcasting aerials.

Climbing up to the **Picota peak** makes a wilder and more interesting walk than Foia, through farms and chestnut coppices. The 30km journey west to Aljezur is a beautiful drive, passing the fragrant and flower-filled villages of Nave, Casais and Marmelete before weaving through pine-covered hillsides.

Monchique is the best place to buy the wooden folding chairs found in hotels and homes around the country. This simple design was brought to Portugal by the Romans and is considered evidence of a Roman presence in Monchique. José Leonardo Salvador, the 'Monchique Chair Man', makes them from alder wood and has elaborated on the originals' simple design and even branched out into tables. He is something of a local celebrity, having starred in a BBC documentary. His shop, **Casa Dos Arcos**, Estrada Velha, © 282 912 692, displays his work beautifully. Chairs cost from around 3,000$00 to upwards of 5,000$00. You'll find the 'Chair Man' just outside the centre of Monchique on the road out towards Lisbon. Just out of town on the other side, coming in from the coast, you will see the **Casa Zebra**, which also produces and sells wooden folding chairs.

Facing the main square, Largo dos Chorões, is **Ardécor** (coy about advertising itself, it's the last shop before the road starts rising out of Monchique), stocking some nice handicrafts, clothes, toys and ceramics.

The best place for ceramics is the **Cerâmica Artesanal** in the delightful 19th-century Casa da Nogueira on Rua do Corro, at the back of the parish church. All pieces are handmade and hand-painted on the premises.

At the kite shop **Papagaios** on Rua Caminho do Convento, you can buy huge and unusual kites to fly on the beach. A jolly lady sits behind her sewing machine, ready to help.

Activities and Walks

Experienced walkers might like to pick up a copy of the *Trilhos de Bio-Park Network Monchique* **map** which, in Ordnance Survey-like detail, covers some 300km of trails in and around the Serra de Monchique. Another invaluable aid is the walking tours **guide book** *Algarve* by Sunflower Landscapes. This devotes 4 (out of a total of 20) walks to the Monchique area, graded from easy to moderate, and covering from 6.4km to 11.2km (the latter reaching the summit at Foia). You can buy it in Britain or locally.

If you would prefer to take a guided tour, ask at the Monchique tourist office for local guides, call Susan at **Albergaria Bica Boa** (*✆* 282 912 271, *see* below), or call **Alternativ Tour**, *✆* 0936 500 4337, a local (Portuguese) enterprise which conducts walking (and also cycling) tours in English and other languages. Another English walking group is the **Algarve Walkers**, *✆* 282 449 098.

If you see another group of walkers in the Monchique area the chances are that '*Guten Tag*' will be the most appropriate greeting. There are many Germans here and many are very keen walkers. **Wandern auf den Picota** (Walks on the Picota), is the best known of the German-speaking groups operating in this area. If your Deutsch is up to it, give Ines and Uwe a call on *✆* 282 911 041. The Picota is the mountain peaking at 774m/2540ft, as well as the name of the valley in which Monchique nestles.

The mountains of Monchique are also ideal for exploring on **horseback**. Ask for details at the tourist office.

Where to Stay and Eating Out

Monchique

Rooms at **Residencial Miradouro da Serra**, Rua dos Combatentes do Ultramar, *✆* 282 912 163 (*cheap*), near the main square in Monchique, are clean and tastefully decorated; those at the back have no view. Guests are given a key to the front door, as there is no full-time receptionist in the off season.

There are a couple of reasonable restaurants in Monchique. **Charette** (*moderate–cheap*) is a very Portuguese affair, unfussily bare with lots of chatter and a limited but tasty menu. **Restaurante Central**, 5 Rua da Igreja (*cheap*), is a Monchique institution, tiny and musty with every available surface pasted with letters and messages from countless visitors. It's fun but you'll get better food elsewhere.

Around Monchique

The road to Foia abounds with excellent restaurants and places to stay. A little west of Monchique the delightful **Jardim das Oliveiras**, ℓ 282 912 874, on a terrace in an olive grove. If you want to stay the night (*moderate*) there are three cosy rooms, all with woodburning stoves and local antiques. The restaurant (*expensive–moderate*) serves typical mountain cooking—local sausage, suckling pig, game and specials such as loin of pork stuffed with fig.

The Monchique area is famous for its chicken *piripiri*. Two good places to try it are the **Restaurant Paraiso de Montanha** (*moderate; closed Thurs*), set on a wide terrace with breathtaking views, and the rustic **Agua da Sola** (*cheap*), one of the first places west of Monchique.

Still on the main Estrada da Foia, some 5km from Monchique, is the lovely **Quinta de São Bento**, ℓ 282 912 700 (*expensive–moderate*). Once the holiday home of Portuguese royalty, it has been converted into an award-winning *turismo rural* property, retaining its traditional rooms and throwing open five bedrooms to the public. Even if you don't stay here, do try the restaurant (*moderate, booking essential, ℓ as above*). The owner studies traditional recipes dating back to the 16th century so there is usually something fabuolous to try.

Another good option on the same road is the ★★★★**Estalagem Abrigo da Montanha**, on the Estrada da Foia, ℓ 282 912 131, ✆ 282 913 660 (*expensive–moderate*), a peaceful lodge with a garden full of camellias, mimosas and arbutus. Guest rooms are prettily furnished with iron headboards, and the view from their shuttered windows stretches down to the sea. The restaurant (*moderate*) serves very good local specialities, though the service is rather slow. Dishes include the delicate *assadura* (pork with lemon juice and garlic). The *morgado de figo* is a delicious and unusual dessert made of alternate layers of figs and almonds.

Tucked away well off the main roads, Simply Portugal (ℓ (020) 8541 2207) have many characterful self-catering rustic properties in the Monchique area. Two of the nicest are **Cerca da Cima** (*sleeping 2–4 people*) and **The Stone House** (*2–3 people*). Both have wonderful views—those at Cerca da Cima are breathtaking—and small stone bathing pools, perfect for cooling off, though not for real swimming.

Just south of Monchique, ★★★★**Albergaria Bica Boa**, Estrada de Lisboa, ℓ 282 912 360 (*moderate–inexpensive*) offers pleasant rooms and a mix of Irish and Portuguese cooking.

Chicken *Piri-piri*

You can buy tiny bottles of factory-made *piri-piri* sauce in the supermarket. At the local market stall holders will sell you their 'far superior' home-made variety (usually with oil already added so it is ready for basting). Here is how you make your own *piri-piri* basting sauce.

Ingredients

200ml olive oil
6 chillies (if you can buy the little red piri-piri variety in the Algarve, so much the better)
1 bay leaf
a piece of lemon rind

Simply combine all ingredients in a small airtight bottle or jar and leave for a month! If you can't wait that long, leave it to 'cook' in the noonday sun or on the lowest oven setting you have, for around 3 hours. Leave to stand for at least 24 hours. Then just brush it on the chicken, leave it for a couple of hours, or overnight if you really want the flavour to sink in, and then barbecue.

Silves

Situated among gentle hills beside the River Arade, 8km inland from Lagoa and 26km northwest of Albufeira, Silves was the 30,000-strong capital of the Moorish province of al-Gharb from the mid-11th century to the mid-13th century.

By the 16th century, the river had silted up, the political and commercial heavies had moved on and consequently the population was reduced to just 140. Subsequent earthquakes have destroyed much of the character of the place—the only living monuments to the Moors are the orange and almond groves that surround the town, which is now home to 10,000 people. Since losing its political importance, Silves has been happy to vegetate quietly beside the trickle called the river, though lately it has been enjoying something of a quiet tourist-led renaissance.

History

Idrisi, the 12th-century Arab chronicler and geographer, remarked on the 'fine appearance' of Xelb, a port with 'attractive buildings and well-furnished bazaars', praising the purity of the Yemenite Arabs' language and pronunciation, as well as the region's 'delicate, appetizing and delicious' figs.

For all its opulence, Silves had a troubled history. Soon after the Moors had installed themselves, the city was captured by al-Mu'tadid, of Seville, who planted flowers in the skulls of his decapitated enemies to decorate his palace gardens. Returning to Moorish control, Silves was besieged by Dom Sancho I in 1189. The king had flagged down lusty English crusaders on their way to Jerusalem, promising booty. They set to work in July and August, just when the figs were bursting with ripeness. The parched garrison surrendered on 1 September, and filed out of the stronghold bearing nothing but their clothes—which the Crusaders removed, to the disgust of the king. The allies occupied the city, and spent most of that night torturing the remaining inhabitants into revealing the location of their hidden treasure.

Two years later the Caliph of Morocco recaptured Silves, along with the rest of Portugal south of the Tagus except Évora. The Moors were finally driven out in 1242, during the reign of Dom Afonso III.

Getting There

Silves-Gare is on the east–west **railway** route, © 282 442 310. The station is 2km south of Silves, from which a connecting bus runs every half-hour. Semi-frequent **buses**, © 282 442 338, make the 15-minute journey from Portimão.

Tourist Information

The **tourist office** is in the centre of town, on the Rua 25 de Abril, © 282 442 255 (*open weekdays 9.30am–7pm, weekends 9–12.30 and 2.30–5*). A few yards away in the pretty Praça do Municipio in front of the old town hall is a kiosk, also distributing information on behalf of the municipality.

The **post office** is on Rua Samora Barros.

The daily **market** is off Rua Francisco Pablos and the **gypsy market** comes to Silves on the third Monday of each month.

Silves' **health centre** can be reached on © 282 440 020.

Festivals

A two-week **beer festival** is held in July at the Fábrica do Inglês.

The **Faira da Laranja** is an orange festival held for five days every spring, demonstrating more uses for oranges than you can shake a stick at. The dates change every year; it's best to consult the tourist office.

A Stroll Around Town

The earth-red **cathedral** was built of Algarvian sandstone in 1189, and reconstructed after the Reconquest of 1242. It was the seat of the Algarve's bishopric until 1580, when that honour was transferred to Faro. The Gothic parts of the cathedral have been altered, and although the building is a peaceful place, few interesting architectural features remain. Note the curious gargoyles on the exterior of the apse. Dom João II's coffin was buried here in 1495, having been lined with quicklime to speed the decay of the body. Four years later, it was disinterred: the quicklime had destroyed the shroud and almost burnt through the wooden coffin, but the body was incorrupt. Truly, a miracle. The splinters of the coffin were set aside as holy relics, and the king, placed in a new coffin, was translated to Batalha in central Portugal. Several fine tombs have remained here, including one decorated with a coiled serpent.

Uphill from the cathedral, it's exciting to walk along the top of the thick, rust-coloured curtain walls of the **castle**, built by the Moors on Roman foundations, and restored *c.* 1835. The defences encircle a grove of lemon trees and hibiscus, planted above a Roman copper mine later used for storing grain. The **Archaeological Museum**, Rua das Portas de Loulé (*open daily 10–6 except holidays*), is round the corner from the castle. Built around a large Moorish cistern that once held a year's supply of water, its collection of ancient rocks and broken plates are occasionally glanced at by lines of schoolchildren dragging their feet.

The town's newest attraction is the **Fábrica do Inglês**, a major leisure complex created from a 19th-century English-owned cork factory (hence its name). Opened in 1999, it features a cork museum (only worth seeing on a guided tour when some of the old machinery is demonstrated), six different catering outlets, ranging from high-class seafood to tea rooms, a children's playground and 'Cybernetic Fountains'. The latter come to life on summer nights in a water and laser show with live entertainment and 'street parties'. It's an impressive and attractive place with obvious potential, though during the day and on quiet nights the complex has the sad atmosphere of a white elephant. Call © 282 440 440 to see what's on.

Continue past the Fábrica, on the road to Messines, to see the **Cruz de Portugal**, an ornate 16th-century white limestone cross, 3m high. One side depicts *Christ Crucified*, the other the *Descent from the Cross*.

For beautiful views over Silves and the surrounding countryside, take the road to Messines and turn right after the petrol station. Turn right again if you feel like a hot 3km walk through the orange groves. A ruined mill sits atop a small hill, offering an uplifting panorama over the terraced and cultivated surroundings.

Shopping

Estúdio Destra is housed in a lovely 16th-century building near the castle and is the studio of Kate Swift, a descendant of Frank Swift, who helped revive *azulejo*-painting in the Algarve. Pieces range from individual tiles and small ceramics to wall-sized panels. **Pandora's Box** on Rua Samor Barros (down the steps below the tourist office) has an interesting collection of ceramics, stained-glass lamps, jewellery and local artworks.

On the front, by the river, **Fantasia** is an Aladdin's Cave of merchandise, leather, rugs, carpets and lots of lamps, all from North Africa.

The only hotel in town is the recently refurbished ★★★**Hotel Colina dos Mouros**, ✆ 282 440 420, ✉ 282 440 426 (*expensive–moderate*). Its 57 rooms, some with a great view of the castle, are simply furnished but comfortable, with air-conditioning and satellite televison, and there is an outdoor swimming pool.

Close by are two *residencials*. The **Residencial Ponte Romana**, Horta Cruz, ✆ 282 443 275 (*inexpensive–cheap*), glows in burnt-red sandstone by the river. Inside, the marble staircase leads to very airy rooms, some with a view over the river. There is a popular restaurant (*moderate*), serving good, if standard, Portuguese food in a yard strewn with typical farm bits. Across on the main road **Residencial A Ladeira**, Horta Cruz, ✆ 282 442 870, is a cheaper, more basic alternative.

Estabelecimentos Dom Sancho, Largo do Castelo, ✆ 282 442 437 (*moderate*), next to the castle and cathedral, is at the heart of historic Silves, and includes a large souvenir shop. It's overpriced, but the modern rooms are comfortable, which is more than can be said for the bar's bike-saddle stools.

Better accommodation is to be found outside town. Take the road towards Messines and, not far past the Cruz de Portugal, the **Vila Sodré**, ✆ 282 443 441, has attractive rooms overlooking orange trees. Senhor Silvino gallantly tries to provide 'quality tourism'. His large, '*típico*' restaurant caters only for groups booking ahead; for these he will provide a lovingly crafted regional meal. After another 4km or so, take the signposted turn to the **Quinta do Rio**, Sitio São Estevão, ✆ 282 445 528 (*moderate–inexpensive*), beautifully situated in an orangery in the hills. It has recently been restored by the charming Italian management, who will arrange excursions and horse riding.

Oysters bubble in their tank at the well-known **Rui**, 27 Rua Comendador Vilarinho, ✆ 282 442 682 (*expensive*), which serves fish and shellfish by the kilo in no-nonsense surroundings. *Closed Tues off season.* Just around the corner on **Rua Policarpo Dias**, Tasca do Bene, ✆ 282 444 767 (*cheap*) is a down-to-earth local *tasca* specializing in *petiscos* (snacks), stews, and wine straight from the barrel.

Beautifully located on the castle steps the part-English-owned **Café Inglês**, ✆ 282 442 585 (*moderate*), offers tables out front, inside the traditional old house, or in its lovely courtyard garden. it serves good international-Portuguese cooking and homemade cakes. Live music Sunday afternoons. *Closed Sat.*

Two places worth a look on either side of the Praça do Municipio are **Casa Velha**, ✆ 282 445 491, a basic old-fashioned traditional Portuguese dining room (*cheap*), and the self-service **Pastelaria Destra**, which occupies the foyer of the old town hall and is completely covered with blue and white *azulejos*.

Around Silves

The **Barragem do Arade**, 6km northeast of Silves, is a large reservoir reached by a road lined with incongruously neat box hedges. There is a restaurant at the lake and watersports facilities, but the real highlight is the intensity of the colours of the landscape: the water winds between smooth green and rich brown hills.

The quiet village of **São Bartolomeu de Messines**, 17km northeast of Silves, has grown used to visitors screeching in for a quick look at the **church**, which squats by the main road. The white building edged in rich sandstone is of 16th-century origin, though it has been much restored. Seventeenth-century glazed *azulejos* glow inside the church, which sports twisted-rope Manueline columns. The semi-frequent buses take about half an hour from Silves.

Alte, 28km northeast of Silves, is a flowery little village still touchingly proud of its second placing in a national 'picturesque village' contest. That was in 1938 and Alte is now cannily accustomed to passing tourists, though no less pretty for it. It's also well known for its folk-dance groups, who come into their own in the May Day celebrations culminating in a procession to the village stream in celebration of water. The **parish church** dates from the 15th century and has a fine Manueline portal. An old man acts as guide, running through his patter in French and German and pointing out the 16th-century *azulejos*, the gilt *talha dourada* altar and the European saints depicted in the aisles. The church has a peaceful, shady yard; carob trees fan the benches. At the bottom of the village the stream provides a popular picnicking spot.

Lagos and the Coast West of Lagos

West of the Bay of Lagos development diminishes: Lagos is the only sizeable resort on this section of the coast. With its amber rocks rising out of transparent green waters, lively harbour activity, glitzy marina, funky nightlife and smattering of culture, it's also the most attractive resort west of Faro. Its coastline—the cliffs and their weird outcrops—are best appreciated from the sea, especially around Ponta da Piedade.

The small resorts west of Lagos offer much quieter beaches. In most cases, the original fishing villages have been swamped, but in the village of Salema the locals still pursue a traditional lifestyle. Construction has concentrated on villas and apartment complexes, so no high-rise hotels violate the horizon; brightly coloured fishing boats resting on the sands provide obstacle courses for little children. These low-key resorts are especially popular with English families but a number of young travellers break their monopoly every year, making the nightlife interesting. The farther west you go, the more the balance shifts in favour of the travellers.

The coast west of Lagos is particularly suited to scuba-diving and snorkelling, with calm and very clear waters harbouring shipwrecks and octopuses roaming the rock crevices and vivid watery gardens. It's advisable to wear a wet suit while diving, all year round.

ATLANTIC OCEAN

Raposei

Ingrina

Sagres

Lagos

The Baía de Lagos is one of the widest bays of the Portuguese coast, sheltered on the west by the Ponta da Piedade promontory, and on the east by the Ponta dos Três Irmãos. The harbour town of Lagos commands the bay, on the hilly western bank of the estuary of the River Bensafrim.

Lagos is the principal resort of the western Algarve, particularly popular with Germans and English, attracting a more varied and sexy crowd than Faro or Albufeira. Yet there's still room for the locals to lead their lives without too much interruption. They shop in

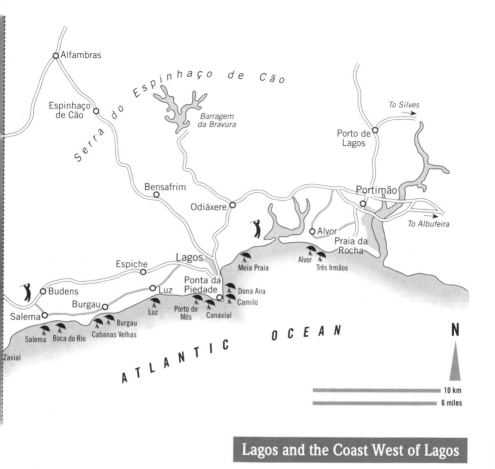

Lagos and the Coast West of Lagos

the market opposite the harbour and let their dogs pick at bones in the narrow, winding streets. The vertical rock cliffs of the coast are pocked with grottoes, which can be explored by boat; the marina at Lagos has a wide variety of colourful craft.

History

The Lusitanian settlement of *Lacobriga* was destroyed by an earthquake, making way for its resettlement by the Carthaginians in 350 BC. When Sertorius took *Lacobriga* from the Romans in 76 BC, it grew into a flourishing town. Many of the early voyages to explore the coast of Guinea set sail from this port—spawning the rope- and sail-making industries—

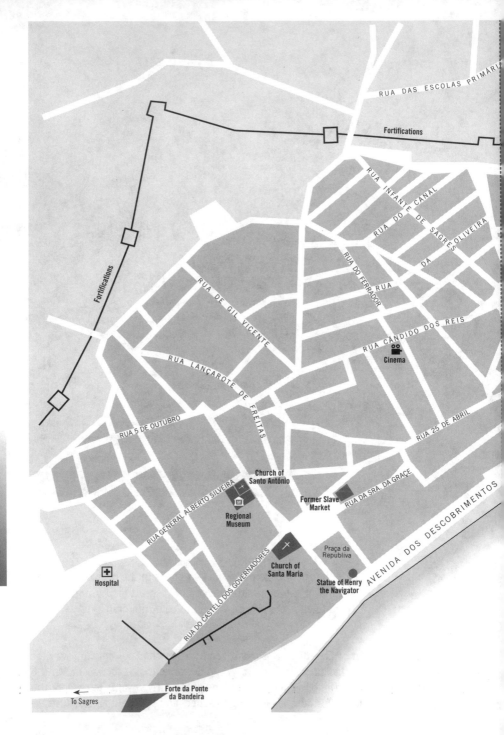

RUA DAS ESCOLAS PRIMÁRI

Fortifications

RUA INFANTE DE SAGRES

RUA DO CANAL

DE

OLIVEIRA

RUA DO FERRADOR

RUA

DA

Fortifications

RUA DE GIL VICENTE

RUA CANDIDO DOS REIS

Cinema

RUA LANÇAROTE DE FREITAS

RUA 5 DE OUTUBRO

RUA 25 DE ABRIL

Church of
Santo António

Former Slave
Market

RUA DA SRA. DA GRAÇE

Regional
Museum

AVENIDA DOS DESCOBRIMENTOS

RUA GENERAL ALBERTO SILVEIRA

Praça da
Republiva

Church of
Santa Maria

Statue of Henry
the Navigator

Hospital

RUA DO CASTELO DOS GOVERNADORES

Forte da Ponte
da Bandeira

To Sagres

RUA DO JOGO DA BOLA

RUA DR A. JOSÉ DE ALMEIDA

RUA DOS CAMACHINHOS

RUA DA CAPELINHA

Praça Luis de Camões

Praça Gil Eanes

RUA DAS PORTAS DE PORTUGAL

Tourist Office

To Faro, train and bus stations

Town Hall

Post Office

Bus Stop

River

N

200 metres
200 yards

Lagos

after Gil Eanes sailed around Cape Bojador in 1434 and found the imprints of the feet of men and camels. Lançarote returned with a report on elephants, whose 'flesh will suffice to satisfy 500 men, and [the Guineans] find it very good'. Lançarote also returned with 235 Moorish slaves, prompting Europe's first slave market. The chronicler Azurara, who ordinarily writes dispassionately, seems genuinely moved: 'What heart, even the hardest, would not be moved by a sentiment of pity on seeing such a flock?'

The last Mediterranean crusade departed from Lagos in 1578, under the command of the ascetic, obstinate 25-year-old king Dom Sebastian, ending in disaster at Alcácer-Quivir (*see* **History**, p.37). Before he left, the king made the town capital of the Algarve, a title it retained until 1755, when Tavira and finally Faro took over. Lagos has survived many battles in its past, including an attack from Sir Francis Drake in 1587, whom the tourist office brochure once passionately described as 'that English pirate'. This has obviously been invaluable training: Lagos withstands its annual invasion from northern Europe with humour and little loss of integrity.

Getting There

Frequent **trains** make numerous stops on their way from Vila Real de Santo António (4hrs), including Tavira (3hrs), Faro (2¼hrs), and Albufeira (1¼hrs). From Lisbon, take the ferry to Barreiro, and catch a train to Tunes. Change at Tunes for Lagos (5¼hrs rail travel).

EVA **buses** arrive from Lisbon (5hrs), and from Vila Real de Santo António (4hrs), via Tavira (3½hrs), Faro (2¼hrs), and Albufeira (1¼hrs), amongst others.

Tourist Information

The **tourist office**, ✆ 282 763 031, is conveniently situated if you are coming by car from the east, signposted just before you get to the centre of town. Otherwise plan on a 15-minute walk. The **post office** is on the Praça Gil Eanes.

The **bus station**, ✆ 282 762 944, is on the harbour front. Turn right at the Rua das Portas de Portugal to get to the Praça Gil Eanes. The best bus stop for the town centre is on the Avenida dos Descobrimentos.

The **train station**, ✆ 282 762 987, is just across the bridge on the left.

The lively main **market** occupies two floors, with fish on the ground floor. It faces the harbour, almost on the corner of Rua das Portas de Portugal. By the bus station on the Avenida dos Descobrimentos, an orderly **Saturday morning market** unfolds on patches of hessian—the usual fruit and vegetables, with rabbits, chickens and odd fish thrown in. The **gypsy market** is on the first Saturday of each month.

The **Totta & Açores bank** on Rua das Portas de Portugal has an automatic change machine which takes most European currencies.

There is a **hospital** in Lagos on Rua do Castelo dos Governadores, ✆ 282 763 034/6/9, or, better still, seek the sevices of MediLagos, by the Motel Marsol on the ring road due north of the old city wall, ✆ 282 760 181.

Around Town

The sculpture of Dom Sebastian in the Praça Gil Eanes portrays him as a spaceman. Although it seems ridiculous to some, this is presumably João Cutileiro's way of updating the myth of Sebastianism, the messianic cult fostered by the Spanish domination of 1580–1640, which hoped for a return of the saviour to restore his people to greatness and prosperity, a cult which lingers even today (*see* **Topics**, p.45).

The Rua Direita runs parallel with the river into the Rua da Senhora da Graça. Portugal's only **slave market** was held where this opens into the Praça da República, under the arches of the Custom House. There should be a memorial, but there isn't, just a small plaque. In the last century, the Portuguese were the first colonial power to abolish slavery. Dom Sebastian is supposed to have put fire in the bellies of his troops by orating from a window of the **Church of Santa Maria**, which overlooks the Praça.

The Rua Henrique Correira Silva leads inland to the tiny **Chapel of Santo António**, whose gilt woodwork is among the finest and most ebullient in Portugal. Carved by an unknown sculptor *c.* 1715, the wild animals, monsters, and unlikely vegetation surround scenes from the life of St Anthony—preaching to attentive fish, reinstating the foot which a guilty son had cut off in penance. The painted vault was rebuilt in 1769, following an earthquake. Aesthetes will pay their respects to the grave of Hugo Beattie, an Irish colonel whose motto was '*Non vi sed arte*'.

Leading off the chapel, the **regional museum** (*open daily 9.30–12.30 and 2–5; closed Mon and holidays*) mixes oddities, works of art, and ethnography. Pickled freak animal foetuses, colonial hair picks, and a funky pair of 19th-century sun-glasses vie for attention with a fantastical 17th-century embroidered altarcloth, the 16th-century vestments used at Dom Sebastian's last Mass in Portugal (on Meia Praia beach), and Lagos'

charter of 1504. Other displays include octopus pots, corkwork from Silves and a selection of Algarvian chimneys. You don't have to be Santa Claus to get a kick out of the Algarve's chimneys, which were introduced into the whole country from the south. The Algarve's pretty latticed flues hark back to Moorish times; the white oblong structures puff out lace-like smoke. Some wear a cockerel weathervane on top, while others, for instance the chimneys of Olhão, are box-like.

Go back, past the Church of Santa Maria, and on the front of the Praça da República, facing the Avenida dos Descobrimentos ('the Discoverers' Avenue') is a large **statue of Henry the Navigator**, prince and patron of the Great Discoverers who made Lagos his headquarters during these halcyon years (*see* p.140 and pp.49–50). His palace is thought to have been just behind where the statue now stands, or rather sits, but it was lost in the Great Earthquake of 1755.

Across the road however is an ancient survivor, the **Forte da Ponta da Bandeira**, built in the 17th century. It has little historic importance but houses a small exhibition and restaurant, and is worth the small admission fee for its views alone.

Beaches

Heading west, the cove-beach closest to town is the oft-photographed **Praia Dona Ana**. It can be too small for the crowds that flock here in the summer. Tour boats stitch their way amongst the caves—they tout for business by the Forte de Ponte da Bandeira and on the Avenida dos Descobrimentos. Or you can just approach one of the fishing boats; that's what they're there for. **Praia do Camilo** is even smaller, though just as pretty, with strange rock formations rising out of the warm green water.

Just east of Lagos, **Meia Praia** is flat and four kilometres long—so if you walk far enough you can escape the crowds, or visit Alvor. It can be reached by car from several places along the coast. There is a watersports centre at the western end of Meia Praia (that's the bit nearest the town) which teaches windsurfing as well as hiring out windsurfs, jet bikes and waterskis. The 18-hole Palmares **golf course**, *see* p.18, is situated near Meia Praia.

A headland juts south into the sea amidst a collection of thickly twisting rocks. This is **Ponta da Piedade**. It has excellent views, and the grottoes formed by the terracotta orange rocks look particularly impressive viewed from the luminous sea.

Praias do Canavial and **Porto de Mós**, towards Luz, are small stretches of body-dotted sand which are marginally quieter than the other beaches in Lagos and very popular with young Portuguese.

Around Lagos

The **Barragem da Bravura reservoir**, 15km inland from Lagos (from Odiáxere take the left turn on to the small Rua do Barragem), makes a worthwhile diversion. The later stages of the route are beautiful, with rusty soil and a curiously Mexican feel. If you want somewhere to picnic, the scenery is prettier before you get to the dam itself, which is choppy, banked by trees and running pitifully low on water.

Sports and Activities

One of the best-looking boats is the *Bom Dia*, a two-mast sailing boat which offers **trips round the grottoes**. Tickets can be bought at the marina or by the river. If you're interested in **deep-sea** and **big-game fishing**, the *Espadarte do Sul* is a bluewater fishing boat with a friendly crew and good equipment, ☏ 282 761 820. A seven-hour fishing day costs 11,000$00, including lunch. Prospective catches include tuna, blue marlin and many species of shark.

Shopping

Lagos has two treats for antiques lovers. On the main street, Rua 25 de Abril, **Casa do Papagaio** is something of a Lagos institution with its delightful junk-shop-cum-museum atmosphere and resident *papagaio* (parrot). Much more refined is the **Casa da Barroca**, on the often overlooked Rua da Barroca, which runs parallel to 25 de Abril. Near Papagaio on Rua 25 de Abril, the trendy **Olaria Nova** is a welcome change from the usual tired old tourist ceramics and souvenirs, with some unusual modern pottery plus top quality jewellery, clothing and accessories.

Where to Stay

luxury

The clever irregular design of the ★★★★**Hotel de Lagos**, Rua António Crisógono dos Santos, ☏ 282 769 967, ✉ 282 769 920, sprawls over three acres of Lagos hilltop, offering spacious, well-furnished bedrooms which overlook the town, the swimming pool or a courtyard filled with lush exotics and birdsong. The cavernous main dining room serves good food, and guests enjoy fringe benefits such as membership of the Duna Beach Club at Meia Praia and reduced green fees at nearby golf courses. Smooth, helpful service, impressive facilities and a more discerning class of tourists help distinguish the hotel.

Less pricy, but offering good value in the centre of town, **★★Pensão Mar Azul**, 13 Rua 25 de Abril, ℭ 282 769 749, @ 282 769 960, is very pleasant and well maintained. Most rooms have private bathrooms. Under the same ownership, **★★★★Albergaria Marina Rio**, Avenida dos Descobrimentos, opposite the marina, ℭ 282 769 859, @ 282 769 960, is very well kitted out (including a pool) and efficiently run. However, it's mostly devoted to German block-bookings, making it difficult for the independent traveller to get a look-in. It's worth contacting them anyway: rooms are sometimes available and some have good views over the harbour and marina. Another option is **★★★Pensão Lagosmar**, 13 Rua Dr Faria da Silva, ℭ 282 763 523; it's clean and friendly in a quieter part of town.

inexpensive–cheap

★★★Pensão Dona Ana, Praia Dona Ana, ℭ 282 762 322, makes a good cheaper option on the road above the beach. It's largeish, busy and very sociable. The English-owned **★★★Pensão Rubi-Mar**, 70 Rua da Barroca, ℭ 282 763 165, is pleasant and good value. You could also try **★★★★Pensão Sol e Sol**, 22 Rua Lançarote de Freitas, ℭ 282 761 290, a modern and spotlessly clean establishment. There are **very cheap** rooms to be had in people's houses; ask at the tourist office or hang around the bus stop and wait for the touts.

A lively **campsite** called **Trinidade** sprawls on the Ponta da Piedade road, ℭ 282 763 893. It attracts a young party crowd. The other campsite is 1½km from Lagos towards Porto de Mós, called **Imulagos**, ℭ 282 760 031, but beware—during 2001 it may be closed for major renovation.

Solares de Portugal

It is expected that the **Casa Pinhão** will be open during 2001. Ask at the tourist office for details.

Eating Out

expensive

Dom Sebastião, 20–22 Rua 25 de Abril, ℭ 282 762 795 (*reservations recommended*) is usually humming with activity. It's a split-level tavern with a dragons'-tooth floor, a black-beamed ceiling, leatherbound menus, and very good fish and seafood. *Closed Sun in winter*. Next door, **Os Arcos**, ℭ 282 763 120, spills out on to the pavement. The service can be curt although the food is often excellent. Inland from the Praça Gil Eanes, the wood-beamed **Alpendre**, 17 Rua António Barbosa Viana, ℭ 282 762 705, serves very good food, but the leather armchairs dispel intimacy, the menu is rather too large to find one's way around, and smoochy Muzak plays in the background. Fillets of sole are *flambéed* with vermouth. *Reservations recommended; closed off season.*

O Galeão, 1 Rua da Laranjeira, ℭ 282 763 909, is very smart. Go for the *arroz de tamboril*: succulent pieces of firm monkfish cooked with rice, herbs, sausages and tomatoes.

The Algarve is a bleak place for vegetarians so it's worth knowing about **Mediterraneo**, Rua Senhora de Graça, ☎ 282 768 476 (*moderate*). Tables spill out on to the corner of a pretty little pedestrianized street, or you can squeeze into the attractive cosy interior. Dishes span the world with several vegetarian options. *Closed Sun, Mon and Dec–Mar.* Close by, the trendy **Café Xpreitaqui Nature**, Rua Silves Lopes, is also a good place for non-meat eaters, with excellent quiches, salads, and the best selection of juices, shakes and coffees in town. *Closed Sun.*

Slightly off the tourist trail, **O Escondidinho** ('the hideaway'), Beco do Cemitério, ☎ 282 760 386 is a simple grilled fish restaurant but portions are huge and the atmosphere jovial, verging on boisterous. *Closed Sun.* Close by, **O Alberto**, 27 Largo Convento Senhora da Glória, ☎ 282 769 387, has an open kitchen where you can watch waiters burning themselves on the hot plates. On Rua 25 de Abril, teeming with bars and restaurants, is the friendly **O Lamberto**, ☎ 282 763 746, a first-floor establishment with a nice terrace, good food and a buoyant atmosphere.

Restaurante Piri-Piri, 15 Rua Lima Leitão, ☎ 282 763 803, is deservedly popular. The large portions are expertly cooked and served by courteous waiters. Usually the half-portions are enough; try the *peixe espadarte*—grilled swordfish served with an onion and butter sauce.

Adega da Marina, 35 Avenida dos Descobrimentos, ☎ 282 764 284, is a huge, barn-like dining room with a beamed, vaulted ceiling, long refectory-style tables, fishing nets, anchors, and a swordfish. The garrulous clientele is mostly Portuguese and the high quality of the food matches the atmosphere. Tucked away at the top of town, small, plain **Ritinha**, 25 Rua do Canal, ☎ 282 763 791, is popular with local families and has no menu in English. There's also unpretentious **Oceano e Lagos**, Rua José Afonso, which serves good seafood to a loyal clientele.

Bars, Entertainment and Nightlife

There is a cacophony of bars. Largest, and the best of the young and trendies, is the family-run **Mullens**, 86 Rua Cândido dos Reis, ☎ 282 761 281, with a stone floor and black benches. Mullens doubles as a restaurant (*moderate*) and the food is good. There is a whole bevy of noisy bars at the end of **Rua 25 de Abril**. At night you'd have to be deaf or incredibly drunk to miss them. The classiest of these is **Bon Vivant**, with its Gaudí-esque decoration—look skywards for its rooftop terrace.

If you're after a bar where the locals drink, pop into friendly **Ferradura**, Rua 1 de Maio. At lunchtime, snacks such as sausage, shellfish and a bowl of stew are on the menu. *Closed Sun.* Fancy a cup of tea? Back on Rua 25 de Abril, **A Casa Amarela** has 21 different varieties, 10 coffees, 7 types of juices, as well as 40-year-old ports and *medronhos* to taste. Just pull up a a wicker chair.

At the **cinema** on Rua Cândido dos Reis, opposite Mullens, there is a 10pm show nightly during which you can drink beer or do pretty much anyting else you fancy, so long as you don't put your feet on the seats. *Closed Thurs.*

The **Centro Cultural de Lagos**, Rua Lançarote de Freitas, ✆ 282 763 403, holds art exhibitions and music recitals for culture vultures.

West of Lagos

Luz

Backed by bare cliffs, Luz is popular with English families, and there is even an English primary school here. Luz was probably idyllic once; the older villas are large, rambling affairs on the cliff above the beach, with 'Private Property' signs everywhere. The rest of the resort is Anglo-continental, though there is a little patch of sky above the church that's still Portuguese.

Getting There

Semi-frequent buses run from Lagos (15 mins), but you may have to walk from the highway.

The handsome 400-year-old **fortaleza**, at the end of the beach promenade, is now a restaurant (*see* below) but curious visitors who want to take a peek inside are always welcome (within opening hours).

Praia da Luz is a long stretch of sand backed by apartments and a handful of restaurants and bars. Red-faced teenagers weave around at night. The two large, popular complexes which dominate the resort, the Ocean Club and Luz Bay Club, provide plenty of water-sports and tennis facilities, though the long-established Anglo-German Luz Bay diving club has recently decamped a few kilometres east to Porto de Mós, near Lagos, and now calls itself Blue Ocean Divers, ✆ 282 782 718.

Where to Stay and Eating Out

 Apartments comprise most of the accommodation. An alternative is the large, sugary-pink ★★★★**Hotel Belavista da Luz**, on the road to the beach, ✆ 282 788 655, 🖷 282 788 656 (*expensive*), which is quite plush and very comfortable with good-sized rooms and smooth service; another is the ★★★**Residencial Vila Mar**, 10 Estrada de Burgau, 1km west of the parish church, ✆ 282 789 541 (*moderate*).

There are two **campsites**, one situated a couple of kilometres north of town at Espiche, ✆ 282 789 431, and another about 1½km east of the beach, called **Valverde**, ✆ 282 789 211.

Whether or not you plan to dine, do call in for coffee at **Fortaleza da Luz**, ✆ 282 789 926 (*expensive*) whose ancient bare brickwork is adorned with shields, weapons and armour, a fine antidote to all those bathing suits. Dinner by candle-light cannot but be romantic, and the food is generally very good. The lunchtime menu is quite different, with pizzas and vegetarian dishes included (*moderate–cheap*), and you can eat them outdoors on the *esplanada*, with great views of the coast and a lovely garden. At lunchtime on Saturdays there's jazz and a barbecue.

At the far end of the beach, set back a block or two, **O Português**, Rua da Praia, ✆ 282 788 804 (*moderate*) has an open-plan kitchen and a warm atmosphere. The food is of a high quality, especially the grilled fish, and the wine list is distinguished. *Closed Thurs.*

Entertainment and Nightlife

There is a **cinema** in Luz, at the main commercial centre on the left as you head for the beach. It screens the latest releases on weekends at 10pm, charging around 550$00.

Burgau

Eighteen kilometres west of Lagos, Burgau is small and mostly undeveloped, with cobbled streets running down to the beach hemmed in by scree. The small fishing community is almost extinct save a few colourful boats.

Getting There

Semi-frequent buses run from Lagos (15mins), but you may have to walk from the highway.

Beaches

Praia do Burgau is backed partly by the Burgau Beach Bar, partly by sharply sloping cliffs. The smooth, clear water is ideal for children and there are lots around, mostly English.

A couple of kilometres west of Burgau is **Praia das Cabanas Velhas**, a long beach similar in character to Burgau, reached by taking the old road through fields dappled with fig trees, verdant in winter, scorched in summer. A smaller beach lies to the right over some rocks, backed by low scrub-carpeted cliffs. Popular with local families and holidaymakers in the know, it is busy in the summer though it can bear crowds better than the village beach.

Where to Stay

 If you want entertaining accommodation, head for **Casa Grande**, ✆ 282 697 416, ✉ 282 697 825, *www.nexus-pt.com/casagrande* (*moderate*). It's a rambling old place, built in 1912, tatty at the edges but comfy, and with bags of character, mostly injected by Sally the chatty English owner. She is a great source of information as well as enormous fun. The restaurant (*expensive–moderate; open evenings only; closed Sat, Sun*) is a wooden barn with tile-topped tables, extravanagant murals and occasional live music. The interesting Portuguese- international menu includes several delicious vegetarian dishes.

Set between Luz and Burgau, the **Casa Rosa Montes** (*book with Simply Portugal, ✆ (020) 8541 2207*) is nominally a hotel, but has the atmosphere of a friendly guesthouse, and is an oasis of peace and quiet. The modern building is handsomely arcaded and traditionally decorated. Rooms overlook the lovely garden and swimming pool, and beyond to hills and fields. The old couple who run it speak hardly any English but are so accommodating that it hardly seems a problem. Self-catering apartments (sleeping 2–3 people) are also available.

Eating Out

For the best typical Portuguese food head for **O Celeiro**, ✆ 282 697 144 (*expensive–moderate*) on the highway near the village of Almadena, a couple of kilometres east of Burgau and 10km west of Lagos. It's a busy, rustic restaurant arranged around a wood-burning stove, with copper implements hanging from the walls. The menu is a joy, adding a flamboyant touch to typical dishes, and the fairly extensive wine list represents most regions in the country. You could sample a 1981 red from Borba in the Alentejo, costing around 6,000$00. Do book in advance. If you're feeling adventurous, ask for the menu of specialities, which must be ordered at least 24 hours ahead. It includes *galo de cabidela com arroz*— a cockerel cooked in its own and served with rice, or *cabrito no forno à antiga* which is kid baked in a traditional oven.

Salema

Seventeen kilometres east of Sagres and 22km west of Lagos, Salema is a rickety fishing village with a sheltered bay, whose rock cliffs fall to a sweep of smooth sand. Development is noticeable and growing all the time, but there is still a happy mix of locals and beach people. The 2km road from the highway passes through a beautiful ravine banked with wild flowers. At the beach, an alley flanked by low and humble houses leads to the left, while to the right a road rises steeply up the cliff with development groping upwards from here.

The Parque da Floresta **golf course** (*see* p.18) is 16km west of Lagos, near Budens in the hills above Salema.

Getting There

Semi-frequent **buses** run from Lagos (45mins), but you may have to walk from the highway.

Beaches

Praia da Salema is popular with travellers as well as English and German families. Head to the right of the beach and the colourful fishing boats for more sand and less clutter; to the left, the beach is littered with debris from the houses and restaurants. The smell of the charcoal grill of the restaurant Mira Mar wafts around invitingly.

Praia da Boca do Rio, a couple of kilometres east of Salema, is lovely and a bit quieter, with easy access. It's good for diving when the water is calm; there is the wreck of a French ship some 300 metres off-shore. When the waves are up, surfers take over.

Where to Stay and Eating Out

Perched high above Salema beach, but sufficiently far back not to be affected by any noise, is **A Maré**, ✆ 282 695 165, *www.algarve.co.uk*. Run by a very friendly English couple, it is far and away the best place to stay in Salema. The breakfast room is light and airy and all bedrooms are tastefully decorated with personal touches throughout. The top room is a gem, with a wonderful view and a good music system.

Various houses have **very cheap** rooms to let: walk down the Rua dos Pescadores to the left of the beach; signs are stuck in windows, for example at No.91.

There is a pretty **campsite**, Quinta dos Carriços, ✆ 282 695 201, near the ravine. It is about 1½km away, heading towards Salema from the main road.

There are a few places to eat. At the beachside, **Atlântico** (*moderate*) has tables outside and serves delicious fresh tuna in a variety of styles. Also popular is **Boia**, 101 Rua dos Pescadores (*moderate–cheap*), with a beach terrace and a couple of vegetarian dishes. Good breakfasts are served in the bar.

There are a couple of **bars** (and a nice gift shop) on Rua dos Pescadores.

Raposeira and Around

Getting There

Semi-frequent buses go from Lagos, taking almost an hour to reach the highway.

A small and very ordinary little village about 11km north of Sagres and 27km west of Lagos, Raposeira has narrow, cobbled streets and a couple of cafés slumber in a sleepy haze. Three kilometres to the east crouches little white 13th-century **Chapel of Nossa Senhora de Guadalupe**, where Henry the Navigator is supposed to have worshipped.

Beaches

Two lovely, quiet **beaches** lie some 4–6km south of Raposeira, calling for a hire car or sturdy legs. **Praia da Zavial** is a crescent-shaped bay with sand stretching way back. It's not too big but very picturesque. **Praia da Ingrina** is a tiny cove flanked by rocks creating a deep pool of water. Both beaches have restaurants and their calm waters and easy access make them particularly suitable for children. There is a **campsite** near Ingrina, ✆ 282 639 242. From here you can walk to Sagres, around 7km, without seeing a single house.

Sagres and the West Coast

This unspoilt stretch of coast is a haven for the independent traveller, with some good-value accommodation, often in people's houses, no monster hotels, and miles of beautiful, empty beaches. The raw weather and stark scenery deter those who spend their holidays baking; this coast is windswept, keeping the air piercingly fresh and making stiflingly hot days bearable. The sandstone cliffs of the south coast stage a gloriously vivid ochre finale on the beaches of Sagres before being superseded by a mixture of hard limestone and folded layers of jagged black slate.

The majority of the travellers and foreign settlers along this coast are German, attracted by the relaxed lifestyle. The English don't make it much further than Lagos and its easy delights. But beware, these beaches are a less suitable location for a family holiday: the undertow can be very strong and a lot of the quieter beaches have no facilities or lifeguards, so care must always be taken when swimming, especially with children.

The area west of Burgau up to the Alentejan town of Odemira is a protected zone known as the Vincentina Coast. The government exerts tight planning controls despite heavy lobbying by big firms and pressure from the American, German and British governments. In 1998 the Vincentina Coast became a nature reserve, aided by a massive cash injection to prevent excessive development.

Among the endangered species represented in this area is the last pair of **ospreys** in the Iberian peninsula. Fifteen years ago there were three pairs nesting in the cliffs, but human encroachment on their habitat has led to their disappearance. The last of Portugal's **rock doves** inhabit the cliffs around Cape St Vincent, as do fifteen pairs of **peregrine falcons**. Curiously sea-attracted **storks** also nest here, eschewing their normal urban habitat. **Otters** like the salt marshes and sometimes the sea, where they fish, for example in Praia da Bordeira. All sorts of **amphibians** inhabit the small ponds found in the coastline plateau between October and April, migrating solely to reproduce in these temporary waters. The rarest species in the Iberian Peninsula is the beautiful **lynx**, which can be found in the Monchique and the Espinhaço de Cão ranges and comes down to roam the coast, preferring dunes with lots of scrub.

Mass tourism is not the only enemy here: the government has made itself particularly unpopular in Sagres with its unsightly renovations of the fortress (*see* p.142) and by erecting the navy's giant antennae on an important wildlife habitat, a biogenetic reserve between Tonel and Beliche beaches. Do respect the area by acting responsibly; walk or drive only on existing tracks; don't collect plants, fruit or minerals; take your litter with you and don't start fires. Freelance camping can also be destructive to the natural habitat—use the many campsites provided.

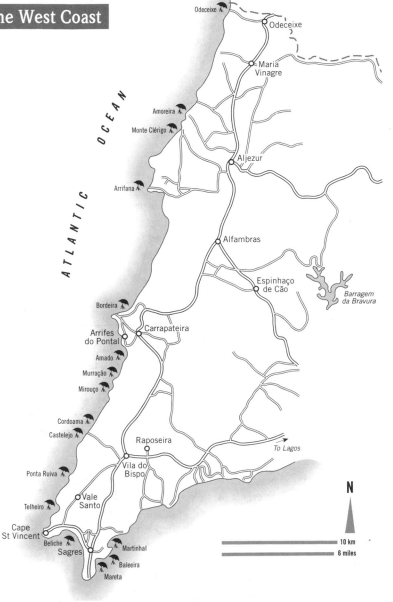

Odeceixe

Odeceixe

Maria
Vinagre

Amoreira

Monte Clérigo

Aljezur

Arrifana

Alfambras

Espinhaço
de Cão

Barragem
da Bravura

Bordeira

Arrifes
do Pontal

Carrapateira

Amado

Murração

Mirouço

Cordoama

Castelejo

Raposeira

Ponta Ruiva

Vila do
Bispo

To Lagos

Vale
Santo

Telheiro

Cape
St Vincent

Beliche

Martinhal

Sagres

Baleeira

Mareta

ATLANTIC OCEAN

N

10 km

6 miles

Sagres

On a barren rock promontory pelted by northwesterly winds, 34km west of Lagos, the unexpected village of Sagres harbours the spirit of Portugal's groping exploration down the west African coast: a small peninsula some 300m wide juts out from the coast, and on this Henry the Navigator founded his school of navigation.

The wind and the sea are his only true monuments. The insubstantial and sprawling modern village of 3,000 inhabitants appears deceptively large from a distance, disappointing close to. On the road to Sagres, the countryside becomes barer and the sky wider, and the wind picks up the sweet smell of the gum cistus that is so prolific on this part of the coast. The approach heightens the feeling that this is the *Fim do Mundo* (End of the World), as was supposed by the ancients who were convinced that from Sagres Point (the western headland and the most southwesterly point in Europe) one fell into a seething pit of serpents and scaly monsters. Indeed the road ends at Sagres: there is no way to leave here except back the way you came.

The village is laid along three parallel streets popular with noisy morning motorbikers. In the square, lined by cafés and a bar, travellers with stories to tell and ham rolls to eat sit outside the Café Conchinha, occasionally playing a guitar as the wind whips up whirlpools of dust and napkins. Along the headland, fishermen with rods like interplanetary receivers lean against the walls at the top of the cliffs catching anchovies, bream and snook—some of these locals scratch a living from fishing off the cliffs or scraping barnacles (*perceves*) from the rocks in winter. At the other end of the village the harbour glints bright blue as fishing boats unload their catch from these fertile waters.

History

In 1437, the Infante Dom Henrique, **Henry the Navigator**, son of Dom João I and Philippa of Lancaster, was obliged to leave his younger brother Dom Fernando as a hostage for the return of Ceuta to the Moors. Crushed by shame, a lesser man than Henry, as his pupil Magellan later remarked, 'would have hidden himself with seven yards of sackcloth and a rosary of oak-apples, to die in the wilds of the Serra de Ossa.'

But Henry found a more useful outlet for his ascetic tastes: he devoted himself—and his revenue as Duke of Viseu, Governor of the Algarve, monopolist of the soap and tuna-fishing industries, and Governor of the Order of Christ—to encouraging and financing the exploration of the west coast of Africa. He built the town on Sagres Point in 1443 for purely altruistic reasons: when Sagres had no settlement and no resources, ships rounding the headland would be surprised by Atlantic storms and shelter in the cliffs, only to lose crews to starvation. So the Vila do Infante was built to provide shipping provisions and spiritual succour, with a couple of churches and a cemetery. Henry then founded a **school of navigation** there, gathering astronomers and astrologers, geographers, cartographers, Jews, sailors and wandering Arabs, who were able to give first-hand accounts of their travels. Jaime Cresques, whose father had produced the Catalan atlas, was an early recruit. Azurara, the 15th-century chronicler of the Portuguese court, records that multifarious races visited Sagres 'to see the beauty of the world'. It was here that the first caravels were built in secret, constructed of Alentejan oak and caulked with pine resin. These revolutionary new designs contributed greatly to Portugal's seafaring prowess.

The infrastructure of trade developed so quickly that, when Cadamosto arrived here in 1454, one of Henry's secretaries showed him 'samples of sugar from Madeira, dragons' blood, and other products', and explained that any merchant could take part in the Infante's trading ventures, on the following conditions: if the merchant provided both ship and cargo, he must pay Henry one-quarter of all he brought back; if the Infante provided the caravel, but the merchant provided the cargo, Henry was owed half of the returns; if nothing was brought back, the Infante would bear the expenses. Such was the volume of trade that at Sagres the apprentice Columbus wrote, 'The Torrid Zone is not uninhabitable, for the Portuguese are sailing to and fro in it every day.'

Prince Henry died in 1460, a few decades short of witnessing Portugal's greatest triumphs: Bartolomeu Dias' successful navigation around the Cape of Good Hope in 1488 and Vasco da Gama's discovery of the route to India at the turn of the century. Henry also missed Columbus' unexpected visit to Sagres in 1476, when pirates sank the convoy of ships with which he was sailing between Genoa and England. Wounded, he swam the few miles to shore. Two years later, Columbus sailed from Lisbon to Madeira and within a year he married a local girl, the daughter of the governor of Porto Santo. He first submitted his plans to reach the East by sailing west to Dom João II, who set up a committee to study its feasibility and rejected it on the grounds that the calculations were wrong.

The entire library of Henry the Navigator was destroyed when Sir Francis Drake called in at Sagres and set fire to the place, as he sailed home after burning Cadiz in 1587.

Getting There

EVA buses run frequently from Lagos (1hr).

Tourist Information

The official **tourist office** is a short walk away from the popular square of Praça da República, Rua Commandant Matoso, ✆ 282 624 873. *Closed Sun, Mon*). **Turinfo** is on Praça da República, ✆ 282 620 003. Being a private company, they have a vested interest in the advice they offer; for rooms it may be better to make your own arrangements. They usually make the accommodation situation sound desperate, but a quick walk around the square and the town will unearth a plethora of clean and cheap rooms. They also hire out bikes and mopeds, and arrange fishing trips and 'jeep safaris' inland and up the west coast. If you don't have your own transport, it is worth taking their **West Coast jeep tour**, which takes in Cape St Vincent and Vale Santo and hugs the coastline between Sagres and Bordeira beach along rough tracks difficult for a normal car to negotiate. The trip lasts all day; the guide does his best to provide information about the unique vegetation of the area (though working in several languages makes his job more difficult) and a hearty lunch is included in the price, around 7,000$00.

The **post office** is on Rua do Mercado, which runs parallel with the main road into Sagres.

The **market hall** is next door, selling fruit, vegetables and fish on weekday mornings. The monthly **gypsy market** hits Sagres on the first Friday of each month, occupying a field in front of the post office.

There is a **diving school**, ✆ 282 624 736, at the harbour at the bottom of the steps to the left, with tuition, equipment hire and the usual services. The clean, very clear waters around Sagres, boasting 15 metres' visibility and water temperatures never less than 15°C, attract a variety of fish, octopus and crustaceans in the rocks; the sea bed displays its most impressive foliage in August.

Go right down to the harbour front for boat trips on the Estrela-do-Rio which goes to Cape St Vincent and beyond. If you are lucky you may spot dolphins on the way.

The Fortress (Fortaleza)

The mighty fortress which occupies the rocky plateau was completed in 1793—not that you'd know it now. Astonishingly, a few years ago the Ministry of Culture agreed to its development and, despite a national campaign for its conservation, covered it with an unsightly layer of now cracking concrete. Some old buildings (of no historical importance, so it was claimed) were demolished to make way for a **café-restaurant** and an **exhibition block**—both built in an ultra-modern boxy style that won few allies. The exhibition hall is given over to temporary shows, usually art or photography, while upstairs you can log on to one of several computers or other interactive displays which tell you about the flora, fauna and history of Sagres and the fortress. In 2000 the fortress was painted white, to the astonishment of the locals who foresaw that in a matter of weeks the salty air would set the paint peeling.

The principal ancient surviving buildings are the simple 14th-century **Chapel of Nossa Senhorita da Graça** (*open to the public*), and outside the main area, a squat white buttressed building known, confusingly, as the **Auditorium** (*closed to the public*). It used to be the supplies and ammunition store and its current appearance goes back to its last renovation, in 1793. In the courtyard the most intriguing feature is the huge, flat wind compass, discovered in 1928. Named the **Rosa dos Ventos**, it is believed to date back to Henry the Navigator, though no one knows how it was used. Despite the government's efforts to destroy Sagres' most striking piece of history, a powerful energy still survives here.

As the wind blows you through the fortress, take care not to irritate Henry's thickset, bushy-haired ghost. Azurara, his chronicler and panegyrist, reports that 'His aspect...was severe; when anger carried him away—rarely—his countenance became terrifying.' Nor should you try to outfright his ghost, whose 'heart never knew fear other than the fear of sin.'

The jagged cliffs overlook impossibly clear, green waters, offering an exhilarating walk along the coast. The landscape becomes increasingly barren, until even the cacti fade away and the ground harbours white limestone boulders tearing through the red earth, while clumps of sticky gum cistus shelter wild onions which bloom with elegant white flowers. From the fortress, walk out to the edge of **Sagres Point** and try not to get swept to America, to its left. The **lighthouse**, which boasts the most powerful lamp in Europe, is sometimes open to the public (*at the whim of the lighthouse keeper, no set times*). If you are allowed up the steps, leave him a small tip. If the cool breeze gives you goosebumps, check out the good-value sweaters sold from stalls lining the approach to the lighthouse.

Beaches

Sagres has some beautiful beaches, with stunningly rugged cliff faces, no development and regular visits from playful dolphins. The waves can be impressive, making the beaches popular with the local Portuguese as well as Australian surfers stranded in southern Europe. Most of the young locals relish the waves, but tourists must be wary of the strong current; lifeguards are present only between June and September.

The southernmost beach east of Sagres Point is **Mareta**, to the right of and below the main square. Waves break against rocks on which people bask like lizards. It is popular with young families. **Baleeira** beach is by the harbour and nice enough. **Martinhal** is a five-minute walk away and beloved of windsurfing groupies; there is a windsurfing school here. The other beaches easily accessible from the town lie to the west of Sagres Point. As you approach **Tonel** beach, you pass by some giant burnt-orange rocks of Martian aspect. The beach is sandy and the waves powerful—an ideal combination for surfing and hanging out. To the right you can clamber over the rocks to reach a lovely small beach colonized by nude Germans and privacy-seeking couples. **Beliche** beach is a beautiful secret about 4km down the road from Tonel, with imposing cliffs that have formed many caves and coves. The water here is the warmest, clearest and calmest and there is good shelter from the wind, though the long, steep stairs down may not suit the very young, very old or terminally unfit. The second beach fosters some discreet, quietly unintimidating nudity. A family of falcons nests in the cliffs.

To the north of Sagres on the west coast are a couple of virtually deserted beaches which are difficult to reach without your own transport. Take the road to Cape St Vincent and, just after it swings left to the Cape, turn right on to an untarmacked road. From here drive on until you reach a dust track on the left, leading to the small settlement of Vale Santo. Take the path left to reach **Telheiro**, where a freshwater stream trickles into a green valley above the beach. The climb down is steep, and your companions are likely to be Portuguese surfers. The path that leads a little way north arrives at **Ponta Ruiva**, a beautiful and accessible, gently curving bay; the schist above gives way to a headland of deep ochre sandstone reaching into the sea. This sandstone was used to build Silves castle (*see* p.119), or so they say. Surfing competitions have been held here and, apart from the surfers, the only people you will find here are very adventurous families.

Care must always be taken when swimming, as the currents are strong. There are no lifeguards or facilities of any description anywhere near the northern beaches.

Where to Stay

Peacefully located on the headland between the fishing harbour and Mareta beach, **Pousada do Infante**, ✆ (direct) 282 624 222, ✉ (direct) 282 624 255; central reservations ✆ 218 442 001, ✉ 218 442 085 is a large modern villa with a colonnade, chimneys and, most significantly, a fantastic view across the beach to the promontory and its fort. Bedrooms are comfortable and public areas are bright and airy, with large windows and interesting tapestries. The dining room (*expensive*) is rather formal but not too stuffy and the food is usually good, with regional specialities, including anchovy caught just below the Pousada. Whet your appetite by wandering to the edge of the cliff and spotting shoals of fish swimming free. A small swimming pool and tennis court help justify the luxury price tag.

Almost next door is the smart ★★★**ApartHotel O Navegante**, Rua Infante Dom Henrique, ✆ 282 624 354, ✆ 282 624 360 (*expensive*). Clean, with polite staff, its small-roomed gadgety apartments are furnished in inoffensive modern style. The building is arranged around a shady pear-shaped swimming pool. Like all the hotels here, it's being overrun by package-tour operators. The best thing about the ★★★**Hotel da Baleeira**, Baleeira, ✆ 282 624 212, ✆ 282 624 425, with its coffin-shaped swimming pool, is its location overlooking the harbour and its wonderful views stretching east to the cliffs of the Algarve. Rooms are spick and span, though package tours block-book. For more fabulous ocean views, head for ★★★★**Residência Dom Henrique**, Sítio da Mareta, ✆ 282 620 003 (*moderate*), on a cliff above the Mareta beach. Some of its clean, simple guest rooms overlook the beach, and you can hear the surf from the conservatory. The little restaurant serves grilled squid. The newish ★★★**Residencial Sagres**, Beco da Olaria, Baleeira, ✆ 282 624 612 (*moderate*), is located in the centre of Sagres and only has views over scrubland. Still, it's a clean and friendly place with a balcony to each room.

Sagres' **campsite** is about a kilometre inland from the village, ✆ 282 624 351.

There are very cheap rooms to let in people's houses—ask Klaus at Rosa dos Ventos (*see* 'The Fortress' *above*) about **Casa Marreiros**, which has clean, airy rooms and a large communal kitchen.

Eating Out

On the way to the Pousada do Infante stands Sagres' best restaurant, **Vila Velha**, ✆ 282 624 788 (*expensive*). Dutch Lia painstakingly prepares the traditionally inspired dishes served in huge portions in the rustic dining room. Her affable Portuguese husband supervises the smooth service and brings the fresh fish of the day to your table for inspection. The special house menu for two people is good value, with six courses costing 5,000$00 per person. *Bacalhau à casa* is cooked with mashed potato, cream, bacon and shrimps. The three vegetarian dishes are very good, as is the house wine. *Evenings only; closed Mon.*

Opposite the turning for Vila Velha on Rua da Baleeira is **Carlos**, ✆ 282 624 228 (*expensive*), a large, sugary-pink and typically Portuguese affair serving reliably good food to visitors and enthusiastic locals alike. The ubiquitous fish soup is superior and the grilled *cherne* (grouper) is very good and very large. If it's on the menu, go for the marvellous *lulas recheadas*, squid stuffed with rice, herbs and pork meat. The house wine is worth a slosh.

Fortaleza do Beliche, ✆ 282 624 124 (*expensive*) is in a little fort about a third of the way along the road from Sagres to Cape St Vincent. Run by Enatur, the *pousada* people, it's decorated in 'Navigator style', with maps and fake candelabra. The waiters are smartly dressed and courteous; the food is okay, though the menu is limited, unadventurous and overpriced. You can also stay here (*expensive*) but beware the high turnover. If you do decide to tarry, choose Room 4 with a great sea view.

Bossa Nova, Rua Citie Matoso, ✆ 282 624 566 (*moderate*) is a large, airy restaurant with a covered terrace where German hippies happily rub shoulders with children dressed in Marks & Spencer's best. The food is pricey given that it's mainly pasta and thick-crusted pizzas—you pay for the atmosphere—but the vegetarian options are cheaper. Avoid the tropical curry.

Practise your Portuguese ready for the **Flying Bar Marisqueria**, Sitio do Botelha, ✆ 282 624 762 (*cheap*) is near Topas disco, and devoid of tourists. The restaurant is small and plain; you can sit in the bar or outside in the colourful garden. Choose your shellfish from the tank; eat octopus in tomato sauce, three sorts of crabs, clams and cockles cooked with garlic and herbs, or *arroz do mariscos* (seafood rice), which may take some time to prepare (for a minimum of two people). A treat every time. **Rosa dos Ventos** on the main square, ✆ 282 624 480 (*cheap*) is a bar serving a full range of good-value snacks and meals; here, they understand salads in a way most Portuguese don't. Children are fascinated by Klaus, the ponytailed owner. They follow him around, like rats after the Pied Piper, and demand rides on his motorbike. In the evenings a happy mix of international (mainly German) travellers and locals get drunk and fall out (and often over) at 2am to stagger off to **Topas** disco, which is great fun. To get there, take the main road to Lagos and take a left signposted for *Topas* and *Flying Bar*. Follow the road to the end for about 10 minutes to Topas.

Around Sagres

Vale Santo

On the way to Cape St Vincent, after the sharp bend to the left, take the dirt track right into the wilderness. Vale Santo is about 6km northwest of Sagres and may have been settled before people gravitated to the fishing village at Baleeira; there is a well-defined 15th-century road to the Cape and evidence of water use. The handful of long ramshackle white farmhouses squat amidst wide, amber plains of hayfields and low, hardy *camarinha* and rosemary bushes. It's very eerie and deserted but there are signs of life: chickens peck the rusty soil, cattle stand penned in by rickety wooden fences, and the round outdoor ovens are blackened by baking. The air hangs heavy; the dogs don't bark; there isn't a tree in sight. The only ingredient missing is Clint Eastwood, squinting.

Cape St Vincent

The invigorating headland on the brink of Europe stands on raw, limestone cliffs, rising 60m out of the sea, 6km west of Sagres. There is no settlement to speak of, but the land mass announces itself with one of the most powerful lighthouses in Europe, inhabited by seven families, and a ruined monastery.

The landscape is hardy, dominated by gum cistus, rosemary and juniper bushes, but in springtime colourful wild flowers peek through cracks in the rock. On the way from Sagres to the Cape, you'll see the fragile white cistus roses, poppies bearing tissue-thin scarlet blooms, and small purple pimpernels twisting through rock crevices. In the summer, white sea daffodils appear while red and bright pink bougainvillaea climb the walls alongside the deep purple flowers of the clematis. There are at least three plant species named after the Cape and indigenous to this area alone: *Biscutella vincentina*, *Scilla vincentina* and *Centaurea vincentina*.

Many birds of prey stop here on their autumn migration path for a feed and a rest. The easiest to spot are the gannets, casting large shadows as they circle and plunge down to pluck their meal from the waves. Starlings and blue rock thrushes are common, and cooing rock doves can occasionally be seen above the lines of tourists assembled, as if for a school photo, at sunset.

The Romans called this the *Promontorium Sacrum*; at sundown the sun appeared a hundred times larger than elsewhere, and hissed as if it were being quenched. (A freak of atmospherics continues to magnify some of the sunsets, and occasionally the sun appears to yield a green flash as it vanishes.) In later times, when the body of St Vincent arrived from Valença in a boat guided by ravens, the promontory became a Christian shrine and for centuries boats dipped their sails as they passed. The shrine has gone, but the ravens remain (although some of them are believed to have accompanied St Vincent's body on its removal to Lisbon in 1173). A later resident was rather more lively: Henry the Navigator lived and died on the site where the lighthouse stands, commuting to his school of navigation at Sagres. In 1693 these seas bore a naval battle between the French and the combined British and Dutch fleets, and it was here that the British fleet under Jervis and Nelson battled the Spanish in 1797. Sustained by the royal gift they had received when docking in the Tagus (400 bullocks, 400 sheep, chocolate, China tea and 56 pipes of wine) the British were victorious, and Jervis became Count St Vincent. In 1833 Sir Charles Napier, on behalf of Portugal's Maria II, defeated her uncle Miguel's squadron despite having half the number of guns. The waters at the Cape seem to carry memories of these battles, especially when moaning and sighing through the **blowhole** on the headland.

There is no public transport between Cape St Vincent and Sagres.

Vila do Bispo and Around

Ten kilometres north of Sagres, on a junction of the west and south coast roads, lies a serene little town with a sunny central square and a lovely white church. Behind the fine Manueline doorway the interior blazes with giltwork, painting and 18th-century blue *azulejos*. Otherwise there's nothing much here except the district town hall and the nearest police station to Sagres. A walled cemetery stands in burnished, flat fields across the highway and is visible from the square. It is a scene direct from a western—you could be in New Mexico. There is a *pensão* opposite the church: **Pensão Mira-Sagres** (*cheap*), which is perfectly adequate, despite the strangely musty smell. Alternatively you could ask for rooms at **No.18 Praça da República** (*very cheap*), next to the bank, or at the restaurant on the same side of the square.

The best place to eat is the plain and large **Café Correia** (*moderate*), next to the post office, opposite the church. Their *caldeirada* (fish stew) is very good. *Closed Sat.*

Several kilometres west of Vila do Bispo rises the **Torre de Aspa**, a plateau 156m high, thick with tall clumps of cistus which infuse the air with their heavy, sweet aroma. On a clear day, the views stretch from the west to the south coast. By the little tower itself sits a mysterious, smiling Portuguese granny, knitting under an umbrella.

Around this area are a collection of **megaliths**, dating from the Neolithic Age and thought to relate to a fertility cult since they are sited near the finest agricultural land. The easiest one to reach is the *Pedra Escorregadia* (slippery stone), a lump of limestone resembling Obelix's menhir. From Vila do Bispo, take the potholed old road alongside the highway to Sagres and turn left when it goes under the highway. After the tunnel turn right and the stone is immediately on your left. The surrounding spirits have been frightened away by the roar of traffic.

Beaches

For two of the most stunning beaches in the Algarve, look no further than the **Praias do Castelejo** and **Cordoama**, 5km west of town. The beaches stretch for miles, and large waves throw a constant film of spray on to the stark slate cliffs. There's plenty of space to escape from other bathers or the few hardy hippies who camp here (although officially camping is discouraged and campers may be moved on). Each beach has a busy restaurant serving good, cheap food. Access is difficult without a car, as there are no buses and the walk over dusty hills can be rather gruelling.

North of Cordoama, **Praia da Barriga** is a small and quiet beach, reached by a dust track winding through wooded hills which escaped a fire that recently singed the surrounding forest. The cliffs are low, forming curious shapes. There are no facilities or lifeguards.

At **Praias do Mirouço, Murração** and **Amado**, jade waters lap black cliffs stacked high into the sky while lower-strata rock extends out into the sea. All of these beaches are deserted as they are a good 6 to 9km north of Castelejo and hard to reach, especially the smaller cove of Murração, which involves a very steep climb. Again, there are no facilities or lifeguards here; these beaches are not suitable for young children. About a kilometre inland of Mirouço, a hundred yards left of the main road, a small **pine forest** rises unexpectedly from the low vegetation and freshens the air with its scent. It's a good place to picnic.

It is worth following the cliffs for the 3km walk to Praia da Bordeira: the coastline landscape is quite diverse, with clumps of pine giving way to gangs of eucalyptus and acacia trees on starkly dry ground, trodden by ponderous cattle escorted by a flock of sprightly white egrets. You eventually emerge onto cistus- and scrub-covered heath, alive with the chirruping of insects. **Arrifes do Pontal**, midway between Amado and Bordeira beaches, is a minuscule fishing community with little reference to the 21st century. A handful of bamboo and marram grass huts for storing equipment are scattered precariously down the cliffs. There is no beach so the small fishing boats are pulled out by a winch to rest on a wooden platform when the sea is restless.

Praia da Bordeira is unusual for this coast in being backed by shifting dunes, rather than cliffs, which fall away on either side of the curving bay. Behind the beach a stream becomes an estuary, which frequently metamorphoses into a lagoon nurturing young fish, and is the feeding ground for many birds such as the white stork. The beach has easy access and is calm and quiet: ideal for children. There are no facilities.

Carrapateira

This lies small village 23km north of Sagres and is favoured by a few very laid-back German travellers. There are some private rooms for rent in people's houses: ask at the café in the square. The valley to the east of Carrapateira is hazily beautiful: green fields bloom with an abundance of wild flowers and goatherds slumber in the shade of cork trees while the creatures roam. For a lovely walk to Bordeira beach, follow the stream jewelled with water-lilies and diving kingfishers.

Arrifana

This small, lacklustre settlement sits above the beach, 49km north of Sagres and 8km west of Aljezur. There is a handful of restaurants, all remarkably similar; **Brisamar** has the best views. At the end of the village the ruins of the *fortaleza* offer magnificent views.

There is a **snack bar** (*cheap*) overlooking the beach itself at the bottom of the winding road. Eat a generous portion of prawns on the terrace while admiring the tough beauty of the beach. The rounded hills of the coastline, green with glistening cistus, drop in sheer slate-grey cliffs to a smooth bay backed by shingle and dotted with small stacks, against which breaking waves foam. A weird cone-shaped rock, the *Pedra da Agulha* (Needle Stone), protrudes from the sea.

Ask for rooms at the **Restaurante Fortaleza**.

Aljezur

A very small town 50km north of Sagres, Aljezur straddles a broad river valley. The older part hugs the hillside, while newer houses bake quietly on the other side of the valley through which only a small stream trickles. The ruin of an old Moorish castle watches over all. The area was originally settled by the Moors in the 10th century and was recaptured by the Portuguese in 1246. The conqueror was Dom Paio Peres Correia, a master of the Knights of Santiago, one of the best-known chivalric orders in southern Portugal. A dashing and notable figure in the Algarvian reconquest, he captured the castle without a fight when a Muslim maiden opened the gates to admit his troops one clear night. The defending soldiers were cooling off on the beach.

Getting There and Around

EVA **buses** run semi-frequently from Lagos (¾hr). There are two buses a day to Arrifana and Monte Clérigo on Mondays and Thursdays only.

The sleepy **tourist office** is at Largo do Mercado, ✆ 282 998 229. They can help with private rooms and villas. The **post office** and **banks** are on Rua 25 de Abril, the main road in from Lagos. The **market hall** is behind the tourist office and sells fresh fish, fruit and vegetables every weekday morning. The **gypsy market** descends on Aljezur on the third Monday of every month.

Perhaps because it is sandwiched between the foothills of Monchique, the Espinhaço de Cão range and the Atlantic, Aljezur has a forgotten feeling about it, especially palpable at the castle on a hot day. If you are suffering from a headache, make a trip over the river and visit the 18th-century church that houses the skulls of the last two Moors killed in Aljezur: lay your hands on them to be instantly relieved.

The views from the **castle** are splendid: from the top you can see the two parts of the town, divided by a vivid green patchwork of cultivated land. In the distance, the hazy purple hills of Monchique seem to occupy another age, and on the other side soft green hills are dotted with cattle and provide peeks at the sea. Late afternoon is the quietest time to visit.

Beaches

Praia do Monte Clérigo is a nice family beach which you can drive right up to, 5km northwest of Aljezur. It is overlooked by holiday homes and small-scale developments; there are a couple of beachfront restaurants and bars.

For **Praia da Amoreira**, which is about 7km northwest of Aljezur, turn left off the main road by the yellow sports hall rather than at the next turning, which takes a longer route over a rough dirt track. A lovely long beach near a stream, Amoreira is flanked on the left by gentle grass-topped cliffs and backed by scrub-heavy dunes. The crouching slate cliffs to the right are marvellous to explore, especially when the tide is low. This is a fun beach for children as there are many small caves and shallow pools in the rocks. A restaurant serves standard fare at the usual prices. It can be busy, but only by west-coast standards.

There are no hotels in Aljezur. The nearest is about 5km southwest of the town in Vale da Telha tourist village, a large-scale development with a **campsite**, villas and a hotel. The modern ★★**Hotel Vale da Telha**, ✆ 282 998 180 (*moderate–inexpensive*) looks like a row of matchboxes. Long, dark corridors lead to decent-sized bedrooms with small bathrooms and tiny balconies, and it's all very clean. The restaurant and pool are round the back.

There is a **campsite** at Serrão, 3km north of Aljezur on the way to Amoreira beach, ✆ 282 998 612.

Restaurante Ruth on Rua 25 de Abril, ℭ 282 998 534 (*moderate*) draws locals from miles around to sample its fresh seafood. The snow-haired owner is very friendly and the menu small. Go for the fresh fish of the day, or *perceves* (barnacles) if you can. The *ementa turística* is particularly good value.

Odeceixe

The road winds 71km from Sagres, descending through eucalyptus woods to offer glimpses of Odeceixe snugly settled in the crook of the surrounding hills. The river that runs alongside marks the boundary with the next province, the Alentejo. The green and well-cultivated land infuses the village with a gentle peacefulness that soothes the soul. In the tiny central square old men sit under the tree to talk, unconcerned by the rainbow-attired travellers slouching past. The **shop** opposite the post office has a bit more to offer than the usual hippy favourites of leather bracelets and tie-dyed T-shirts.

Beaches

Praia de Odeceixe lies a beautiful 4km walk west of the village and is reached by a good road that runs alongside the river and farmland. There is a tiny settlement at the beach if you want to stay here; the restaurant across the road offers cheap rooms. The river cuts through the beach to empty itself into the sea; the water's warmer for swimming at this point. Black cliffs rise out of sand blackened by powdered slate. Rose quartz runs through the rocks like the luminous trail of a celestial snail. Young German travellers camp on the far side of the river.

Semi-frequent **buses** take an hour and a half from Lagos.

 The tourist office at Aljezur (*see* p.149) can supply you with a list of approved accommodation, though you needn't worry about finding rooms—touts will approach you with offers. **Pensão Luar**, Rua da Vàrzea, ℭ 282 974 194 (*cheap*) is at the bottom of the village on the road to the beach. It's clean, with lovely views over farmland and hills from the front-facing rooms.

There is no shortage of good food in Odeceixe. **Snack-Bar Stop** (*cheap*) in the square combines this with a good place to sit and watch the action: in season this is likely to be provided by the makeshift German hippy commune (though action isn't a strong point); out of season, by the locals chasing a diseased dog.

Taberna da Gabão, Rua da Gabão (*moderate–cheap*), has a mainly Portuguese clientele clamouring to fill its large, barn-like interior, where the waiter grins at solitary diners. Good food comes in large portions: try *feijoada com polvo*, a huge helping of beans cooked with octopus, sausage and parsley, served with rice. Prices rise slightly in high season.

Trips into the Alentejo

The Algarve is bordered by the Alentejo, Portugal's largest province, covering almost a third of the country. It's easy to hop across for a day or three, and the region offers rich rewards to travellers in search of the heart of Portugal.

The appeal of the Alentejo lies in its austere beauty: its strong, pure colours and vast, arid spaces. The climate is fiery—in summer temperatures can rise to 34°C in Évora, and a stultifying 40°C in Beja. The red earth is planted with wheat fields which sprout green in spring and mellow into a summertime beaten gold beneath the peculiarly clear blue sky. Stripped cork-oaks line the roads, showing a deep ochre where the harvested bark is blackening again. Flat-topped ilex oaks dot the countryside, pruned into a canopy to shade livestock and produce acorns for the animals to eat; the smaller branches make some of the world's finest charcoal. Brilliant, whitewashed settlements punctuate the plains, offering a profile of oblong chimneys wide enough to hoist and smoke a pig in. The horizon is interrupted by white grain silos like giant test-tube racks, for this is the granary of Portugal—although yields are a quarter of the EU average. Most of the country's cattle and sheep graze here too, but the Alentejo supports just 12 per cent of the country's population.

The lovely city of **Évora** unites the rich history and romance of the Alentejo; its appeal is such that a single visit is seldom enough, and most travellers who make the journey want to return there. Across near the Spanish border is **Monsaraz**, a time-warp hilltop village slap bang in the centre of an area rich in the evidence of megalithic culture. Due south of Évora stands **Beja**, the capital of the Lower Alentejo and a good stopover point en route to **Serpa**, brilliantly whitewashed and under-visited, and **Mértola**, which clusters around a castle overlooking the stunningly beautiful banks of the lazy River Guadiana. The castle walls have recently been renovated, leaving nesting spaces for the rare lesser kestrel.

Day or weekend trips into the Alentejo add an extra dimension to a holiday in the Algarve; detailed here are the most remarkable and convenient places to visit. The lovely city of Évora is rich in history and memorable; its walled streets have been declared part of the World Patrimony by UNESCO. The environs of Évora are sprinkled with the remains of megalithic culture and also include Monsaraz, a beguiling little hilltop village. Due south of Évora stands Beja, a good stopover point en route to brilliantly whitewashed, undervisited Serpa. From Serpa it's a short hop to Mertola, taking in the Pulo do Lobo waterfall, overlooking the lovely banks of the gentle River Guadiana. The Algarve is a mere slither south, so Serpa or Mertola could be reached on a day trip from Tavira or the eastern Algarve.

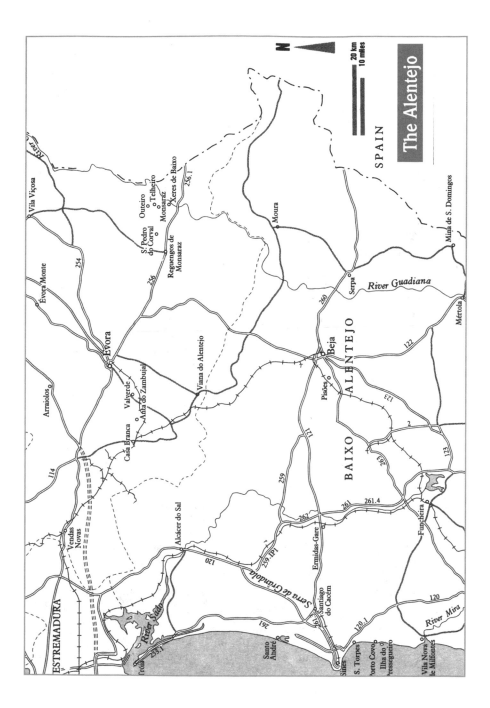

The Alentejo

Cork and Olives

The plains of wheat around Évora and Beja yield to fields peppercorned with cork-oak or olive trees, both short, small-leafed and gnarled. Portugal is the world's largest producer of cork. The bark, up to 10cm thick, is cut from the trees every nine years: the trunk and branches are ringed in 2–3m sections with a light axe, and then cut straight down one side. If the weather is too dry, the cork shatters into many pieces; if the weather is too wet and cold, the tree dies of shock. The flayed trunks are a shrieking salmon pink, which blackens with time. Olive trees are shaken until they yield their crop as well as their dignity; mechanized shakers are now edging their way in, requiring a new strain of less tenacious trees.

What to Eat and Drink

The Alentejo is a splendid place for pork; the pigs are herded under oaks whose acorns give the meat a wonderful flavour. Traitionally, home-made *chouriça* sausages (chopped pork with garlic and sweet-pepper paste), *paios* (loin of pork) and *morcela* (blood sausage) are smoked over oak wood, whereas *presunto* (salted ham) is cured in sea salt for around a month. Two popular local dishes use cubed, marinated loin of pork: for *Porco à Alentejana* it is stewed with clams; for *Migas à Alentejana* it is fried with pork fat and served on top of or alongside a golden slice of bread mixed with water, beaten and fried.

Lamb, too, can be superb. Try *borrego assado* (pot roast, usually with a delicious sauce) or *ensopado de borrego*, a 'soup' dish served in a tureen with stale bread in the base covered with tasty broth. The meat is eaten last. Olive oil and garlic are widespread, and bread is predominant, appearing soaked in *açorda* soup with poached eggs, coriander, garlic and sometimes fish, pork or cockles.

Serpa produces wonderful curd cheese made from ewe's milk, usually served with salt and pepper or with honey. there ar other local cheeses, but be warned that in maturity they can be overpoweringly strong. Strict vegetarians will be glad to note that the coagulating agnt is an infusion made from the dried flower of the cardoon thistle, not rennet. Check for '*cardo*' in the list of ingredients.

The Alentejo produces some of the world's finest honey. When the bees have been communing with lavender their honey is labelled '*rosmaninho*'. Desserts tend to be very sweet, mainly composed of sugar, cinnamon and egg yolks, an echo of monastic life in the days when there was a surfeit of yolks because the whites were used to purify wine.

The wines of the Alentejo are vastly superior to those of the Algarve. Portugal's most recently Demarcated Region, in the east of the Alentejo, incorporates the towns of Reguengos de Monsaraz, Redondo, Borba and Vidigueira, producing full-bodied, mouth-filling red wines, matured in cement *depósitos* (except for J.M. da Fonseca's Tinto Velho, from Reguengos). The internationally acclaimed, prizewinning reds approach a powerful 13.5°, while the whites, which are less successful, reach 12.5°.

History

The history of the Alentejo has been shaped by landholding and irrigation. The soil is thin and dry, transport costs are high, and there are few mountains or rivers: hence the Romans introduced huge farms known as *latifúndios* some time between 202 BC and 139 BC. They built 18 dams in the south of Portugal, irrigating fields of wheat planted among olive trees, where pigs grazed when the land lay fallow. Wine production was concentrated on the river valleys and along the main road from Lisbon to Beja via Évora.

The Moors made few changes to the pattern of landholding—though pig breeding declined, given the Koranic injunction. Merchants and representatives of the caliph invested their wealth in land, so in the Alentejo, towns grew into concentrations of absentee landlords. When the Alentejo was conquered from the Moors, vast tracts of land were doled out to the military orders, though the king retained all important cities and towns. Urban Moslems were compelled to reside outside the town walls, and rural Moslems were milked by heavy taxes—between a third and a half of Moslem town dwellers fled to southern Spain. Dom Sancho I (1185–1211) tried to offset this depopulation by encouraging emigration from Flanders.

From the 14th century, the maritime trade offered rich rewards to speculators, and Alentejan agriculture suffered from lack of investment. The seaports and the cities enthralled villeins, who continued to leave the land. Portugal began importing wheat in the early 16th century. It was not until chemical fertilizers were introduced in 1884 that heathland was brought under new cultivation. Salazar was keen to increase wheat production, but his schemes of 1929 and 1958 met with little success.

The landless rural workers of the Alentejo were the sinews of civilian support for the Revolution of 1974. In July 1975, a law called for the expropriation of properties with more than the equivalent of 500 ha of dry land or 50 ha of irrigated land. (Two years later, the limit was raised by 40 per cent.) In October 1975 *latifúndias* around Beja were occupied by workers. Roughly 900 cooperatives were established—and are currently being dismantled, or falling apart due to lack of initiative and lack of governmental backup. Although most local government is still Communist, the right wing holds the purse strings in Lisbon, and is reinstating the landowners.

Getting There and Around

Call © 800 296 296 and then press 2 for helpful travel information in English, Mon–Sat 9am–midnight, Sun 9am–8pm.

By bus: Buses from Faro take two hours to reach Beja, which serves as the lovcal hub. From there, buses wind their way to both **Mértola** (¾hr; get off at the São Domingo mines) and **Serpa** (½hr)—there are no direct connections between the two.

By train: There is one train a day up from the Algarve, from Vila Real de Santo António to **Beja**. From the other end of the Algarve, a train departs from Lagos. Most Algarvian towns and resorts are taken in on the way. From both departure points, change at Tunes. Frequent trains connect Beja to Évora.

By car: The best way to explore the area is by car; it's worth hiring one for a few days as public transport is slow and irregular (but do check carefully that you may take the car out of the Algarve—some smaller companies do not have assistance facilities further afield). Most of the major roads are good and many have three lanes. In the east, roads are narrower, though there's very little traffic. If you do get stuck behind a cork-bark-laden truck, be patient! From Faro it is an easy 3hr drive to Évora, and from Beja to Évora takes about an hour.

Évora

Some 77km north of Beja and just over 250km north of Faro, Évora is one of the joys of Portugal. Unspoilt and memorable, it occupies the gentle slopes of a wide hill on the Alentejo plain, surrounded by olive groves, wheat fields and vineyards. Its 55,000 souls rank it as one of the country's largest cities, but just 13,500 live within the encircling walls, so it feels more like a small town. It is this inner town that was declared part of the World Patrimony by UNESCO in 1986. Walking its clean, cobbled streets, you come across arches and arcades, whitewashed *palácios* and Renaissance fountains, which together give Évora a wholeness in spite of the range of its monuments.

Houses stretch under the arches of the aqueduct, and it is around here that life is played out. Artisans tap out their trades, making pine coat-hangers or tables; old ladies tend a couple of cratefuls of fruit or vegetables. In winter, children keep themselves warm with fleecy sheepskin jerkins, while old men prefer faded, habit-like capes.

History

Évora's history is as fertile as the title Pliny the Elder gave it—Ebora Cerealis. It was a political centre of Roman Iberia, and its townspeople have been able to claim Roman lineage since *c.* 61 BC, when Julius Caesar sent a group of his countrymen to mingle with the natives. Évora may have been the headquarters of Quintus Sertorius, who was sent to govern Hispania and bit the hand of his imperial master when he attempted to make the province independent, around 80 BC. (Sertorius had a pet albino fawn, which he swathed with gold necklaces and earrings, and taught to nuzzle his ear as if it were whispering to him. He ordered that good news should be delivered to him secretly, so he could pretend that the doe had brought it to him from the goddess Diana.)

The Visigoths came, and then the Moors, who stayed from 711 to 1165. In the 12th century, Idrisi, the Arab geographer, described Évora as a large walled town with a great mosque and a castle, surrounded by fertile countryside rich in wheat, fruit and vegetables. The Moors were expelled by Gerald the Fearless, an ingenious outlaw who drove lances into the outer wall of the city to form a staircase, which he mounted by night. Dom Afonso Henriques made Gerald castellan of the town, and he is depicted on the town's blazon.

In 1166 Dom Afonso Henriques issued Évora with its first charter, in Latin, stating that every man who had a house, a yoke of oxen, 40 sheep, an ass and two beds was obliged to keep a horse and turn it out for military service. When there was a brawl among villagers, wounds were to be taxed, and those who caused them fined according to a fixed penalty.

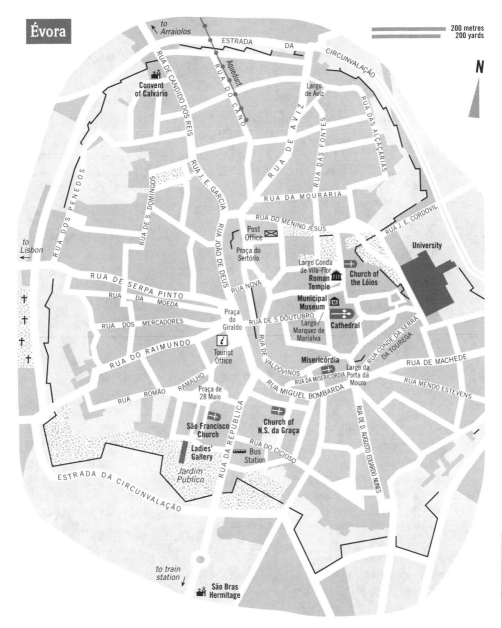

to
Arraiolos

ESTRADA   DA

Aqueduct

RUA DO CANO

RUA DE CANDIDO DOS REIS

Convent
of Calvário

RUA DE AVIZ

Largo
de Aviz

CIRCUNVALAÇÃO

RUA DAS ALCAÇARIAS

N

200 metres
200 yards

RUA DOS PENEDOS

RUA DE S. DOMINGOS

RUA J. E. GARCIA

RUA DAS FONTES

RUA DA MOURARIA

RUA DO MENINO JESUS

RUA J. E. CORDOVIL

to
Lisbon

RUA JOÃO DE DEUS

Post
Office

Praça do
Sertório

Largo Conde
de Vila-Flor

RUA NOVA

Roman
Temple

Church of
the Lóios

University

RUA DE SERPA PINTO

RUA   DA   MOEDA

RUA DOS MERCADORES

Praça
do
Giraldo

RUA DE 5 DOUTUBRO

Municipal
Museum

Largo/
Marquez de
Marialva

Cathedral

RUA CONDE DA SERRA DA TOUREGA

RUA DO RAIMUNDO

Tourist
Office

RUA DE VALDEVINOS

Misericórdia

Largo da
Porta da
Mouro

RUA DE MACHEDE

RUA DA MISERICORDIA

RUA MENDO ESTEVENS

RUA   ROMÃO

RAMALHO

Praça de
28 Maio

RUA MIGUEL BOMBARDA

São Francisco
Church

Church of
N.S. da Graça

RUA DE D. AUGUSTO EDUARDO NUNES

Ladies'
Gallery

RUA DA REPUBLICA

RUA DO CICIOSO

Bus
Station

ESTRADA   DA   CIRCUNVALAÇÃO

Jardim
Publica

to train
station

São Bras
Hermitage

The Renaissance and After

Évora flourished from the 14th century to the 16th century, enjoying the regal attentions of the locally based House of Avis. The *Cortes* (parliament) was summoned here, and great artists duly followed. Together they produced a wealth of noble palaces and artworks, and in 1559 Cardinal Henrique founded a university. In 1490, Évora hosted the splendid celebrations for the marriage of Afonso, son of Dom João II, to Infanta Isabel of Castile. For this, a wooden hall 44m high and 180m long was built in the garden of the Church of São Francisco, and hung with striped Moroccan cloths. Dancers and musicians were recruited from the Moorish quarters of neighbouring towns, and the whole neighbourhood was scoured for spare beds, each of which was marked, so its owner could identify it, before being carried to Évora. But an outbreak of the plague just before the jamboree obliged guests to leave the town for 15 days until the September moon.

Decline set in with the Spanish seizure of the throne in 1580, following the death of Dom Henrique, last ruler of the House of Avis. The limelight left Évora's limewash as future monarchs kept nearer to Lisbon, and its Jesuit university was duly closed by Pombal in 1759. After the 1974 Revolution the town became the centre for agrarian reform, thus circling back to Pliny's denomination.

Tourist Information

The **tourist office**, 73–4 Praça do Giraldo, © 266 702 671 (*open April–Sept Mon–Fri 9–7, Sat–Sun 9–12.30 and 2.30–5.30; Oct–March 9–12.30 and 2–5.30*), is a short walk uphill from the **bus station** (© 266 769 419 for Express buses).

The **train station**, © 266 702 125, is less than 1km southeast of town: walk straight ahead and up the Rua da República to get to the Praça do Giraldo.

The **post office** is in the Rua de Olivença (*open weekdays 9–7, Sat 9–1*), uphill from the Praça do Sertório.

The best way to get around Évora is on foot: the points of interest are not far apart, there are no steep hills, and the one-way traffic system is maddening.

The Roman Temple and Around

Portugal's best-preserved Roman monument stands at the highest point in Évora. The Roman Temple dates from the late 2nd or early 3rd century AD, its granite Corinthian columns topped with local marble. Although it is popularly known

as the temple of Diana, scholars now think the sanctuary may have been dedicated to the god Jupiter. Perhaps his indignation at the slight resulted in the building's conversion into the municipal slaughterhouse, until 1870. In the interests of conservation, visitors are requested not to climb on the temple. The neighbouring **sculpture garden** is the best place to watch the sunset.

The Church of the Lóios

Open daily 10–12.30 and 2–6; adm; joint ticket available with the Palace of the Dukes of Cadaval museum; © 266 704 714.

The church of the Lóios (St John the Evangelist), to one side of the Roman Temple, features the country's most captivating employment of *azulejos*—it would be a great pity to leave Évora without seeing this stunning church. Built on the site of the Moorish castle, the monastic church was founded by Rodrigo Afonso de Melo, Count of Olivença, in 1485, for the Canons Secular of St John the Evangelist, who were nicknamed 'Lóios'. The entrance is through a Flamboyant Gothic portal, while the single nave serves as the pantheon of the de Melo family, whose Gothic and Renaissance tombs include that of Dom Francisco, in the transept, attributed to Chanterène. He tutored the sons of Dom João III.

But one's attention is captured by the very beautiful *azulejos* which subtly complement the internal architecture, with *trompe l'œil* tiles mirroring high windows. The main panels show scenes from the life of St Lorenzo Giustiniani, patriarch of Venice. Created in 1711, they are the master work of António de Oliveira Bernardes, who presided over the golden era of Portuguese tile production.

From Aristocrats to Students

Downhill in the same road, the two tall towers and courtyard of the **Palace of the Dukes of Cadaval** (*open 10–12.30 and 2–6; adm*) incorporate a small museum. A finely painted *Virgem do Leite* (the Virgin of the Milk), from the workshop of Frei Carlos, is stared at by portraits of grim-looking ecclesiastics, whose faces are all the same. There are also two Flemish bronzes and an equestrian portrait of the third duke by Quillard, a pupil of the artist Watteau, *c.* 1730. One room is devoted to old parchment books and manuscripts.

In the street behind the Lóios and the palace, the **university** is rather disappointing. Arranged around a two-storeyed classical cloister, it was founded in 1559 by Cardinal Henrique, the future regent, to satisfy the Jesuits' wish for a university they could control, as Coimbra had successfully resisted their influence. But the new foundation never achieved its rival's size or breadth of studies. The corridors are lined with Baroque *azulejos* and all the doors are conveniently numbered, which saves the three thousand students from getting lost.

The Municipal Museum

Open Wed–Sun 9–12.30 and 2–5.30, Tues 2.30–5; closed Mon, Tues morning and hols; adm.

Opposite the Roman Temple, the Archbishop's Palace, reconstructed in the late 17th century, now houses Évora's museum, with important collections including sculpture and 15th–16th-century Flemish and Portuguese paintings. One of the earliest sculptures is the Roman fragment of a vestal, clad in a diaphanous marble skirt. Two tombs are outstanding: one can almost feel the softness of the pillows supporting Fernando Cogominho's effigy, and the warmth of the dog at his feet; the simple, classical cenotaph of Bishop Dom Afonso de Portugal is one of Nicolas Chanterène's most elegant works. The Frenchman was married in Évora, and here he established a school of sculpture through which he was able to introduce the sculptural aspects of the Italian Renaissance to Portugal. The museum's modern sculpture includes a disturbing representation of three baby boys fighting, made by Teixeira Lopes in 1910 from a single block of marble. Aggression finds expression rather than representation in João Cutileiro's disembodied women.

Upstairs, note the delicate triptych of the Passion enamelled on copper in Limoges in 1539. Primitive paintings by 16th-century Flemish and Portuguese artists working in Portugal are juxtaposed. Both groups relish colour, but on the whole the Flemish Frei Carlos and Francisco Henriques have a greater depth of feeling and grasp of perspective than Gregório Lopes, Garcia Fernandes or the Master of Sardoal.

The museum's star attractions are the 13 panels of the *Life of the Virgin* from the cathedral. The panels are by anonymous members of the Bruges School, working under one master, *c.* 1500. They were created in Portugal—there is a typically Portuguese plate in the *Nascimento da Virgem* (the Birth of the Virgin)—with the probable exception of the one larger panel, though Italian Renaissance buildings are used in the background. Saints Ana and Joaquim, the parents of the Virgin, are pictured with a cartoon-like castle, and she is pregnant at her marriage (*casamento*).

The Cathedral

Open July–Sept daily 9–6; Oct–June daily 9–12.30 and 2–5.

Behind the museum, the **cathedral** seems half-fortress, half-church. Its irregular façade is closest akin to that of the Sé Velha in Coimbra, a good example of the transition from the Romanesque to Gothic styles. According to the chronicler André de Resende, it was begun by the second bishop in 1186, on the site of a mosque, 20 years after the Moors were initially expelled from Évora. Perhaps it served as a mosque again when the Moors retook the town (1192–1211). Construction probably continued through the 13th century.

The bearded gentlemen flanking the portal are the Apostles, standing on ledges of human figures and fantastical animals. These fine medieval Portuguese sculptures were probably commissioned between 1322 and 1340. They all look similar, except St Peter and St Paul, who are the progeny of Telo Garcia of Lisbon.

The interior is very brown; the obtrusive white mortar binding the stonework gives it an oddly Victorian feel. The chandeliers hang on giant rosaries. Because they were considered insufficiently dignified for an archiepiscopal see, Ludwig, the Italian-trained architect of the Convent of Mafra, rebuilt the chancel and high altar in 1718, including a lovely sculpture of the crucified Christ. Ludwig is buried here.

The Cloister and Sacred Art Museum

Tickets down to the cloister and up to the Sacred Art Museum are sold just inside the entrance portal (*open the same hours as the cathedral; adm*). The stunning Gothic cloister of *c.* 1323 is pierced by open circles with almost Moorish designs. Sculptures of the Evangelists stand at the corners of the quadrangle, but the most moving sculpture panels the tomb of the 14th-century Bishop Pedro, whose long head is supported by angels. A terrace above the cathedral's west entrance leads to the museum. Filled with a number of reliquaries and embroidered vestments, it features a late 13th-century French Madonna whose seated ivory body parts to reveal scenes from her life. Introspection indeed. Near her is a 16th-century weathervane, looking more like a witch than an angel.

Fifty-six steps spiral to the roof terrace, which has wonderful views.

Central Évora

Walking down the steps by the cathedral, and continuing in the same direction, the **Largo da Porta da Moura** is a pleasant place to come upon. It is arranged around a Renaissance orb-fountain whose walls are rippled, presumably by centuries of buttocks. Behind them the Cordovil House sports a hybrid Manueline-Mudéjar porch. The beautiful modern building at the upper end of the square comprises the Courts of Justice.

The Rua 5 de Outubro, opposite the cathedral, leads down to the **Praça do Giraldo** and its 15th-century fountain, shaped like a *cataplana*. This is a focus for low-commotion time-passing.

The Rua da República runs downhill from the Praça, from which a road to the left, behind the bus station, opens on to the strange late Renaissance façade of **Nossa Senhora da Graça**, which was worked in part by Diogo de Arruda (a founding master of Manueline architecture and creator of the famous Tomar chapter house window) and is topped by four disgruntled giants in the process of standing up. The nave has fallen down three times.

The Church of São Francisco

Open daily 9–1 and 2.30–6; adm to Capela dos Ossos.

The Rua da República continues downhill past the back of the Gothic church of São Francisco, reconstructed 1460–1501. Gargoyles spew moss down its plastered sides. The church is entered through a gigantic, dizzying porch. As in the cathedral, the mortar is eye-catching. The single nave is daringly high and wide, while the chancel is a jumble of styles including a beautiful 18th-century neoclassical altar. The church hosts Évora's freakiest monument, the **Capela dos Ossos** (Bone Chapel), on ground level. Half-close your eyes and the walls seem built of flint: the truth is more disturbing. For the walls are composed of over 5,000 monks' bones. Femurs, tibias, skulls: all are arranged rather neatly, but the effect is macabre, and the mummified skeleton strung on one wall is gruesome. A notice at the entrance proclaims *'Nós ossos, que aqui estamos, Pelos vossos esperamos'*—'We bones here are waiting for your bones'. Less threateningly, the chapel's three founding fathers are commemorated with an epitaph of 1629. Note the plaits of hair near the entrance desk, offered as *ex votos*.

The **Museu de Artesanato** (Handicrafts Museum), opposite, houses temporary exhibitions, some of which are well worth visiting.

luxury

Pousada dos Lóios, Largo Conde de Vila Flor, © 266 704 051, 266 707 248 (category CH), next to the Roman temple, is in a wonderful and memorable location, the old Lóios monastery, which first offered hospitality to travellers in 1491. Now blue habits have given way to the blue blazers of the reception staff. The monastery was founded by Dom Rodrigo de Melo, who became the first Governor of Tangiers. The building centres on a two-storeyed cloister: the upper level has been glassed in. Guests pass through here to get to their snug bedrooms, which are scattered with Arraiolos rugs. Morning church bells ring loud in some rooms. A swimming pool is available for use. In warm weather, the ground level of the vaulted cloister is set with dining tables (note the double-horseshoe Manueline doorway). Otherwise, you'll be in the grand hall under iron chandeliers. The food does justice to the setting, and non-residents are welcome. You might try the *migas à Alentejana* (fried pork with fried bread).

moderate

Situated southeast of the town walls, **Albergaria Vitória**, Rua Diana de Lis, © 266 707 174, 266 700 974, is a comfortable, modern set-up, where the uniformed staff work efficiently and seem to enjoy doing so. Rooms have balconies.

****Pensão Residencial Riviera**, 49 Rua 5 de Outubro, © 266 703 304, 266 700 467 (*moderate–inexpensive*), is all right, but a bit tacky. The breakfast room is homey, though.

***Hotel Dom Fernando**, 2 Avenida Dr Barahona, © 266 741 717, 266 741 716, is a modern complex which tries to incorporate typical Alentejan styles, notably in the arched ceilings. The rooms are large and comfortable, if somewhat soulless.

***Hotel da Cartuxa**, Travessa da Palmeira 4–6, © 266 743 030, 266 744 284, is large and modern and conveniently situated just within the walllls of the city, within easy walking distance of the historic centre. Its restaurant, Cerca Nova, serves traditional food, and parking is a bonus.

***Évorahotel**, Quinta da Cruzeiro, Apartado 93, © 266 734 800, 266 734 806, is a large modern hotel with well-equipped rooms, all with balconies.

Hotel Ibis, Quinta da Tapada, Urb da Muralha, © 266 744 620, 266 744 632, is one of a rapidly expanding group of reasonably priced hotels with basic but reliable accommodation.

inexpensive

***Pensão Diana Residencial**, 2 Rua Diogo Cão, © 266 742 972, 266 743 101 (off the road running between the cathedral and the Praça do Giraldo), is comfortable and well established in a solidly built house, with high ceilings and strong furniture. There's a friendly, chatty atmosphere, especially at breakfast.

★★★**Pensão O Eborense 'Solar de Monfalim' Residencial**, 1 Largo da Misericórdia, ℂ 266 702 031, ◈ 266 742 367 (down the steps by the cathedral, take the second right), occupies a grand 16th-century house, with a whitewashed loggia and sympathetic décor, from cartwheels suspended to hold lights in the breakfast hall to old photographs hung in corridors that head off at odd angles. Room 112 is especially nice.

In the 16th century, the Count of Lousã built himself a town house, which is now the ★★**Pensão Policarpo Residencial**, 16 Rua da Freiria de Baixo, ℂ/◈ 266 702 424 (down the steps by the cathedral, turn left and go past the Misericórdia church). The place is atmospheric, with granite columns and open-air corridors. Room 101 is particularly attractive; rooms 102 to 109 are furnished with bright and flowery Alentejan furniture, right up to the pelmets. After 109 the rooms are plainer and not so special. The breakfast room is barn-like and lovely. Parking is available, and some of the staff speak English.

cheap

In one of the parallel streets running downhill from the Praça do Giraldo, ★★**Pensão Manueis Residencial**, 35 Rua do Raimundo, 1st floor, ℂ 266 702 861, is small and decent, with adequate rooms.

Another of these streets contains ★★★**Pensão Giraldo**, 15 and 27 Rua dos Mercadores, ℂ 266 705 833, which has high ceilings, plenty of wooden furniture and hot water, but is dingy in parts.

There are very cheap **rooms to let** in people's houses. The tourist office can provide a list. There is an **Orbitur Campsite**, Estrada de Alcáçovas, ℂ 266 705 190, ◈ 266 709 830, which is quite pleasant and open all year.

Out of Town

A farm's stables and servants' quarters have been converted into an inn, ★★★★**Pensão Monte das Flores**, 4km southwest of Évora, on the road to Alcáçovas, ℂ 266 749 680, ◈ 266 749 688 (*expensive*), that attracts young and beautiful Portuguese, keen on horse-riding at 5,000$00 per hour. That is the main appeal. When not in the saddle, you may sit on musty armchairs in the dauntingly large sitting room or on ponyskin wallseats in the bar. Bedrooms are furnished with flowery Alentejan furniture. Pork and steak dishes are popular in the dining room.

Solares de Portugal

There are many houses under this scheme in and around Évora; the tourist office can provide full details, but the pick of the bunch are highlighted opposite.

Quinta da Nora, Estrada dos Canaviais, 3km from Évora, ℂ 266 709 810, ◈ 266 733 781 (*moderate*) is a charming farmhouse with beautiful grounds, a swimming pool and a vineyard. The six rooms have lovely, heavy furniture and beamed, sloping ceilings. The lounge has its own panel of dazzling *azujelos* and Arraiolos rugs. Ridiculously good value.

Casa de S. Tiago, 2 Largo Alexandre Herculano, ✆ 266 702 686 (*moderate*) is a 16th-century town house dating from the reign of King Manuel I. The rooms display a happy mixture of the simple and the grand, while always feeling comfortable.

Quinta da Espada, Estrada de Arraiolos, 3km along the Arraiolos road, ✆ 266 734 549 (*moderate*) means 'The Sword Estate'—legend has it that Gerald the Fearless, who liberated Évora from the Moors, hid his sword here. Perhaps it is still lurking in the beautiful grounds, which are distinguished by an aqueduct. Still, the house looks like a typical Alentejan farmhouse, albeit very prettily furnished.

Eating Out

expensive

Humberto is the patron saint of hunting, and **Cozinha de Santo Humberto**, 39 Rua da Moeda, ✆ 266 704 251, ✉ 266 742 367, in one of the parallel streets which run downhill from the Praça do Giraldo, is an atmospheric place to celebrate him. The 300–400-year-old building incorporates a trough, now grilled over, which was formerly used for storing wine. Collections of glass, plates and kettles adorn the walls. The *calducho* is good, but the desserts aren't riveting. *Closed Thurs.*

Run by two brothers and sometimes a third, **Fialho**, 16 Trav. das Mascarenhas, ✆ 266 703 079, ✉ 266 744 873 (*reservations recommended*), near the theatre, has received a lot of hype, and has a good reputation for regional cooking. Thirty years ago, the prostitution in this side street was so obtrusive that ladies feared they would compromise themselves by coming here. All that's changed now. It's decorated as a tavern, with lots of local pottery and bizarre deer-foot coatpegs. Chairs are leather with bosses, and a huge display of fruit rests under the wood-beamed ceiling. Pork, lamb and game in season are specialities of the large menu. *Closed Mon.*

O Aqueduto, 13A Rua do Cano, ✆ 266 706 373, ✉ 266 706 373, near the aqueduct, glows with a warm yellow light. It is well run, with plenty of black-tied waiters serving good-quality regional dishes. Shrimps are displayed on a table, bay leaves are stored in tall pots over the earth-coloured floor, and down a couple of steps six huge vessels dwarf the tables they surround. The choice includes *migas com carne de porco* (pork with breadcrumbs).

Luar de Janeiro, 13 Trav. do Janeiro, ✆ 266 749 114, ✉ 266 749 116, has giant bottles of wine on the bar, setting the tone for this small restaurant with copper pots, a stag's head and sundry trophies lining rough upper walls. The bow-tied waiters are friendly and the good food comes priced by the kilo. *Closed Thurs.*

The restaurant of the **Pousada dos Lóios** (*see* 'Where to Stay') is open to non-residents.

moderate

Close to the main square, **A Muralha**, 21 Rua 5 de Octubro, ✆ 266 702 284, is inevitably popular with tourists, but has a pleasant lively atmosphere and a short menu of superbly cooked local dishes. *Closed Sun.* You can also eat good traditional food at the **Monte das Flores** out of town (*see* 'Where to Stay').

cheap

Sobreiro, 8 Rua do Torres, © 266 709 325, near the Calvário Convent off the Rua Cândido dos Reis, comes as a great relief—there is not a bow tie in sight. The interior setting is plain and rustic, with wooden farm equipment on the walls, and bread-bowls made of cork complete with bark. It fills quickly and empties early, but the service is constantly efficient. Most of the locals choose *cozido à portuguesa*: assorted boiled meat does not make a pretty dish, but it's tasty. *Closed Wed.*

Around Évora

Arraiolos

Set among low hills 21km north of Évora, benath the circular walls of a castle, the village of Arraiolos is famous for its **carpetmaking**, consisting of a single cross-stitch in magically beautiful patterns.

Getting There

Arraiolos is a ½hr bus ride from Évora or a ¾hr bus ride from Estremoz. The service runs frequently enough to make an easy day trip.

The hilltop **castle** was built by Dom Dinis in 1310, and the soldier Nun' Álvares Pereira lived here at various times between 1415 and 1423. Only the circular walls remain intact; they give the feeling of a giant animal pen. The white conical buttresses of the **convento dos Lóios** stand 500m to the north of town, surrounded by birdsong. The monastery was given to the Brothers of St John the Evangelist in 1526, and contains tiles dated 1700.

Arraiolos Carpets

The tradition started at the local convent of Lóios in the 17th century, when silk or linen was embroidered with local wool. By the third quarter of that century, the carpets were being exported to other parts of the country. The patterns were inspired by various sources, all sprinkled with a little popular imagination: Portugal's Moorish heritage, the carpets of Herat and Isfahan brought back by the discoverers, and legendary tales of Persian exoticism, which contributed tiger and deer, peacocks and doves. France and Germany contributed the fleur-de-lis and the double-headed eagle respectively, in shades of red, blue, yellow and green. At the beginning of the 18th century, embroiderers shrugged off Oriental influences to incorporate palm trees, figures in traditional costume and huge floral or leaf sprays, considered by many to be the finest designs. From the start of the 19th century, the ripples made by Aubusson carpets reached Arraiolos; a hundred years later the carpets were echoing azulejos (tiles), or blooming with floral designs on fawn or dark blue backgrounds. You can see a good selection at the permanent exhibition in the Town Hall.

A number of workshops in Arraiolos produce carpets, all of which have their own showrooms. It's cheaper to buy them here than anywhere else: prices currently average out at 30,000$00 per square metre, half of which goes to the hunched sewers. Cushion covers are an alternative, at around 7,000$00 each. A showroom that exports worldwide is D. Nunes Álvares Pereira, Rua dos Moínhos de Vento, 3 7040 Arraiolos.

Monsaraz and its Megaliths

Getting There

With the advent of more and more tourists, special day trips are available from many towns, but for up-to-date information on regular buses and trains dial the Portugal Telecom freephone on © 800 296 296 and then press 2 for an English-speaking assistant.

Tourist Information

Monsaraz' **tourist office**, Largo D. Nuno Álvares Pereira, © 266 557 136, is in the square near the pillory.

The walled hilltop village of Monsaraz has held off centuries of development—its medieval streets retain a peculiar magic. You can feel its allure a couple of kilometres away, where the only visible parts of the settlement are its castle and the Igreja Matriz.

The four parallel cobbled streets of Monsaraz offer massive views of the plains of the Alentejo, peppercorned with olive and cork trees. The low, bulging houses are white-washed or built of chaotic grey slate, with mellow terracotta roofs and terracotta jugs used as gargoyles, and whimsical iron dachshund doorknockers. Bitches with distended teats sprawl in the shade, and women wearing black trilby hats sit outdoors and crochet. For cosmetic reasons telephone wires have been buried, and cars are excluded from the walled precincts between 11am and 8pm in summer, 11am and 6pm in winter.

Monsaraz was taken from the Moors in 1167 and in the same year was given to the Templars. The joy of the place comes in absorbing the village and its life—there are a couple of churches but, with the exception of a damaged 14th-century marble tomb in the **Igreja Matriz**, they contain little of interest. To the left of that church, the **Paços do Concelho** contains a 14th-century fresco depicting a good and a bad judge: the latter has a devil on his shoulder and is accepting a bribe. Vertical lines scratched into the inner side of the entrance gate were used for measuring material on market days. At the other end of town, the **castle** forms part of a chain of fortresses built by Dom Dinis in the 14th century. Part of it has been converted into a bullring.

Just outside the village walls the **Capela de São João Baptista** is emerging from beneath a mountain of soil and sheep manure. Renovation is bringing to light paintings of the saint's life.

Sited in a subsidiary settlement below the castle walls, the best feature of ★★★★**Estalagem de Monsaraz**, Largo de S. Bartolomeu, ✆ 266 557 112, 🖅 266 557 101 (*cheap*), is a wonderfully peaceful and private sinuous garden, backed by natural rock. Below is a swimming pool. Public rooms are decorated in a rustic style, with copper pots and painted plates, and onions suspended from wood beams. The small-windowed bedrooms have heavy furniture and may be dirty. Some of the bathrooms are squashed and ramshackle. The restaurant serves simple food such as liver (*figado*). If it is full you may like to try the recently renovated **Convent da Orada**, ✆ 266 557 381, 🖅 266 557 381, a huge building with awesome echoing corridors, beautiful marble bathrooms and spacious bedrooms.

Solares de Portugal

Dom Nuno, 6 Rua Direita, ✆ 266 557 146 (*moderate–inexpensive*), is near the church square, a surprisingly large old house, artistically and comfortably decorated, with stone floors, wooden ceilings and Renaissance doorways. Some of the eight rooms offer fantastic views from their fat beds with handmade bedcovers. A collection of keys hangs on the wall of the galleried sitting room like musical notes. There are very nice modern bathrooms, and a small bar—it's good value.

Casa Dona Antónia, ✆ 266 557 142 (*cheap*) is the only house on the upper road bearing bougainvillaea. Its seven rooms have recently been renovated. All have TV and air conditioning, most have a shower or bath, and there's one suite.

Outside Monsaraz, the **Horta da Moura**, Apartado 64, 7200 Reguengos de Monsaraz, ✆ 266 550 100, 🖅 266 550 108 (*expensive*) is an impressive converted farmhouse set in extensive grounds, with rough white walls, beamed ceilings and terracotta floors. It's a luxurious base for exploring the Guadiana—by bicycle, on horseback or even horse-drawn carriage. The many other facilities include tennis. The mellow dining room serves well-cooked regional specialities.

Eating Out

Lamb is the local speciality, and it can be mouthwateringly delicious. Treat yourself to a fine red wine from Reguengos.

moderate–cheap

Restaurante Casa de Forno, Travessa Sanabrosa, ✆ 266 557 190, has a great atmosphere. *Closed Tues.* **Restaurante O Alcaide**, Rua de São Tiago 16, ✆ 266 557 168, is a small restaurant with excellent food. Arrive early to bag a window seat overlooking the plains. *Closed Thurs.*

Pretty **Restaurante Santiago**, 3 Rua de São Tiago, ✆ 266 557 188, serves delicious food. In good weather sit and enjoy your meal on the terrace. *Closed Wed.* **Zé Lumumba**, on the upper road, ✆ 266 557 121, is short on atmosphere but the food is good and there's a terrace. *Closed Mon.*

Porco Com Ameijoas à Alentejana

This recipe is a mouthwatering combination of the products from the Alentejo's rolling pastureland and coastline.

Ingredients (*serves 4*)

> *700g pork, cubed*
> *500ml dry white wine*
> *2tsp paprika*
> *1 bay leaf*
> *2 cloves*
> *5 garlic cloves, crushed*
> *60g butter*
> *2 onions, sliced*
> *4 medium tomatoes, chopped*
> *1kg clams, washed, scrubbed and soaked (change the water once*
> *or twice and discard any which are open)*
> *2tbsp parsley, chopped*

Marinade the pork overnight in the wine, paprika, bay leaf, cloves and three of the garlic cloves.

Heat half the butter in a large saucepan, add the tomatoes, onions and remaining two garlic cloves. Cook gently until the onions soften. Add salt and pepper. In another pan, heat the rest of the butter. Drain the pork, reserve the marinade and brown the pork in the butter on a medium heat. Once browned, add the marinade and cook until it reduces. Add the clams to the tomato mixture and cover the pan. Cook for about 5 minutes on a high heat until the clams open and then turn down the heat and cook for a further minute.

Add the pork to the clams, sprinkle with the parsley, garnish with lemon, and serve with boiled potatoes or rice, a green salad and some crusty bread.

Out of Town

expensive

If the idea of a closer communion with the local culture appeals, head for **Herdade do Esporão**, ✆ 266 519 750, ✉ 266 519 753, on the outskirts of Reguengos de Monsaraz. Follow signs from the railway. The 400ha vineyard is one of the country's finest. There are guided tours of the *adega*, and a shop, as well as an attractive and rather worthwhile restaurant. Booking is essential for the tour and lunch. *Closed Mon and eves.*

moderate

Sem-Fim Restaurante Bar and Galeria de Artes, 6A Rua das Flores, Telheiro 7200-181, ✆ 266 557 471 (*open for dinner Thurs–Sun and lunch at weekends*) occupies an old oil press, with tables placed around the machinery. A faint smell of olive oil lingers. It can be a little chilly, so be prepared, but the food is excellent and the service attentive.

Around Monsaraz: Megaliths

The Alentejo was a centre of megalithic culture between 4000 and 2000 BC, and the area between Reguengos de Monsaraz, 36km southeast of Évora, and Monsaraz, 16km farther east, preserves some good examples of menhirs (tombs with large flat stones laid on upright ones) and a cromlech (a circle of upright stones), which can all be visited on a circular tour around the two towns. (The name '*reguengos*' denotes what was once a royal estate, yielding to the Crown a quarter to a fifth of the produce of the soil.) The tourist office produces a glossy booklet detailing the megaliths and their locations.

Some 8km east of Reguengos de Monsaraz, just past S. Pedro do Corval, and about 50m to the left of the road, stands **Lovers' Rock**. It's a natural-standing knobbed fertility stone, just shorter than the trees around it. On Easter Monday, hopeful local single ladies roll up their left sleeves and pelt the rock with fist-sized stones. If a missile stays atop, a baby is due within a year. The base of the rock is littered with disappointments. It is also said that the number of throws it takes to get the stone on top is the number of years before you marry. And we have seen a happy bride and groom having one of their wedding photos taken by the stone.

Off the road from Telheiro (where there is a whitewashed fountain dated 1422) to Outeiro, a menhir is visible across the fields, about 5½m high. Local farmers found the **Menhir da Bulhoa** lying flat and chopped off a third of it to make an olive-oil press. Decorated with faint zigzag patterns and stars, it is considered too oval and tapering to be a credible phallus, and was probably erected in memory of a chief, or as a geographical marker.

Five kilometres from Monsaraz, on the road to Xeres de Baixo, the **Cromlech do Xerez** stands 300m to the right. Fifty stubby menhirs are arranged in a square, with a great big phallic one in the middle. The splendid central member of the group weighs 7 tonnes. Probably a place for ritual prayer and meeting, it's best seen when the sun is low, casting long shadows from the clusters of natural shrub-studded boulders in the surrounding ploughland. Fertility in an agro-pastoral economy was related not only to people, but also to the land and flocks.

Those interested in ceramics should stop in the small village of **São Pedro do Corval**. It is renowned for its 30-plus workshops.

Beja

Some 175km north of Faro, Beja occupies the highest point of the plain which separates the catchment areas of the Rivers Sado and Guadiana. The principal town of the Lower Alentejo, Beja is prosperous, purposeful and pedestrian in its new parts, and pleasantly lackadaisical in its old parts. Here old people in low houses wait and watch at their street-level windows, and the streets are paved with dragons'-teeth and egg-shaped cobbles.

Beja's main appeal is as a useful stopover point on the way up to Évora: it's certainly worth spending a few hours here.

History

At the beginning of Beja's history the town was named Pax Julia to commemorate the peace between Julius Caesar and the Lusitanians. It was a commercial centre made up of freemen and foreigners, who practised a variety of Eastern religions: inscriptions have been found dedicated to Cybele, Isis, Serapis and even Mithras. Of the brilliant Muslim court that followed, few traces now remain—only the tiles which wall the *convento*. In the mid-15th century, Afonso V made Beja a duchy. Traditionally, it was granted to the second son of the king, until Dom Pedro IV decided that the second-in-line should be Duke of Oporto, and the third-in-line Duke of Beja. During the French occupation, most of Junot's army was stationed in the Alentejo. In June 1808 something snapped, and several French soldiers were killed in a riot in Beja. Junot ordered reprisals; 1,200 Bejans were killed in a street battle, and the French commander was moved to report: 'Beja no longer exists, its criminal inhabitants have been put to the sword and their houses pillaged and burned.'

Beja still exists, although its charms are limited to those of the *convento*-museum.

Tourist Information

The **tourist office** is at 25 Rua do Capitão J.F. de Sousa, *©* 284 323 693 (*open June–Sept Mon–Fri 9–8, Sat 10–1 and 2–6; Oct–May Mon–Fri 10–6, Sat closed 1–2*), just outside the medieval town walls, not too far from the museum. The **bus station**—*©* 284 313 620 for EVA buses—is in the southeast of town (walk down the street flanking the odd modern Casa da Cultura), while the **railway station**, *©* 284 325 056, is in the northeast.

The Castle and Around

Open daily 10–1 and 2–6; it costs 220$00 to climb the 160 steps to the top of the tower but entrance to the castle is free.

The castle, yet another of Dom Dinis' fortifications, stands on the edge of medieval Beja. Ivy covers its courtyard buildings. The philosophical castellan will show visitors the thick-walled keep, and the balcony holes positioned for pouring boiling olive oil on assailants. The building's 40m height allows the luxury of three Gothic windows, and very big views.

In the 18th century, the castle walls supported 40 towers, but they were torn down at the end of the 19th century. Stepped bungalows follow what remains of the wall of the castle.

To one side of the castle is the church of **Sant'Iago**, with pillars of 18th-century *azulejos*. To the other side, the **Igreja de Santo Amaro** houses the **Museum of Visigothic Archaeology** (*open Tues–Sun 9.30–12.30 and 2–5.15; closed Mon and holidays; adm, which also gives admission to the Convento de Nossa Senhora da Conceição*), with artefacts mostly from the 7th–8th centuries well displayed amongst the whitewashed arches of the church. Downhill from the castle, on the Lisbon road, stands the **Hermitage of Santo André**. It is not held in great respect locally, despite its foundation in the reign of Dom Sancho I to commemorate the capture of Beja from the Moors in 1162.

The porch of the mid-15th-century **Misericórdia**, at one end of the Praça da República, was originally a meat market: as if to prove it, the stonework is nicked like pigskin. Now workmen eat sardines there, and the church itself is used as a small craft exhibition and sales centre.

The Convento de Nossa Senhora da Conceição

The convento de Nossa Senhora da Conceição houses the municipal **museum** (*open Tues–Sun 9.30–12.30 and 2–5.15; closed Mon and hols; adm, which also gives adm to the Museum of Visigothic Archaeology*). In the 17th century this was the home of that deserted and reproachful correspondent, Mariana Alcoforado, authoress of the five *Love Letters of a Portuguese Nun*. Her chevalier quit Beja at the end of the Portuguese war with Spain (1661–8). The originals of her letters to him have never been found, but they were published in French in 1669, and later translated into English: 'I do not know why I write to you. You will only take pity on me, and I don't want your pity. I despise myself when I think of all that I have sacrificed for you. I have lost my reputation...' By the grille where the lovers blew kisses, a flippant curator has displayed Roman *ampullae* created to hold tears, and a nippled jug for a baby.

The Conventual Building

The conventual building, founded in 1459, is a good example of the transition from Gothic to Manueline style; the structure and the ogival arches are Gothic, while the decoration betrays the later influence. The dusty chapel features lots of giltwork and, fourth on the right, an all-marble side chapel dedicated to John the Baptist, though his image was removed in the 19th century. His life is portrayed in good tiles dated 1741, and there's a silver shrine for him and his namesake the Evangelist. A little marble tomb contains the bones of Dona Uganda, the first abbess. The cloister runs the length of the chapel, lined with uneven tiles from various periods, through to the extraordinary, exuberant *Sala do Capítulo* (the chapter house), decorated with a dense combination of paintwork and tiles. The painted panels are a bit kitsch, but the ceiling is great. Each pattern of carpet tiles has a single eccentric, because the Moors who made them believed only Allah could be perfect.

The Museum

In the museum's collection, three 16th-century paintings are outstanding: *São Vicente*, from the school of the Master of Sardoal; a Flemish *Our Lady of the Milk*, breast-feeding; and a Portuguese *Descent from the Cross*. Note too an 18th-century polychrome sculpture of *Nossa Senhora dos Dores*, unusually detailing her toenails, teeth and tears; and a blue and white Ming bowl decorated with horsemen, the name of its first owner and the date of acquisition. There are two curious tombs. One is a stone half-barrel, built for a vintner. The other is Roman, with a little wolf, stating that now the land will be lighter.

The capital on display near the entrance is the largest in Portugal and was found as recently as 1981 in the cellar of Os Infantes restaurant. There are more within the region that remain in situ as they are very worn and cannot be removed easily.

luxury

Pousada de São Francisco, Rua do Nuno Alvares Pereira, ℂ 284 328 441, ✆ 284 329 143 (*category CH*), is one of Portugal's newest *pousadas* and opened in November 1994 after two years of careful restoration. The modern comforts inhabit the 13th-century convent built by Dom Afonso III and much added to since. One of the first to begin additions was Dom Dinis, who, in a bargain with God typical of ancient monarchs, promised to build a chapel if he defeated the Moors in an important battle. His victory spawned the Chapel of Tombs, a small and perfectly formed Gothic chapel restored with the rest of the building and displaying some Roman and medieval relics. In the 19th century, the convent was converted to be used as an army barracks.

The hotel has a cavernous entrance and banqueting hall, all covered in 18th-century marble and shining splendidly. The ground-floor cloister surrounds a courtyard built around a Moorish well (if you want to visit the underground cistern, just ask the reception). Other delights of the original building include an 18th-century chapter house with its ceiling panels alive with saints, and a peaceful restaurant (*expensive*) situated in the old stables, serving a small international menu, a fun children's menu and daily regional specialities under a multi-domed ceiling. There is also a tennis court and swimming pool, and a playground for the kids. The bar spills tables on to the grass: peacocks strut in between.

Upstairs, the large and very comfortable rooms are converted monks' cells, complete with their original arches. Throughout, the *pousada* is decorated with great luxury and understatement, and the rooms are draped with heavy cream curtains. There is one suite, which is like a large London flat for one. You can easily gain access to the bell tower from where the good views take in Beja's public gardens.

The staff are very helpful, the service absolutely impeccable and the whole is grand without being intimidating. The entire hotel is light and airy and as calm and peaceful as you could want.

moderate

★★★**Hotel Residencial Melius**, Avenida Fialho de Almeida, ℂ 284 321 822, ✆ 284 321 825 (*moderate*), is on the edge of town with modern comfortable rooms and good service. The hotel is part of a complex that includes a cinema, gym, garage and lots of yellow bordering. ★★★★**Pensão Residencial Cristina**, 71 Rua de Mértola, ℂ 284 323 035, ✆ 284 329 874 (*moderate*)—around the corner from the beginning of the road to the Algarve—is functional and very clean behind tinted glass doors. Rooms have thick, patterned curtains, TV and phone, with small bathtubs.

inexpensive

Further down the same road, ★★★★Pensão Residencial Santa Bárbara, 56 Rua de Mértola, ℂ 284 322 028, ✆ 284 321 231, provides clean, satisfactory rooms, with stand-up balconies and telephones.

In the central elongated square, near the Misericórdia, ★★★**Pensão Residencial Coelho**, 15 Praça da República, ✆ 284 324 031, @ 284 328 939, is a very decent, solid sort of place. Rooms come with showers rather than baths. Fun and characterful ★★★**Pensão Residencial Bejense**, 57 Rua Capitão J.F. de Sousa, ✆ 284 332 512 (near the tourist office), is basic but clean. A gaudy selection of knick-knacks adorns every available space; not all rooms have bathrooms. There is a **campsite** behind the football ground, off Avenida Vasco da Gama, ✆ 284 311 911, @ 284 311 929.

Solares de Portugal

Monte da Diabrória, Estrada Nacional 121, Beringel (4km along the road to Lisbon, on the right), ✆ 284 998 177 (*inexpensive*) is a huddle of picturesque farm buildings close to a game reserve. Inside, the rooms are rustic and characterful, with animal skins splayed on the floors, and roaring fires. **Horta do Cano**, ✆ 284 326 156, offers tennis, swimming, clay-pigeon shooting and riding.

Eating Out

Small and whitewashed, **O Portão**, 1 Travessa da Audiênca (off the Rua dos Infantes, which runs between the Praça da República and the museum), ✆ 284 329 030 (*moderate*), serves carefully prepared and often very good food. MTV by satellite makes conversation a bit difficult. Hope that the *bacalhau à Gomes de Sá* is a dish of the day. *Closed Sun.*

In the square next to the museum, **Alentejano**, 6–7 Largo dos Duques de Beja, ✆ 284 323 849 (*cheap*), is full of locals in old leather jackets and gregarious students, sitting under the fake wood ceiling and enjoying their meat, rice and potatoes. Portions are large, prices reasonable and the service fast and efficient. *Closed Fri.* **Os Infantes**, 14 Rua dos Infantes, ✆/@ 284 322 789 (*expensive–moderate*), has a good reputation and a cosy interior with stone arches leading from one room to another. Try the *ensopado de borrego* (lamb stew) and their superlative regional sweets. *Closed Wed.* Nearby **A Floresta**, Largo dos Duques de Beja, ✆ 284 329 578 (*moderate*), is popular with locals. The roast lamb is very good, as is the *bolo de rala*, a cake from Beja made with almonds. *Closed Mon.*

Along the street from the tourist office, **Luís da Rocha**, 63 Rua Capitão João Francisco de Sousa, ✆ 284 323 179 (*moderate–cheap*), is plain and unexciting though it's over a hundred years old, the tables adorned only by single carnations. Unusually for Beja, there are several fish dishes on the menu, but the speciality is *cabrito à pastora* (boiled kid). *Closed Sun.*

Dom Dinis, 11 Rua Dom Dinis, ✆ 284 325 937 (*moderate–cheap*), specializes in charcoal-grilled food and regional dishes. *Closed Thurs.*

The large **A Esquina**, 26 Rue Infante D. Henrique, ✆ 284 389 238 (*moderate*) serves regional dishes and is popular with local people.

The peaceful and dazzlingly white little town of Serpa is 28km southeast of Beja and 50km north of Mértola, where the plains give way to smooth, undulating hills. There's something quintessentially Portuguese about the place—its 8,000 souls appear to live a life untainted by anything other than the Moors, who left 750 years ago. Kids stare at visitors, who seem to be invisible to the old people ruminating beside 2,000-year-old olive trees near the Botanic Gardens. Serpa boasts Portugal's Whitest Street, cobbled and quiet, and also some of the country's finest ewes' milk cheese.

Tourist Information

The **tourist office** is at the bottom of the steps to the citadel at 2 Largo Dom Jorge de Melo, ℂ 284 544 727 (*open daily 9–12.30 and 2–5.30*).

The **bus station** is at Av Capitães de Abril, ℂ 284 544 740.

In and Around the Walled Town

The western approach to Serpa is very striking—the plain, flat façade of the Solar (manor house) of the Counts of Ficalho is built into the town walls, supplied by a slender aqueduct and chain pump, beside the conical late 13th-century Gates of Beja. The **Solar** was built in the 17th century by the Bishop of Guarda, a native of Serpa and a member of the Melo family. It remains in private hands.

The Castle Hillock

Within the town walls, a wide staircase near the tourist office leads up to the castle hillock, first inhabited by the Celts in the 4th century BC. Gnarled olive trees camouflage equally gnarled time-passers on the cobbled terrace fronting the clock tower and the Gothic **Igreja Matriz** (*open daily 9.30–12.30 and 2–5.30*), whose pale grey capitals are carved with mythological beasts. Beside the church, a huge dislocated chunk of wall perches dramatically above the entrance to the **castle** (*open Tues–Sun 9.30–12.30 and 2–5.30; closed Mon*). It has been there since 1707, when part of Dom Dinis' fortification was blown up by the Spanish Duke of Osuna during the War of Spanish Succession. The wall blooms with wind-blown flowers, and, high above passers-by, a lemon tree ripens beside the boulder. Behind them, a cockerel weathervane has been peppered with pot-shots.

Elsewhere, the crenellated castle walls are intact, offering beautiful views of the town's terracotta roofs and palm trees, to the wide-open country beyond. When things got too dangerous for the 13th-century residents of Serpa, they abandoned their houses within the castle's outer walls, and rumbled their carts through the zigzagged principal entrance gate of the inner line of defence, which is now visible from the ground floor of the **castle's museum**. Its extensive collection of prehistoric remains includes the tools of daily life employed by *Homo erectus*; Christian artefacts include a life-size rendition of the Last Supper in plaster of Paris.

A Stroll Round the Town

The great pleasure of Serpa is wandering the irregular streets of the walled town, around the Rua da Figueira (fig tree) and the Rua da Parreira (trellis). Housed in the old municipal market, off the Largo do Corro, is the **Ethnographic Museum** (*open Tues–Sun, 9–12.30 and 2–5.30; closed Mon*). It displays the tools of cobblers, tinsmiths, cart-makers, cheese-makers, basket-weavers, tailors, carpenters and blacksmiths. There's a huge Sheffield bellows and an enormous hand-turned and -operated band-saw that makes you tired just looking at it.

The short Rua de Lampreia runs north from the Largo; at its end, turn right and then left into the Rua da Ladeira to get to the **Convento de Santo António** (*open daily 9–6*) founded in 1463 and abandoned at the time of the 1974 Revolution, when it was occupied by students. Now it is annexed to an old people's home. Its most interesting feature is a series of 18th-century *azulejos* of the life of St Francis, who is shown letting down a rope to help some decidedly naked and breasty people out of Hell, while a winged Christ flies heavenwards with his cross. Cats wander about the church, communing with the angels carved on the retable.

Serpa is full of surprises and none more so than at the **Watch Museum** (*open Tues–Fri 2–5.30, weekends and hols 9–12.30 and 2–5.30; closed Mon; with guided tours on the hour; adm*), a magnificent private collection housed in the 17th-century Convento do Mosteirinho, just off the Praca da Republica. Its 1,600 mechanical watches, all in working order, make it the largest European collection outside Switzerland. This fascinating assemblage includes two 200-year-old sun watches used by shepherds in the fields, a 1676 Hamleys of London double-cased silver watch, a Beatles limited-edition wristwatch boxed in a miniature guitar, and watches used by American astronauts. The Gran Sonnérie by Edward East (1630–70) displayed here is considered to be the oldest timepiece in the world.

Returning to the Largo do Corro, the Rua A.C. Calisto becomes the Rua do Calvário. Turn right into the Alameda da Correia da Serra for the compact **Botanic Gardens**, fronted by a Roman road running alongside three tremendous olive trees reputed to date from the time of Christ. Gnarled and hollow, they are among the largest in Portugal, with a diameter of about two metres. But it was not always thus: the trees were moved in from the countryside about a hundred years ago. The Garden itself is haphazard, and offers welcome shade under huge, colourful trees. Do note the cork beehive in the corner, made from a circle of cork bark topped with more cork, which is typical of many still used in the region.

Where to Stay

The **Pousada de São Gens**, Alto de São Gens, ✆ 284 544 724, ✉ 284 544 337 (category C), 2km south of town—turn right where the houses stop—is on a mount of olives, and the modern building is well designed to exploit the enormous views of endless, chequered yellow and brown plains. Bedrooms are equipped for the heat with air-conditioning and terracotta floors. Bathrooms are pleasant, and there's a swimming pool. The public rooms are habitable, with a fairly elegant dining room featuring a rustic menu. The roast leg of pork is very good, while an *à la carte* choice might be stewed hare in white rice or partridge with nuts. Pastries are home-made.

Occupying a corner slot next to the supermarket, **Pensão Residencial Beatriz**, 10 Largo do Salvador, ✆ 284 544 423 (*inexpensive*), offers spacious, clean, air-conditioned rooms, complete with bathroom and TV. Comfortable, if rather plain.

There are very cheap rooms to let above the restaurant **O Casarão**, 15 Rua do Calvário, ✆ 284 549 682. There are also rooms to let at **Monte da Portela Nova**, Estrada de São Bras, ✆ 284 544 778, ✉ 284 544 487. **Camping Municipal de Serpa**, Largo de São Pedro, ✆ 284 544 290, ✉ 284 540 109, is open all year, with the large As Piscinas restaurant-bar 50m away.

Solares de Portugal

Herdade do Topo lies 12km south of Serpa on the road to Mértola at Monte do Topo, P.O. Box 29, ✆/✉ 284 595 133 (*moderate*). The farmhouses focus on the stables: this is a stud farm, set in 800 hectares of land and breeding only Lusitano horses. Dressage and traditional Portuguese riding are their specialities, though the elegantly simple rooms and beautiful countryside are reasons enough to visit.

Eating Out

The best place to eat inexpensively is the small and cosy **Cuiça-Filho** at 18 Rua das Portas de Beja, ✆ 284 549 566 (*cheap*). One of the more imaginative dishes on the menu is the tasty *arroz de polvo* (octopus rice) and Alentejan specialities.

Also near the tourist office there's the **Alentejano**, Praça da República, ✆ 284 544 335 (*moderate*), with brick arches, a blue ceiling, and an almost Italianate feel to its first-floor restaurant. It specializes in long, smoky lunches for business types. **Restaurante O Zé** in Praça da República, ✆ 284 549 246 (*moderate–cheap*) is simpler, despite the silver walls and the spotlights which reveal it to have once been a disco, and it's always busy, featuring good *gazpacho*, a delicious *migas* and local cheese. **Adega Molho O Bica**, Rua Quente 1, ✆ 284 549 264 (*cheap*), is another place to go for a warm welcome and to try regional pork specialities (*see* p.154)

The **Cervejaria Lebrinha**, 6–8 Rua do Calvário, ✆ 284 549 311 (near the Botanic Garden), has superb draught beer and a restaurant.

Mértola

The delightfully slow little town of Mértola creeps up the steep bank of the curvaceous River Guadiana, at its confluence with the River Oeiras, 58km north of Castro Marim and 50km south of Beja. The gritty soil around Mértola hampers agriculture, but the habitat is suitable for partridges, rabbits, hares, foxes and wild boars. The subsoil is rich in copper, sulphur and iron, but the deposits at Mina de São Domingos are exhausted.

Modern Mértola is architecturally nondescript, but in the old quarter tiers of tiny low houses crowd between the river and the castle. They are best appreciated from within the castle walls. The most comfortable place to pass the time is by the lower wall in the old quarter, which runs parallel to the flow.

Mértola is a great base from which to explore the beautiful banks of the Guadiana and its tributaries, which are covered with pink oleanders. Both sides of the river have been designated a nature reserve. Downstream, the river is serene and happy, smooth enough to mirror its own green banks. Pond terrapins peep out at visitors, storks rap undeterred, and snakes serpent themselves away in terror.

History

The Phoenicians sailed up the Guadiana and founded a settlement here, which became an important commercial centre for themselves and the Carthaginians. The Romans made Mirtilis grand because it occupied a key defensive point on their road from Beja to Castro Marim; it minted coin between 189 and 170 BC. The Moors called it Mirtolah, and built walls around it in the 12th century. These failed to prevent Dom Sancho II conquering the town in 1238. He handed it to the Order of Sant'Iago, to settle and defend.

Tourist Information

The **tourist office** is at 13 Rua da Igreja, in the old part of town, ℭ 286 611 190 (*open Mon–Fri 9–1 and 2–6*), and sells nice wooden handicrafts. Be sure to ask for the excellent map of the town. The **bus stop** (ℭ 286 612 157) is a short walk away from Rua da Republica up the Rua Serrão Martins.

It is now possible to take **boat tours** from Mértola for varying distances. As the river is tidal at this point the trips are dependent on the vagaries of the river and there are no scheduled times—it is worth asking at the tourist office for details.

Around Town

Dominating the uppermost point of town, the **castle** dates from 1292, though it's dramatic only when seen from the southern approach to Mértola, silhouetted above the Moorish town walls. Just downhill, an 11th-century mosque has been converted into the **Igreja Matriz**, without substantially altering the structure. The pineapple-top merlons are typically Mudéjar, but the cylindrical towers which buttress the church are native. A bell tower now performs the muezzin's function, and within the church an altar stands in front of the *mihrab*, the niche which indicates the direction of Mecca. The square church has five naves, with 13th-century Gothic vaulting. Between the church and the castle, extensive excavations are revealing a sizeable Roman villa and fortifications, including a large cryptoporticum.

Descend the steps at the entrance to the Old Quarter to find a flourishing **weaving workshop**, which uses designs that date back centuries. It's a great place to find gifts at reasonable prices, be they woollen blankets or wall hangings, or cotton or linen mats and runners.

Further downhill, the **town hall** has recently discovered its Roman foundations. These have been adapted into a well-designed museum, with various Roman artefacts and sculptures. Around the corner, the small **municipal museum** contains Moorish pottery, excavated bones, and puppet-like figures—who required only the upper half of their bodies, because their nether regions were hidden by clothes.

The town advertises several other small museums, all of which are worth visiting. The **Islamic, Roman and Sacred Art Museums** (*open 9–12.30 and 2–5.30*) are situated in the south of the old town. The key for the **Paleo-Christian Museum**, on the north side of town, is available from the tourist office.

A door in the town walls gave access on to the fortified **jetty**, which was probably built by the Moors from Roman materials. Now only stacks remain. The Guadiana is narrow enough for fishermen to shout across on a Sunday afternoon, as they mend the nets normally buoyed in arcs. Reproduction **jewellery** and new designs with an Arab or Roman influence is made in a workshop near the jetty. Pieces are worked in copper, brass or silver; gold designs can be made to order.

A bridge crosses the River Oeiras just south of Mértola. On ledges under the arches, nesting boxes have been placed for the rare lesser kestrels that make Mértola their home. These birds, which bear a striking resemblance to large swallows, are always in evidence during the summer, hawking for insects above the castle and convent and circling the steppe lands by day; some accept these specially provided nesting boxes, while others prefer to make their own selection from the many holes in the old castle walls.

Just over the bridge you can visit the **Convent of São Francisco** (*open daily 2–6; adm*), owned by a Dutch family and renowned for its modern-art exhibitions. The gardens are planted with loquats. The convent, like the old quarter of Mértola, is adorned with white storks' nests—the birds are in residence and rearing their families in the summer.

Around Mértola

Seventeen kilometres east of Mértola lie the old copper mines of **São Domingos**. Known to the Romans, they were rediscovered in 1857 and worked by a British firm and some 7,000 dependants until 1966. Then the mines closed and the population was decimated. Now it's something of a ghost town, an ideal setting for a Tarkovsky film. São Domingos was once illustrious enough to be the first town in Portugal to have telephones, trains and electricity. More importantly to the Portuguese, it was the first town that allowed foreign players in its football team: two Englishmen played for the town in the 1920s. Enquire at the tourist office for details of buses from Mértola.

Twenty-five kilometres north of Mértola, the **Pulo do Lobo waterfall** (translates as Wolf's Leap) can be reached by following the road from Mértola to Beja and turning right after about 5km. Go straight through the little village of Corte Gafo de Cima and carry on up until you can turn right for the village of Amendoeira da Serra. The waterfall is about 5km along a dirt track from here. This is a better road than the one from Serpa, which is really quite rough after the village of São Brás. Within the high gorge, over the millennia the river has cut a 15m-deep, 2m-wide channel through the slate. When in full flood, it is a spectacle not to be missed, and on a sunny day the spray makes rainbows in the valley, which is composed of creepy rock formations—a powerful and primeval place.

Where to Stay

Pensão Beira-Rio, Rua Dr Afonso Costa, ✆ 286 612 340 (*cheap*), is down by the river, with a good view only slightly spoilt by the small factory opposite, and very nice new shared bathrooms with plenty of hot water. The garden is full of sweet-smelling orange trees. This is preferable to **Pensão San Remo**, Av. Aureliano Mira Fernandes, ✆ 286 612 132 (*cheap*), in the square opposite the bus depot, which is decent but a bit soulless. The back rooms have neither view nor sunshine, though this keeps them cool. The hot water is plentiful, though, and the pastelaria next door serves good coffee, toasted sandwiches and delicious cakes. **Oasis**, 104 Rua Dr Afonso Costa, ✆ 286 612 071/405, ✉ 286 612 701 (*moderate–cheap*), has panoramic views over the river. All rooms are air-conditioned, and at the time of writing private bathrooms were due to be installed. **Casa Rosmaninho**, Rua 25 de Abril, ✆ 286 612 432/286 612 005 (*moderate–cheap*), has rooms equipped with private bathroom, TV and air-conditioning.

Out of Town

Pensão São Domingos, Rua Dr Rocha, Mina de São Domingos, ✆ 286 647 187, is useful if you're visiting the mine at São Domingos and want to stay in the village. Nine of the 19 rooms have private bathrooms, and all are basic but comfortable. Its restaurant specializes in regional cuisine.

Solares de Portugal

Casa das Janelas Verdes, below the castle on Rua M. Francisco Gomes, ✆ 286 612 145 (*inexpensive*) is a peeling townhouse, comfortable and well run, with pretty rooms and great views of the river.

Eating Out

There are no really interesting restaurants in Mértola; most have plain menus, little atmosphere and reasonable food. The **Restaurante O Alengarve**, Av. Aureliano Mira Fernandes, ✆ 286 612 210 (*cheap*), in the square opposite the bus depot, is one of the better ones. *Closed Wed.* The best is probably **Restaurante Boa Viagem**, at the top of Rua Dr Afonso Costa by the roundabout, ✆ 286 612 483 (*cheap*), which has a surprisingly large menu (for Mértola) of Alentejan and Algarvian specialities. *Closed Sat.* **Restaurante Migas**, Mercado Municipal, ✆ 286 612 811 (*moderate–cheap*), is a small, attractive restaurant serving typical regional food. For something more exotic, at least in season, try **Restaurante Avenida**, Rua Dr Afonso Costa, ✆ 286 612 458 (*moderate–cheap*), which serves *javali* (wild boar), *veada* (venison) and *avestruz* (ostrich), with lamprey (at a cost) as well as charcoal-gtrilled fish and meat. **Adega da Casa Amarela**, Além-Rio,

© 286 618 026 (*moderate–cheap*) on the far side of the river is considered locally to be one of the best restaurants around. Look for the yellow house. *Closed Mon.*

Out of Town

Ten km from Mértola on the road to Serpa (and Mina de São Domingos), **O Alentejo**, at the centre of the village of Moreanes, © 286 655 133 (*moderate–cheap*) is a cheerful place specializing in traditional dishes, with a superb *javali à Alentejana* (wild boar, Alentejo style). *Closed Mon.*

House of Burgundy

1128/39–85	Afonso (Henriques) I
1185–1211	Sancho I
1211–23	Afonso II—Uracca (1220)
1223–48	Sancho II
1248–79	Afonso III
1279–1325	Dinis—Isabel of Aragon (1282)
1325–57	Afonso IV
1357–67	Pedro I—Blanca of Castile (1328)
	—Constanza of Castile (1336)
	—?Inês de Castro
1367–83	Fernando—Leonor Teles (1372)

House of Avis

1383–5	João I (Regent)—Philippa of Lancaster (1387)
1385–1433	João I (King)
1433–8	Duarte
1438–81	Afonso V
1481–95	João II—Leonor (1471)
1495–1521	Manuel I—Isabel of Castile (1497)
	—Maria of Castile (1500)
	—Leonor of Spain (1518)
1521–57	João III
1557–78	Sebastião (Sebastian)
1578–80	Cardinal Henrique
1580	António, Prior of Crato

House of Hapsburg

1580–98	Philip II of Spain (I of Portugal)
1598–1621	Philip III of Spain (II of Portugal)
1621–40	Philip IV of Spain (III of Portugal)

House of Bragança

1640–56	João IV
1656–67	Afonso VI—Isabel of Savoy (1668)
1667–83	Pedro II (Regent)—Isabel of Savoy (1668)
	—Maria of Neuberg (1687)
1683–1706	Pedro II (King)
1706–50	João V—Maria-Ana of Austria (1708)
1750–77	José
1777–92	Maria I—Pedro III (1760)
1792–1816	João VI (Regent)—Carlota Joaquina of Spain (1784)
1816–26	João VI (King)
1826–8	Pedro IV
1828–34	Miguel
1834–53	Maria (da Glória) II—August of Leuchtenberg (1834)
	—Ferdinand of Saxe-Coburg-Gotha (1836)
1853–5	Ferdinand (Regent)
1855–61	Pedro V

Rulers of Portugal to 1910

1861–89	Luís—Maria-Pia of Savoy
1889–1908	Carlos
1908–10	Manuel II

If you have a basic knowledge of Latin and French or Spanish, you should be able to make sense of written Portuguese, which is a Romance language. Pronunciation is another matter: Portuguese is diabolically difficult to speak. Plunge on in. The Portuguese are far too polite to make fun of your attempts, and most people will be delighted that you've made the effort. (Also, they are fond of reminding visitors that Portuguese is the seventh most widely spoken language in the world.) English is not uncommon in the cities and tourist areas, but it's just as alien to the Portuguese as their language is to us; French is a more useful lingua franca, since the Portuguese learn it as their second language.

Some anthropologists reckon that the Portuguese made their pronunciation as different as possible from Spanish, to emphasize their own identity. It may take several flagons of local wine before you can get your tongue around the vowels. A single stressed syllable (denoted by an acute accent or a circumflex) tends to swallow up the rest of a word. The tilde ('~') is most commonly used as 'ão', which produces a nasal 'ow' as in 'cow'. Consonants tend to be slurred. 'C' is soft before 'e' and 'i', but hard before 'a', 'o', and 'u'. 'Ç' is pronounced 's'. 'J' is pronounced like the 's' in 'leisure'. 'G' sounds the same when it comes before 'e' or 'i'—otherwise it is hard, as in 'get'. 'Lh' takes on the sound of 'ly', 'qu' or 'k'. 'S' is pronounced 'sh' when it comes before a consonant or at the end of a word. 'X' also sounds like 'sh'.

Useful Phrases

Greetings

good morning	*bom dia*
good afternoon or evening	*boa tarde*
goodnight	*boa noite*
goodbye	*adeus*
see you later	*até logo*
yes	*sim*
no	*não*
please	*por favor*
thank you	*obrigado (when spoken by a man)*
	obrigada (when spoken by a woman)
excuse me	*com licença*
I am sorry	*desculpe*

Problems and Queries

Please help me	*Ajude-me por favor*
Do you speak English?	*Fala inglês?*
How much is it?	*Quanto custa?*
Where is the toilet?	*Onde ficam os lavabos?*
I am in a hurry	*Tenho pressa*
Why?	*Porquê?*
Where?	*Onde?*
How are you?	*Como vai?*
I'm lost	*Estou perdido*
I don't understand	*Não compreendo*
What do you call this?	*Como se chama isto?*

Asking Directions

Is this right for...?	*Vou bem para...?*
Can you direct me to...?	*Pode indicar-me o caminho para...?*
the railway station	*a estação*
round trip	*ida e volta*
the centre of the city	*o centro da cidade*
bus-stop	*paragem de autocarro*
railway station	*estação ferroviária*
taxi rank	*ponto de táxi*
police	*polícia*
hospital	*hospital*
chemist	*farmacêutico*
museum	*museu*
church	*igreja*
beach	*praia*

Accommodation

a single room	*um quarto simples*
a double room	*um quarto de casal*
with private bathroom	*com banho*
bring me...	*traga-me...*
a towel	*uma toalha*
soap	*sabonete*
toilet paper	*papel higiénico*

Time

What time is it?	*Que horas são?*
when...	*quando...*
...do you open?	*...abrem?*
...do you shut?	*...fecham?*

Language

When will it be ready?	*Quando fica pronto?*
immediately	*imediatamente*
yesterday	*ontem*
tomorrow	*amanhã*
today	*hoje*
this afternoon	*logo à tarde*
this evening	*logo à noite*
one night	*uma noite*
one day	*um dia*
midday	*meio dia*
midnight	*meia noite*
now	*agora*
later	*mais tarde*

Money

Can I have...?	*Pode dar-me...?*
the bill	*a conta*
the receipt	*o recibo*
the change	*o troco*
Can you change...?	*Pode trocar...?*
Do you take traveller's cheques?	*Aceitam traveller's cheques?*
a bank	*um banco*
What is the rate of exchange?	*Qual é o câmbio?*
signature	*assinatura*
notes	*notas*
coins	*moedas*
money	*dinheiro*

Post Office

What is the postage...?	*Quanto é a franquia...?*
on this letter	*nesta carta*
postcard	*bilhete postal*
parcel	*volume*
by air mail	*por via aérea*
stamps	*selos*

Measurements

big	*grande*
bigger	*maior*
small	*pequeno*
smaller	*mais pequeno*
long	*comprido*
short	*curto*
cheap	*barato*
expensive	*caro*
beautiful	*belo*
ugly	*feio*

Everyday Purchases

Do you sell . . . ?	*Vendem . . . ?*
films for this camera	*filmes para esta máquina*
newspapers	*jornais*
books	*livros*
magazines	*revistas*
in English	*em inglês*
ballpoint pens	*esferográficas*
postcards	*postais*

Days of the Week

Sunday	*domingo*
Monday	*segunda-feira*
Tuesday	*terça-feira*
Wednesday	*quarta-feira*
Thursday	*quinta-feira*
Friday	*sexta-feira*
Saturday	*sábado*
holidays	*feriados*

Chemist

Have you anything for...?	*O que têm para...?*
bad sunburn	*queimaduras de sol*
colds	*constipações*
constipation	*prisão de ventre*
diarrhoea	*diarreia*
sore feet	*pés doridos*

Numbers

one	*um*	seventeen	*dezassete*
two	*dois*	eighteen	*dexoito*
three	*três*	nineteen	*dezanove*
four	*quatro*	twenty	*vinte*
five	*cinco*	twenty-one	*vinte e um*
six	*seis*	thirty	*trinta*
seven	*sete*	forty	*quarenta*
eight	*oito*	fifty	*cinquenta*
nine	*nove*	sixty	*sessenta*
ten	*dez*	seventy	*setenta*
eleven	*onze*	eighty	*oitenta*
twelve	*doze*	ninety	*noventa*
thirteen	*treze*	one hundred	*cem*
fourteen	*catorze*	one hundred and one	*cento e um*
fifteen	*quinze*	one thousand	*mil*
sixteen	*dizasseis*		

Colours

white	*branco*
black	*preto*
red	*encarnado*
blue	*azul*
green	*verde*
brown	*castanho*
yellow	*amarelo*

Architectural Terms

Municipal town hall	*Câmara*
Mother church/parish church	*Igreja Matriz*
viewpoint	*miradouro*
pillory	*pelourinho*
villa/country seat	*quinta*
public square	*rossio*
cathedral/diocese	*sé*
manor house	*solar*
keep	*torre de menagem*

Restaurant and Menu Vocabulary

General

the menu	*ementa*
breakfast	*pequeno almoço*
lunch	*almoço*
dinner	*jantar*
the bill	*a conta*
Is service included?	*O serviço está incluindo?*
the wine list	*a lista dos vinhos*

Coffee and Tea

bica	a small, black coffee
chá	tea
galão	a tall glass of white coffee
Nescafé	decaffeinated coffee

Poultry and Game (*Aves e Caça*)

coelho	rabbit
frango	chicken
galinha	hen
perdiz	partridge
peru	turkey

Meat (*Carne*)

anho	lamb	*lingua*	tongue
bife	steak	*lombo*	fillet
cabrito	kid	*porco*	pork
carneiro	mutton	*rins*	kidneys
entrecosto	rumpsteak	*toucinho*	bacon
fiambre	ham	*vaca*	beef
fígado	liver	*veado*	deer
javali	wild boar	*vitela*	veal
leitão	suckling pig		

Fish (*Peixe*)

ameijoas	clams	*meixilhões*	mussels
atum	tuna	*moreia*	moray
bacalhau	salt cod	*navalheira*	small crab
besugo	bream	*pargo*	snapper
búzios	whelks	*peixe espada*	scabbard fish
camarões	shrimps	*peixe espadarte*	swordfish
carapau	shad or horse mackerel	*perceves*	barnacles
carpa	carp	*polvo*	octopus
cavala	mackerel	*robalo*	sea bass
cherne	grouper/brill	*safío*	conger eel
chocos	cuttlefish	*salmão*	salmon
conquilhas	cockles	*salmonete*	red mullet
gambas	prawns	*santola*	spider crab
lagosta	rock lobster	*sardinhas*	sardines
lagostins	crayfish	*sargo*	grey bream
lavagante	lobster	*sapateira*	crab
linguado	sole	*tamboril*	monkfish
lulas	squid	*truta*	trout

Shellfish (*Mariscos*)

amêijoas	cockles	*lagosta*	rock lobster
camarões	shrimps	*lulas*	cuttlefish
gambas	prawns	*polvo*	octopus

Vegetables (*Legumes*)

alho	garlic	*couve-flor*	cauliflower
arroz	rice	*ervilhas*	peas
batatas	potatoes	*espinafres*	spinach
cebolas	onions	*favas*	broad beans
cenouras	carrots	*feijão*	beans
cogumelos	mushrooms	*pimentos*	peppers
couve	cabbage		

Fruit (*Frutas*)

ameixas	plums	*maçã*	apple
ananás	pineapple	*pêra*	pear
figos	figs	*uvas*	grapes
laranja	orange		

Cooking Terms

assado	roasted	*guisado*	stew
cozido	boiled	*mista*	mixed (i.e. salad)
estufado	stewed	*nas brasas*	braised
frito	fried	*no espeto*	on the spit
fumado	smoked	*no forno*	baked
grelhado	grilled		

Other

água	water	*queijo*	cheese
azeite	olive oil	*sal*	salt
cerveja	beer	*vinagre*	vinegar
gelo	ice	*vinho branco*	white wine
manteiga	butter	*vinho de mesa*	table wine
pão	bread	*vinho tinto*	red wine
pimenta	pepper		

History

Boxer, C.R., *The Portuguese Seaborne Empire 1415–1825* (Hutchinson, 1977).
Livermore, H.V., *A New History of Portugal* (C.U.P., 1969).
Marques, A.H. de Oliveira, *History of Portugal* (2 vol) (Columbia, 1972).
Read, Jan, *The Moors in Spain and Portugal* (Faber and Faber, 1974).
Russel, P.E., *Prince Henry the Navigator—the Rise and Fall of a Culture Hero* (Clarendon Press, 1984).
Sanceau, Elaine, *The Perfect Prince* (Livraria Civilização, 1959).
Trend, J.B., *Portugal* (Ernest Benn, 1957).
Ure, John, *Henry the Navigator* (Constable and Co, 1977).

Guides

Port, Len, *Get to Know the Algarve, an Insider's Guide* (Vista Ibérica Publicações, 1994).

Miscellaneous

Gallop, Rodney, Portugal ,A Book of Folk Ways (C.U.P., 1961). Popular anthropology.
Macaulay, Rose, *They Went to Portugal* (Penguin, 1985).
Measures, John and Madge, *Southern Portugal, Its People, Traditions and Wildlife* (Associação 'In Loco', 1995). Knowledgeable descriptions of plants, animals, scenery and country crafts, with colour photographs.
Read, Jan, *The Wines of Portugal* (Faber and Faber, 1987).
Smith, R.C., *The Art of Portugal 1500–1800* (Weidenfeld and Nicholson, 1968). Professorial overview of the arts.
Vieira, Edite, *A Taste of Portugal* (Robert Hale, 1988). Anecdotal cookbook.

Literature

Bell, Aubrey (trs.), *Four Plays of Gil Vicente* (C.U.P., 1920).
Camões, Luis Vaz de, *The Lusiads* (Penguin, 1985).
Garrett, Almeida, *Travels in My Homeland* (Peter Owen/UNESCO, 1987).
Macedo, H. (ed.), *Modern Poetry in Translation 13/14 Portugal* (Modern Poetry in Translation, 1972).
Pessoa, Fernando, *Selected Poems* (Penguin, 1988).
Pires, José Cardoso, *Ballad of Dogs' Beach* (Dent, 1986).
Queiroz, Eça de, *The Maias* (Dent, 1986).
Saramago, José, *Baltasar and Blimunda* (Cape, 1988).

Further Reading

Primary Sources

Azurara, *Chronicle of the Discovery of Guinea*.

White, David and Wise, Peter, *Financial Times Survey*, 30 November 1999.

Main page references are in **bold**. Page references to maps are in *italics*.

Index

Also Available from Cadogan Guides...

Country Guides

Antarctica
Central Asia
China: The Silk Routes
Egypt
France: Southwest France;
     Dordogne, Lot & Bordeaux
France: Southwest France;
     Gascony & the Pyrenees
France: Brittany
France: The Loire
France: The South of France
France: Provence
France: Côte d'Azur
Germany: Bavaria
Greece: The Peloponnese
Holland
Holland: Amsterdam & the Randstad
India
India: South India
India: Goa
Ireland
Ireland: Southwest Ireland
Ireland: Northern Ireland
Italy
Italy: The Bay of Naples and Southern Italy
Italy: Bologna and Emilia Romagna
Italy: Italian Riviera
Italy: Lombardy, Milan and the Italian Lakes
Italy: Rome and the Heart of Italy
Italy: Sardinia
Italy: Tuscany, Umbria and the Marches
Italy: Tuscany
Italy: Umbria
Italy: Venetia and the Dolomites
Japan
Morocco
Portugal
Portugal: The Algarve
Scotland
Scotland: Highlands and Islands
South Africa, Swaziland and Lesotho
Spain
Spain: Southern Spain
Spain: Northern Spain
Syria & Lebanon
Tunisia
Turkey
Yucatán and Southern Mexico
Zimbabwe, Botswana and Namibia

City Guides

Amsterdam
Barcelona
Brussels, Bruges, Ghent & Antwerp
Bruges
Edinburgh
Florence, Siena, Pisa & Lucca
Italy: Three Cities—Rome, Florence, Venice
Italy: Three Cities—Venice, Padua, Verona
Italy: Three Cities—Rome, Naples, Sorrento
Italy: Three Cities—Rome, Padua, Assisi
Japan: Three Cities—Tokyo, Kyoto and
     Ancient Nara
Morocco: Three Cities—Marrakesh, Fez, Rabat
Spain: Three Cities—Granada, Seville,
     Cordoba
Spain: Three Cities—Madrid, Barcelona, Seville
London
London–Paris
London–Brussels
Madrid
Manhattan
Moscow & St Petersburg
Paris
Prague
Rome
St Petersburg
Venice

Island Guides

Caribbean and Bahamas
Jamaica & the Caymans
Greek Islands
Greek Islands By Air
Crete
Mykonos, Santorini & the Cyclades
Rhodes & the Dodecanese
Corfu & the Ionian Islands
Madeira & Porto Santo
Malta
Sardinia
Sicily

Plus...

Bugs, Bites & Bowels
London Markets
Take the Kids Travelling
Take the Kids London
Take the Kids Paris and Disneyland
Take the Kids Amsterdam

Available from good bookshops or via, in the UK, **Grantham Book Services**, Isaac Newton Way,
Alma Park Industrial Estate, Grantham NG31 9SD, ✆ (01476) 541 080, ✉ (01476) 541 061;
and in North America from **The Globe Pequot Press**, 246 Goose Lane, PO Box 480, Guilford,
Connecticut 06437–0480, ✆ (800) 243 0495, ✉ (800) 820 2329.